BUILDING
MENTAL
MUSCLE

BUILDING MENTAL MUSCLE

Conditioning Exercises for the Six Intelligence Zones

David Gamon, Ph.D.
and Allen D. Bragdon

A Division of
Allen D. Bragdon Publishers, Inc.
Cape Cod and San Francisco

ACKNOWLEDGMENTS

The authors drew inspiration and information from many people and publications. Among them Vernon H. Mark, M.D., F.A.C.S.. Among the general works we found most useful were Robert Ornstein's books, some written with David Sobel, especially *Evolution of Consciousness*, and William H. Calvin and George A. Ojemann's book *Conversations with Neil's Brain*. Among those who helped form the manuscript to its benefit, we appreciate the support and skills of Stuart Miller, editor at Barnes & Noble Books, and these graphic artists and designers: Leonard Fellows, Peter Osterowski, Cindy Wood, Bill Young, Carolyn Zellers.

The information in this book is intended to provide insight into how the human brain functions. It is not intended as an aid to neurodiagnosis which must be conducted by qualified practitioners.

Cover design by Cindy Wood

ISBN 0 916410 625

Printed and bound in the U.S.A. by R.R. Donnelley, Harrisonburg

99 00 01 02 M 9 8 7 6 5 4 3 2

This work is dedicated to
all people who keep their
minds active,
especially those who
have used theirs to explore
that fascinating instrument
of survival and delight
— the human brain.

Other books by the authors:

Building Left-Brain Power

Exercises for the Whole Brain

Right-Brain Teasers

How Sharp Is Your Pencil?

What Do You Know?

Can You Pass These Tests?

Visit the BRAINWAVES® website at:
www.mentalmuscles.com

CONTENTS

INTRODUCTION
8

EXECUTIVE & SOCIAL
11

15 What part of your brain causes you to respond as a unique individual? 23 Your right frontal lobe registers negative emotions. 29 How to read deceit. 33 DHEA may make the aging feel young. 37 A type of logic puzzle that often applies to real-life situations. 41 How to make yourself feel happier without drugs. 43 The night a middle-aged man tackled his bureau in his sleep. 47 How self-conscious are you? 51 If you're immoral and lazy, you may not be able to blame your parents. 59 A genetic clue to personality. 65 Physical exercise helps the brain grow.

MEMORY
69

73 "Memory" is, in fact, many processes that occur in different parts of the brain. 77 Imagine a memory-enhancing drug that would make you remember everything. 83 You can still use some kinds of knowledge even if you don't know you have them. 87 A major cause of forgetting. 91 If you want to remember complex data, visualize it. Geniuses do. 99 Background noises, including talk, affect your ability to recall. 103 Why are stories easier to recall than lists? 109 A little stress helps memory. 115 "Now where did I put my Prozac?" 117 Can challenging mental activity forestall age-related cognitive decline? 123 As they age, most people tend to notice problems with their "working" memory. 129 Normal decline of very short-term memory shows up in some tests of older people. 133 New hope for those at risk for Alzheimer's.

EMOTIONAL
137

141 It's cheaper than gin. 143 How distracting thoughts destroy effective mood control. 147 Self-illusions are good for you. 153 How the brain recognizes fear. 157 "Watch two Marx brothers movies and call me in the morning." 161 Would you choose to be more sanguine if it were as easy as taking an aspirin? 173 Why are women more affected by seasonal fluctuations in day length? 177 What is the

brain so busy doing, and not doing, while we sleep? 185 Verbalizing unpleasant experiences helps physical health. 189 Your immune responses and brain are linked together.

LANGUAGE 193

197 Injuries help to map the brain's language regions. 200 A new language area. 205 Women are more linguistically "balanced" than men. 209 Cortisol — as destructive to the brain as cholesterol is to the heart. 213 How a child begins to speak. 217 Educating babies. 219 Around the turn of the first year. 221 The critical window of opportunity. 225 The forbidden experiment. 229 The tragic case of "Genie" from L.A. 234 New technology for testing theories about language processing.

MATH 239

243 Are human infants born with number skills? 247 "Idiot" savants. 249 Brain-changing nutrition and the "post-lunch dip." 253 Lack of sleep reduces problem-solving ability. 257 The genius who thought in pictures but expressed his ideas in math. 261 The magical number 7: how it limits us, and how we can overcome it.

SPATIAL 265

269 Seeing both the forest and the trees: Different parts of the brain are specialized for different visual tasks. 273 Facial recognition depends on visual-spatial processing by the right side of your brain. 279 A gene for visual-spatial ability. 283 Nicotine improves spatial memory, learning, and information processing. 289 "Blindsight," a surprising finding, and other curiosities. 293 Seeing without understanding: Visual object agnosia. 297 A circadian rhythm and sunlight tell us when to sleep.

SOLUTIONS 301

REFERENCES 315

CREDITS 320

INTRODUCTION

Why you need this book

This is a self-help book. It gives you access to recent discoveries about the way your six zones of practical intelligence operate. Your new awareness will give you an edge in using your brain effectively. The exercises are designed to stimulate the cells in different brain zones, some of which you may not use regularly in your personal or professional life. Keeping those cells active prevents their deterioration from disuse caused by ignorance of how your brain functions, by failure to maintain cellular vitality, or because of apathy, laziness or age.

All your cognitive zones must be kept sharp. Most real-world, real-time events are best handled by putting a variety of skills into play, not just one. (For example, to calculate tax and tip on a dinner check, you need both math skills and short-term working memory

EXECUTIVE/SOCIAL ZONE *The front part of the cortex (the wrinkled outer covering of the brain) allows you to foresee goals in the future and take the steps necessary to execute your plans. It also is involved in relating with other people in productive ways — including picking up signals about their attitudes and choosing the most effective responses.*

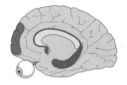

strength, to keep all the numbers accessible as you perform your mental calculations.) Maintaining your cognitive tools gives you an edge by keeping you "in the zone" in another way. A skill used in one domain can cross over into another to enrich the savor of your life and its other incomes. (For example, when you learn the pattern of number intervals in math you may perceive a pattern of musical intervals for the first time and enjoy the music more. Or vice versa.)

Your brain is there to keep you alive. It is your best weapon. Human evolution has equipped you with such an effective toolbox that your brain can find its best tool, adjust it and apply it. The human brain evolved to keep the organism beneath it alive to hunt in groups, to track and to kill stronger, faster, more agile prey — then find its way home again across ancient plains to a cave in a cliff. It has equipped humans to survive ice ages and dry months when deserts crept across their gardens. But these amazing tools can rust.

When brain cells — the ones that carry the messages that built the life you live in — are not used, they get the message that you don't need them to survive. At that moment they begin to get out of

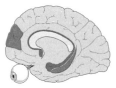

MEMORY ZONE *It is a component of all cognitive skills. The brain codes data it considers useful and stores it in the cortex, often near the sensory area related to each component part of the memory. Before storage, incoming data passes through the brain's interior, more primitive area to take whatever action is required for survival.*

the way, like everything else in nature that isn't required to keep its organism alive. Those unused cells shrink their dendritic "fingers" that evolved to reach out to share information with other cells. At that moment each idled cell cuts you off from some order of a billionth of your capacity to perceive the significance of what's happening around you or to succeed in your goals. Recent research into brain function supports the concept of "Use it or lose it," a phrase that the whisky-voiced actress Tallulah Bankhead once made famous, perhaps in another context. Either way, the idea appears to be a rule of nature.

We hope that some of the information in this book may inspire you to sharpen your mental tools and enrich your life now and as you grow old. (Besides, the information in this book is so fascinating in itself that you could suddenly find yourself the center of attention at social gatherings.) We repeat: Your brain keeps you alive in every sense. It is your best weapon to achieve success and satisfaction.

How this material is organized

This book includes short reports on results of academic research into how the human brain functions, plus tests and mental exercises related to each short report. The editors selected only topics that can be put to practical use in everyday life and that can be understood without scientific background. They clustered the reports into six ways you use your brain: Executive/Social, Memory, Emotional, Language, Math and Spatial. Linked with each text report is a Self-test of brain function you can administer to yourself, or an entertaining Exercise of the brain function related to what you learned from the report.

The Exercises are intriguing challenges, often formatted as puzzles. They are designed to help develop mental skills in two ways:

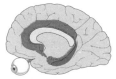

EMOTIONAL ZONE *Our emotional responses, which we are often not consciously able to cause or control voluntarily, tend to be processed in the older, central part of the brain rather than the outer cortex. The brain is primarily a tool to ensure survival, not speculation, so response is often required on a subconscious level.*

LANGUAGE & MATH ZONES *Detailed data that make up the "trees" of the "forest" are mainly processed on the left side of the cortex near the temple. Also nearby the temporal lobe are the parts of the brain that control speech and language — both abstract understanding and motor movements involved in speech.*

First, they will help you to build mental stamina for sustained concentration, much as aerobics builds physical stamina for sustained exertion. The ability to focus attention is an essential first step for conscious memory. Second, the exercises introduce, in an entertaining format, so many different kinds of data — math, verbal, spatial, logic, etc. — that some of it is bound to be new to you. That new data — and more important, the experience you gain in how to organize data so you can locate a solution — will build links among your brain cells that, later, can help you learn new data and spot the most effective pattern to cope with it.

Use the Hints (printed upside down beneath the exercises) when you need a boost to get started solving the task. These exercises are there to stimulate neural activity, not to frustrate it.

Self-tests allow you to investigate a function or phenomenon related to the adjacent article. They do not rely on any prior knowledge. They allow you to observe your own facility in performing tasks similar to those used under scientifically structured, experimental conditions. The evidence from those experiments produced norms against which you can roughly measure your own score. Also, the very process of taking such a self-test, including the need to follow instructions, challenges your powers of concentration and other memory functions, thereby helping to strengthen them, just as the exercises do.

The graphic icons next to the title of an exercise or self-test indicate which of the six practical, cognitive zones will be stimulated.

When answers to exercises or self-tests are necessary they appear in the Solutions section in the back of the book. ("The Lurch" is no place to be left; we've been there often.)

Allen Bragdon and David Gamon — Cape Cod, August 1997

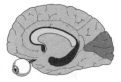

SPATIAL ZONE *The brain processes incoming sensory data about size, proportion, shape, relative volume and other spatial values mostly with neurons on the right side. The colored area in the back of the cortex (right) shows the occipital area, where visual data is first processed, then sent elsewhere to be interpreted.*

executive
& social
function

EXECUTIVE & SOCIAL

This is the most recently-evolved zone of intelligence in the human brain. It functions in uniquely human ways. It works out plans designed to reach consciously-contrived future goals. It selects the paths of social interaction that will bring the greatest long-term benefit. It retrieves data from long-term memory and uses it to construct images of similar data as it might become active in future time. It is the seat of human "character" — that galaxy of consistent responses that involve social reliability and responsibility.

If the textured layer of gray matter known as the cortex is the source of our uniqueness as humans, it's the parts of the cortex behind the forehead — the frontal lobes — that are most responsible for the differences between us and our closest animal relatives. It's this region of the brain, apparently, that is most responsible for self-awareness — the ability to introspect, to ponder, to not only act, but to be aware of the fact that we're acting, to weigh other conceivable actions, to choose not to act, to imagine how the world might be different if we didn't act or if we weren't alive to act. With this comes freedom from materialistic determination, a philosophical preoccupation with the mysteries of life and with death, a sense of beauty, religion — in short, all those interests related to the past, the future and the self that we think of as distinguishing us from other animals.

As the most recently-evolved part of the brain, the frontal lobes also house the most fragile parts of our identity — the faculties that require the most conscious effort and practice, such as logic, planning, monitoring our own behavior, and achieving desired goals. In the process of becoming responsible social beings, we spend much of the early part of life learning how to modify the impulses that come pulsing upward from the lower parts of the brain. For much of the rest of our life, the conflicts between these different systems — between emotion and rationality, libido and intellect, spontaneity and self-control — ensure our financial contribution to the self-help movement and the psychotherapy business.

Conscious, planned, goal-oriented behavior and emotion are not necessarily as conflicting as you might think, however. After all, in order to move towards a goal, it certainly helps to *desire* it. Brain scans show that your left frontal lobe is activated when you feel positive emotions, and the right frontal lobe when you feel negative emotions. Already as babies, some of us have less-than-average activity in one region or the other. If your "positive" frontal region has naturally low activation, you may not have much success in intellectual goal-directed tasks. Some people with frontal-lobe injury lose both their emotions and their decision-making ability; others may become violent criminals. It even seems that "hunches" and "intuitions" — impulses occupying the shadow-world in between rational consciousness and emotion — may have a frontal-lobe locus.

The flip side of the fragility of executive functions is that they are also the most malleable and improvable with practice. The best way to be an expert at organizing information and using it to your advantage is to work at it. Because your frontal-lobe functions are so consciously accessible, this is an easier matter — as long as you're willing to make the effort — than, say, learning to adjust your brain-stem-governed body rhythms.

What part of your brain causes you to respond as a unique individual?

One of the more difficult tasks neuroscience is currently faced with is that of identifying the part or parts of the brain responsible for defining an individual's personality as a unique and stable entity. Lots of progress has been made in associating certain regions of the brain with specific abilities and functions: the hippocampus with the mediation of memory formation, the amygdala with the processing of emotion, areas along the sylvian fissure with various aspects of language. But where is the locus of conscious self-awareness, the site that makes one person have a different identity from another, the region that unites the experiences of an individual human organism into a stable sense of self, despite the fluctuations of mood, affect, drive, and emotion? As Calvin and Ojemann's epilepsy patient asks in *Conversations with Neil's Brain*, "Where is the real me?"

Is identity an illusion?
A point that Calvin and Ojemann make is that this stable sense of self may be less real than we sometimes imagine. There seem to be many different parts of the brain competing for dominance, with any one part winning out at any given moment. Our sense of our unity of consciousness may result from the fact that there's only one winner at any one time.

But if any region of the brain were to be implicated as the seat of identity, it would probably be included in the front third of the brain called the frontal lobe. That area is the most recently evolved. It allows humans to imagine goals for themselves in the future and select appropriate behavior — an ability which suffers when part of the frontal lobe is knocked out of commission by disease or injury, such as a tumor or a stroke.

What happens when you're no longer you?
The most famous and dramatic case of frontal lobe injury is that of Phineas Gage, a promising young railroad construction crew supervisor who, in 1848, had an iron tamping bar shot into his upper jaw and through the midfrontal regions of his

brain. Although he survived and, in some respects, recovered amazingly well, he changed from a soft-spoken, responsible man into a foul-mouthed, erratic, inconsiderate boor. His friends complained that he had changed into a different person — that he was "no longer Gage."

In general, personality-related symptoms of frontal-lobe damage may include changes in drive or motivation, mood, and affect (emotional expression), and in the ability to plan or make decisions. Diminished reliability or foresight, socially inappropriate behavior, depression, euphoria, and lethargy are some of the many complaints that have been reported.

We may understand this wide range of symptoms as due to the other parts of the brain for which the frontal regions serve as association areas. The dorsal frontal system connects to parts of the brain involved in the sequential organization and processing of information. The ventral system connects to emotional regions, including three different limbic systems. The pre-frontal cortex also has strong connections to all sensory regions, as well as to motor regions. This has inspired the identification of the pre-frontal cortex as the "final common pathway," integrating information from a variety of brain regions for the proper motor response.

Awareness is a relationship, not a thing or place

According to some researchers, many kinds of frontal-lobe pathology may be grouped under the umbrella of self-reflective awareness, or the ability to be aware of oneself and one's relation to others and the environment. Based on studies of children, "meta-awareness" — the awareness that one is aware — depends on the relatively late infant development of subparts of the frontal region. The frontal lobe, then, seems to house integration or association regions which are crucial to our stable identity. As is true for so many aspects of cognition, those vexing questions of the source of consciousness and identity may be answered in the associations between many parts of the brain, rather than in one self-contained locus or "module." But, to the extent that we have one, the "driver" of the whole cognitive apparatus — the particular associations that make you different from me — may well be seated, appropriately enough, right up front.

WHAT HAPPENED TO PHINEAS GAGE

These illustrations are computer reconstructions of the skull of Phineas Gage, who lived for 14 years after a crowbar-sized tamping rod entered his cheek, passed through his prefrontal cortex, and exited his forehead. As foreman of a railroad-building gang, he was tamping down explosive charges when a spark set one off. The rod took with it the portion of his brain that nobody knew the function of until then — the part that allows humans to make mental images of what has not yet happened. It is known as an "executive" function.

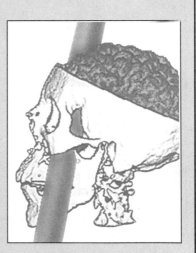

This is the skill that allows chess masters to foresee the results of a move. Business executives use it to plan for expansion. We all use it to plan the route to do a string of chores and to get along with other people.

After he recovered from his accident, young Phineas changed from a kind man and responsible foreman into a foul-mouthed, unreliable social outcast.

EXERCISE: Mixed-up toons

Your frontal lobes plan the best sequence of events to achieve goals. Try to rearrange each of the five sets of mixed-up cartoon panels on pages 18-22 into the most amusing sequences. Replace the incorrect numbers with correct ones.

A

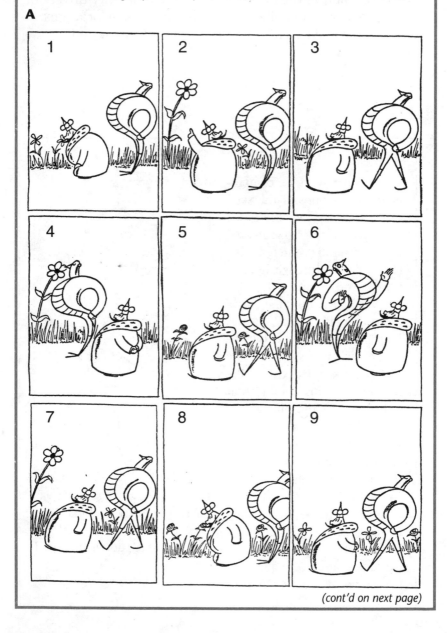

(cont'd on next page)

B

(cont'd on next page)

(cont'd on next page)

(cont'd on next page)

Your right frontal lobe registers negative emotions: how that fact can be useful to you

We sometimes think of our emotional selves — our fears, delights, and outbursts of anger — as diametrically opposed to the cool reason, planning, and logic required for identifying and reaching goals. This is only partly true. Here's why.

Emotions are processed in the frontal lobe

The frontal lobe is a crossroads of the emotional centers of the brain. Negative emotions — disgust, fear, and anger — are registered in the right frontal lobe, and happiness is registered in the left. How do we know? For one thing, these are the regions that electroencephalograph (EEG) readings show to be activated when people are exposed to stimuli that evoke one of these emotional responses — a picture of a dog eating its own vomit, for example.

Emotion and reason are linked

The frontal lobe also controls executive functions such as intention, conscious self-regulation, and planning. People with damage to the left frontal lobe may have difficulty planning a simple sequence of actions and even in initiating voluntary actions, and they may be listless, apathetic, and depressed. Approach-related behavior — movement towards literal or metaphorical goals — requires not only planning a strategy for getting there, but the desire to get moving in the first place.

Low activity in your left frontal lobe correlates with depression

Some people have *low* baseline readings of *left* frontal lobe activity. They may often be labeled as inhibited or shy. Their left frontal lobe also shows low response to positive stimuli — happy scenes in films, for example. People who have an unusually *high* level of *right* frontal lobe activity tend to be anxious and leery of danger. Depression and sadness are usually categorized by most people as negative emotions, along with fear, anger, and disgust. Even so, it seems that depression is better understood, neurally speaking, as a *low* level of activity in the *left* frontal lobe — the "happy" region. It does not show as unusually high activity in the "negative" right frontal area as, for example, anger does.

Does this mean that one side of my body is an eager go-getter, and the other side is an anxious coward?

Since the brain's right hemisphere corresponds to the left side of the body, and the left hemisphere to the right side, you'd expect happiness to be registered more strongly on the right side of the face, and disgust, anger, and fear on the left side. This seems to be true. (It has been speculated that the source of the "enigmatic" effect of the Mona Lisa's smile is that, in her case, it's the left side, not the right side, of the face that is smiling. Thus, the negative side of the face is happy, and the positive side is neutral — resulting in a somewhat inscrutable overall expression.) Some psychologists have argued that the right brain is the dominant hemisphere for emotions in general. This probably has some validity for the *perception* of emotion in other people's faces and other cues, but not for *feeling* the emotion itself.

Even though the left hemisphere does dominate in the *experience* of positive emotion, the right hemisphere seems to be involved in the *recognition* and processing of *both* positive

---

 SELF-TEST: Judgment of emotion; mirror images

There's a theory that the subject of the Mona Lisa is Leonardo himself — i.e., that the painting is a self-portrait. In that case, Leonardo must have been painting his own mirror image. If we flop the image, the effect to most people is dramatic: the picture loses its "enigmatic" quality, and the subject's expression appears to become rather smirking or even lascivious than inscrutable.

Which of the two pictures below is the Mona Lisa with the inscrutable smile and which image has been reversed to reveal Leonardo da Vinci's "lascivious" smile?

---

and negative emotional signals. The right brain als[...] positive facial expressions more than you'd think bas[...] left brain's dominance in feeling positive emotions. Sti[...] left brain does play a role in processing positive signals [...] as experiencing them. Happy faces are recognized better w[...] presented to the right visual field (left brain). Also, films shown in the right visual field tend to be rated more pleasant than ones shown in the left visual field (right brain).

So *that's* why Aunt Mary always thought I liked her fruitcake
It also happens that elderly adults are worse than younger adults at recognizing negative facial expressions — fear or disgust, for example. This finding provides support to the right-hemi-aging hypothesis — that, as we age, the right hemisphere tends to decline more rapidly than the left. Perhaps that's why certain "crystallized" left-brain abilities such as vocabulary size don't decline as fast when we age, compared to certain "fluid" right-brain abilities such as abstract spatial reasoning and facial recognition. In a recent study, young and old adults were asked to assign photographs of faces to categories of emotion ("Happy," "Fearful," etc.). Older subjects performed much worse than younger ones in identifying negative expressions, but as well as younger subjects in identifying happy faces.

Why is it that your negative-processing right brain best reads the "positive" side of another person's face?
Let's face it, the only time you can read the expression on another person's face is when you face each other. But then, the emotion that each side of the brain is specialized to perceive is in the *other* half of the brain's field of vision. In other words, when facing someone head-on, you will tend to have his "negative" side in your field of vision connected to your brain's "positive processing" skills, and his "positive" side in your "negative" field. This seeming contradiction suggests that our brains have evolved to prevent us from viewing and responding to other people in a wholly one-sided fashion.

All this has something of the flavor of a diabolical logic puzzle. If you experience frustration and disgust coupled with a desire to throttle the authors of this article, would we be dealing with right-brain-based withdrawal-oriented, or left-brain-based approach-related behavior?

EXERCISE: Getting on the "right" side of a person

Study the illustrations and the photos on these pages, then answer the following question:

If you were standing face-to-face with a stranger looking directly ahead at him or her, would you be more likely to think that person's face showed the positive or negative aspects of his or her personality?

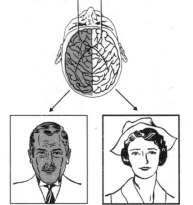

Hint: As demonstrated by the split-image diagram, the left hemisphere of most people's brains processes information their eyes pick up to the right of the midpoint in their field of vision. Similarly, the right hemisphere processes the data to the left. (For example, if your right hemisphere were damaged you might say you saw an angry man in the diagram, not a half-smiling, half-frowning face.)

Even though the left hemisphere is more specialized for the perception of positive than of negative emotion, the right hemisphere does seem to be dominant for the perception of all kinds of emotion.

The right hemisphere processes a person's own feelings of anger, disgust, contempt, fear — the negative emotions.

Each of the two hemispheres of the brain, left and right, controls the physical systems and attributes located on the opposite half of the body.

SELF-TEST: How the brain views faces

Which photo depicts the more disgusted man?

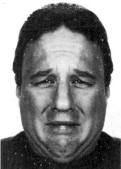

Picture of a man expressing disgust

A Composite picture in which the *right* half of his face appears on right *and* left sides.

B This is a composite picture of the two *left* halves of his face.

A   **B**

Which face is happy? For most people the right side of the brain is dominant for the perception of emotions. When you are looking at a person's face, the part to the left of the nose is interpreted by the right brain.

(Illus. after Julian Jaynes, 1976)

Hint for top photos: Look at the mouth of the man in photos A and B. Which mouth looks more negative? When you sneer, on which side of your face do you curl your lip?

Hint for bottom illustrations: Most people interpret emotions more strongly by what the right side of a person's face looks like — which is what they see on the left as they view that person face-to-face. Try looking at the nose of each and decide which person seems happier. Most people would see face "A" as sad, and face "B" as happy.

SELF-TEST: Right-brain pattern abstraction / abstract reading

Complete the following by filling in a letter, number, or word in each blank. Total time: 10 minutes.

Example: A E I O U

1) 1 3 5 7 _

2) AB CE CD EG EF G__

3) blowhard hardhat hatcheck ____mate

4) astray stray tray ___

5) toner tone ton __

6) stone tone ton __

7) stops ____ top to

8) snit in snot on prod or mode __

9) polygram 12345678 pray 1674 ploy ____

10) gum gun bar bat sun sup lip ___

11) hole pit seed kick punt boat edge shore strengthen hurt ____clever

12) bird crane stretch sprint run snag lozenge mint new note ___ beak

13) 7913 992 488 569 72155 614__

14) Q O M K I _

15) din don fan fen pep pip cod ___

16) 289735 897352 973528 735289 _____

17) bib bib ton not 399 993 pin ___

18) JK KJ LM IH NO G _

19) 37210 2 19903 1 48737 3 52209 9 47391 _

20) retire rite strafe fart inept pen peruse ____

Norms: Age 20-39: 8-12 correct = average
13-16 correct = above average
17-18 correct = superior
19-20 correct = gifted

Age 40-59: 6-10 correct = average
11-15 correct = above average
16-18 correct = superior
19-20 correct = gifted

Age 60-79: 4-6 correct = average
7-10 correct = above average
11-17 correct = superior
18-20 correct = gifted

How to read deceit: false smiles and happy smiles

A long-standing debate in cultural anthropology is whether facial expressions match up with particular emotions on a universal or only culturally specific basis. One piece of evidence cited by proponents of the latter view is that smiles can signal so many different kinds of emotion depending on context: on the one hand, sincere happiness or pleasure, and on the other, any of a number of negative emotions such as embarrassment, chagrin, or malice.

The 19th-century French neurologist Duchenne de Boulogne observed, however, that there seem to be at least two distinct patterns of facial muscle movement which we happen to group together with the same word. One involves both the muscle which parts and raises the lips (*zygomatic major*), and the muscle which raises the cheeks and gathers the skin inward toward the eye socket (*orbicularis oculi*). He identified this as the smile of spontaneous joy. The other involves only the zygomatic major muscle around the mouth. In acknowledgment of Duchenne's insight, University of California researcher Paul Ekman has dubbed the smile of spontaneous happiness a *Duchenne* smile, while the other is sometimes called a false, social, or masking smile.

Parts of your left brain that are active when you make a sincerely happy smile are not active when the smile is false

The brain's electrical activity can be seen and measured in normal, wide-awake, active subjects using electroencephelogram (EEG) equipment. In one experiment, subjects were chosen who could make their faces create the Duchenne happy smile, as actors can. The EEG readings when they were making this genuine smile showed spots of activity in the left hemisphere normally associated with happy feelings. Activity in those areas died away, however, when the subjects changed their faces to show the false kind of smile using only the muscles around their mouth. In other words, the EEG record of their brain activity showed that they were actually *feeling* happier when they were making the Duchenne smile, but not the social smile.

You might think that this effect was due to the subjects' making themselves feel happy in order to produce the Duchenne smile, just as actors will sometimes think of something sad in order to cry. The researchers were careful to prevent this, though, by teaching the subjects to make the different kinds of expression by pointing out to them which muscles they should use; they scrupulously avoided describing the facial-muscle-movement patterns with reference to the emotions associated with them, such as "joy" or "happiness," or even referring to them as "smiles" at all.

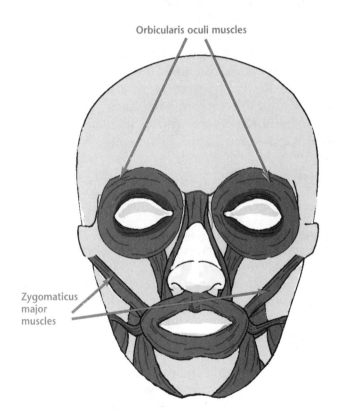

Orbicularis oculi muscles

Zygomaticus major muscles

This is important for at least three reasons. One, it shows that you can, quite simply, make yourself feel happier by smiling — as long as you make the right *kind* of smile! Two, you can tell a sincere smile from a false smile — and, in some cases, tell an honest person from a liar — by paying attention to the muscle around the eye. Third, a certain pattern of brain activity (a cerebral "map" of joy) is indeed biologically linked to a certain pattern of facial movement; those who argue that the link between smiles and emotions is arbitrary and unpredictable are confusing what are, in fact, two fundamentally different *kinds* of facial expression.

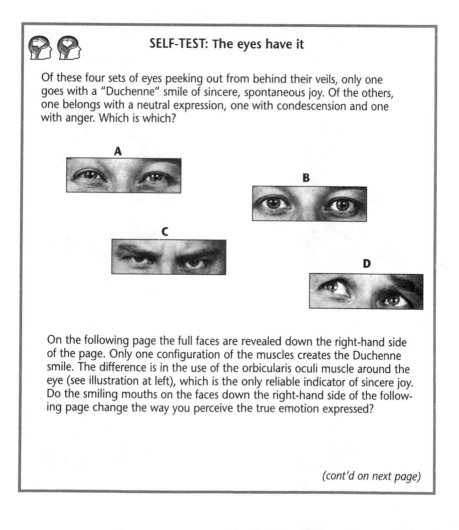

SELF-TEST: The eyes have it

Of these four sets of eyes peeking out from behind their veils, only one goes with a "Duchenne" smile of sincere, spontaneous joy. Of the others, one belongs with a neutral expression, one with condescension and one with anger. Which is which?

A

B

C

D

On the following page the full faces are revealed down the right-hand side of the page. Only one configuration of the muscles creates the Duchenne smile. The difference is in the use of the orbicularis oculi muscle around the eye (see illustration at left), which is the only reliable indicator of sincere joy. Do the smiling mouths on the faces down the right-hand side of the following page change the way you perceive the true emotion expressed?

(cont'd on next page)

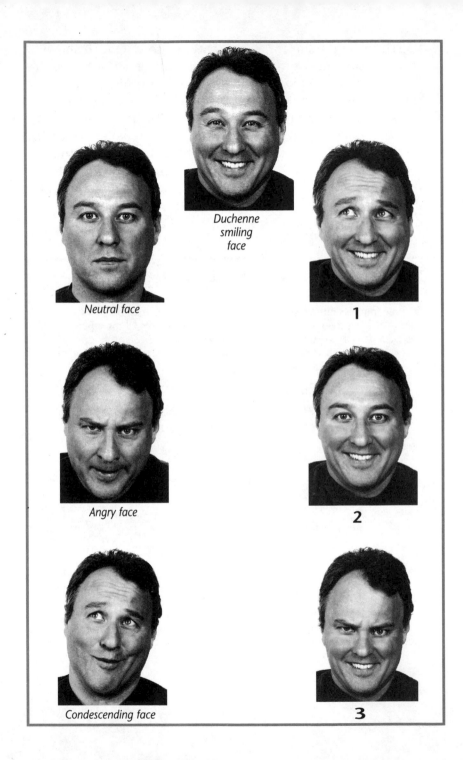

Duchenne smiling face

Neutral face

1

Angry face

2

Condescending face

3

DHEA, a recently tested hormone supplement, may make the aging feel young again

A hitherto mysterious hormone currently stands in the center of a hotly contested battle between competing financial, medical, and intellectual interests, as the medical community tests claims for its ability to cure ills ranging from cancer to depression, and even to reverse the biological process of aging itself. The hormone, which is being promoted as a dietary-supplement wonder drug in health-food stores and even over the Internet, is dehydroepiandrosterone, better known as DHEA.

What is DHEA?

DHEA (and its apparently equivalent "sulfated" twin DHEA(S)) is a hormone produced in the adrenal glands of primates — humans, apes, and monkeys — and a few other species. In humans and apes, levels of the hormone rise sharply during puberty and peak during young adulthood; from then on, DHEA(S) levels drop inexorably until, in old age, only negligible levels are present in the blood.

Why the drop? No one knows for sure. We do know that DHEA is metabolized into sex steroids by various tissues of the body. But that is probably only a small part of the story.

A boost to mood, energy, and memory

In a recent pilot study, middle-aged to elderly men and women with major depressive illness were given DHEA supplements for four weeks. All the patients showed significant mood improvement according to the standard testing instruments, as well as improvements in verbal memory. When treatment was withdrawn, depression and memory returned to their previous levels.

In another recent double-blind experimental study, half of a group of subjects aged 40 to 70 were given pills containing DHEA, while the other half were given placebos. Over 75% of the subjects taking the hormone pill (but less than 10% of the placebo group) reported an improved sense of youthful well-being, including better sleep, more energy, and an enhanced feeling of relaxation and ability to deal with stress. A significant percentage of the DHEA group also reported "marked improvements" in joint pain, stiffness, and soreness. Libido, alas, remained unchanged.

Other studies have shown a correlation between Alzheimer's disease and low DHEA(S) levels. This may be due to the hormone's action against glucocorticoids, which appear to have the potential to cause brain-cell damage. (See "Cortisol," p. 209.)

DHEA as a protector against heart disease and cancer

Several studies have shown a correlation between low levels of DHEA and coronary-artery disease. Administration of DHEA supplements appears to inhibit blood platelet aggregation, and hence to lower the risk of heart attack or stroke. DHEA may also play a role in boosting the immune system: low DHEA levels appear to be correlated with some kinds of cancer, and DHEA supplements can boost production of cancer-fighting "natural killer" cells.

Do we have to grow frail as we grow old?

All of this has intriguing implications. Many of the things that we think of as inevitable by-products of aging — depressed mood, lower energy, memory loss, and increased risk for heart disease and cancer — may result from a correctable drop in naturally produced chemical substances. Why are DHEA levels so high in early adulthood, and why are they so low in old age? It may simply have to do with natural selection for an organism that uses up all its energy and libido in a youthful period of maximal productivity, rather than for an organism that maintains its energy over a long lifetime.

Would it be wrong to override this long-evolved pattern by taking hormone supplements? If DHEA pills are used as a substitute for good old-fashioned physical exercise and self-challenging mental activity, probably so. On the other hand, consider these questions:

Does the fact that most adult humans reduce or stop production of the enzyme lactase, required for the digestion of dairy products, mean that it is "wrong" or "unnatural" to take lactase pills when we eat cheese or drink milk? Or, more dramatically: Does the fact that some humans have an inability to produce insulin mean that diabetics should simply be left to die?

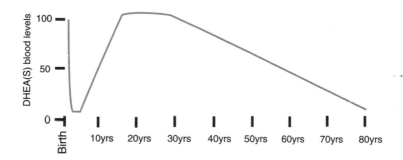

Levels of DHEA(S), the more prevalent "sulfated" form of DHEA, drop dramatically after birth, begin to rise again at about age 7 or 8, peak during the twenties, and then decline steadily.

EXERCISE: A case of confused identity

Part 1.

In the former Soviet Bloc country of "Borduria," someone has committed a series of grisly murders. The culprit has been identified and apprehended — with a couple of hitches. First, the murderer has been identified by an eyewitness, but the identified individual happens to have an identical twin brother. Both are sitting in jail, but nobody knows which one is the real murderer. Under Bordurian law, unless some evidence points decisively to one or the other having committed the murders, both must be set free. Also under Bordurian law, the state prosecutor may ask each suspect only one yes/no question to ascertain his guilt or innocence. However, here's another hitch: one brother is a consistent pathological liar, and the other brother tells nothing but the truth, but nobody knows whether the murderer is a liar or a truth teller.

Prosecutor Multinovic thinks he's figured out what question to ask each of the twins. To each in turn, he poses the following query:

"Did your brother commit the murders?"

Will this question lead him to the murderer?

Part 2.

In response to his question, Multinovic gets a response of "Yes" from the first brother, and "No" from the second.

What can the prosecutor conclude from these answers?

Part 3.

Due to his incompetence, Multinovic is replaced as prosecutor by his assistant Plavac. Under Bordurian law, a suspected murderer may be asked a second yes/no question by a new prosecutor — but the new prosecutor may assume no prior knowledge of the answers to any questions asked by a former prosecutor. In other words, Plavac must start from scratch.

If you were Plavac, what would you ask the twins? Remember, only one question is permitted for each suspect, but the question needn't remain the same from one suspect to another.

Hint: Don't forget that one brother *always* lies, even if it is to his disadvantage. What if in Part 2, the witness were mistaken or both brothers implicated? When you get to Part 3 it would help to start out by asking a question which you and the brothers know the truthful answer to.

A type of logic puzzle that often applies to real-life situations

There are relatively few different formats into which most so-called logic puzzles fit. The characters and situations within which they interact change, but the basic pattern repeats. Once that key is known it is often possible to spot a similar pattern in a dilemma a person must face in reality.

The type of logic puzzle represented by the following brain twisters is as old, probably, as the human cortex. "Familial dilemma" is a variant of the old farmer, fox, goose, and grain chestnut, which we've included in its historically original version on the following page. The "Anders" puzzle is different in detail and structure, but involves essentially the same kind of thinking.

We hope you won't ever find yourself facing these specific situations. The solutions (there are more than one) require a slight reversal of standard procedures. That is why these puzzles translate into real-life situations so applicably.

Like most logic puzzles that require the ability to plan ahead, the solution comes more easily if one can clearly visualize alternative situations. Then it is necessary to hold each of those mini-scenes in mind long enough to evaluate their consequences before retaining or discarding them.

EXERCISE: A familial dilemma

Antonio has invited his mother and mother-in-law to meet at his house so he and his wife can take them to dinner at a nearby restaurant. Since he has the only car, Antonio must drive them all to the restaurant. There are, however, some complications. His car is a Fiat two-seater convertible, so he can only take one passenger at a time. Also, his mother-in-law doesn't get along very well with his mother, and his wife and his mother have a rather tense relationship as well, so he can't leave his mother alone with either his wife or his mother-in-law at any point, either at home or at the restaurant. How can he shuttle them over to the restaurant one at a time and avoid leaving two people who dislike each other alone together? (He cannot leave anyone at a third location either.) (See "Hint," p. 38.)

EXERCISE: Fox, goose, and grain

A "familial dilemma" is a variant of the old farmer, fox, goose, and grain riddle. It goes like this:

A farmer wants to ferry a fox, a goose, and a sack of grain across a river. However, his boat is only big enough to hold one at a time. If he leaves the fox and goose alone together on either bank, the fox will eat the goose. If he leaves the goose and the grain together, the goose will eat the grain.

How can he get all three to the other side?

Hint for a familial dilemma: There are a couple of possible answers, but they both require this: Since Antonio gets along with all three women, but one of them can't get along with either of the other two, what he must do is spend most of his time with that one woman and never leave her alone with either of the others.

EXERCISE: Anders' dilemma

Anders Andert Anderson is off to an outpost in Alaska that is a six-day hike from Shungnak across a desolate expanse of snow and ice. One man can lug only sufficient food and water for four days. As you can see, one man can't go alone because his supplies wouldn't last until he reached his destination. How many people would it take carrying supplies to assure that Anders reaches the outpost and his assistants make it back to Shungnak?

Hint: No matter how many people start out at Shungnak, only Anders has to arrive at the outpost. But remember: Even assistants need to eat, so make sure the others have enough food and water to get them home.

EXERCISE: Menu please

Five old friends had a reunion at their favorite restaurant. Each man ordered something to drink, an entree, and a dessert. John and Mr. Jackson had martinis, and James and Mr. Jones ordered scotch. Mr. Jenkins had cola since he was driving. John and Mr. Jennings ordered steak. Joe and Mr. Jenkins had roast beef. For dessert Joe and Mr. Jordan ate chocolate cake, while Jerry and Mr. Jenkins had pie. The other man had ice cream. No two men sitting next to each other were served two things the same. Who had pheasant and what did Jake eat?

Hint: The location and name of each man has been given here:
1, Jackson; 2, Jones; 3, Jordan; 4, Jenkins; 5, Jennings.

How to make yourself feel happier without drugs

As every actor knows, the facial expression and body language depicting any emotion can be faked. The emotional response itself, however, is usually not in the control of the person experiencing it. Emotional arousal is usually subconscious, even though many of the outward manifestations of arousal can be modified consciously by the cortex.

There is strong evidence that people are able to change mood by changing their facial expression, posture, and style of movement to reflect a different emotion from the one they are currently feeling. If someone feels depressed, for example, they can try to look and behave as if they were happy — the result will be that they actually begin to *feel* happier. The patterns of muscle and nerve action that produce an expression of happiness, in this example, also trigger other neurological changes that help a person feel happier in reality.

One element of facial expression that is a tip-off to emotional arousal is difficult to counterfeit but is easily observed by another person. Research on emotional response mechanisms conducted at the University of Chicago in the 1960's under the direction of Eckhard Hess revealed that the dark pupil in the center of the human eye grows larger when that person's interest has been aroused. Like many other physical symptoms of emotional arousal, including those measured by lie-detector polygraphs — increased heart rate, perspiration, skin temperature, for example — changes in the size of the pupil are not under the conscious control of the individual.

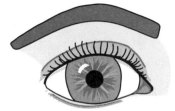 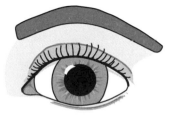

SELF-TEST: Interested?

Most people think that a look of aroused interest makes a person appear more attractive to others. To test this theory for yourself, look at the two faces below and select the one which appears more attractive to you, the one on the top or on the bottom.

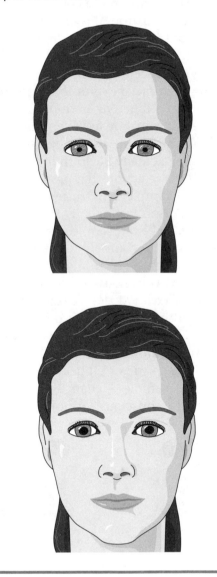

Hint: Pupils of the eyes grow larger when a person is aroused by emotional interest.

The night a middle-aged man tackled his bureau in his sleep

In a recent study, brain scans of subjects moving a joystick in a certain pattern or simply imagining moving it in the same pattern revealed that about 80% of the circuitry used when physically moving the joystick is also used in the purely imaginary exercise. This shows that mentally picturing a physical action such as swinging a golf club or playing the piano activates most of the brain circuits used when actually performing the action, thus strengthening the brain cell connections needed for expert performance (see "What is the brain so busy doing...?" p. 177).

The role of REM sleep in reinforcing learned behaviors

In REM sleep (a phase during normal sleep in which the eyeballs move rapidly beneath the closed lids), we act out movements mentally but not physically. Normally, neurons in the spinal cord that send messages to the muscles are shut down. This makes it physically impossible to move our bodies in response to signals from the brain stem, which sends messages to muscles. (A middle-aged man with a neurological disorder is reported to have injured himself by tackling his chest of drawers while replaying a college football game in his sleep — probably during the REM phase.)

Dreaming rehearses new experiences to aid recall of them when needed

Given that the proportion of REM sleep in the sleep cycle is increased during periods of particularly active learning of new tasks, dreaming and learning seem to be linked. We've probably all had the experience of performing some repetitive physical task all day long — typing, running a cash register, house painting, sandblasting, or what have you — only to dream about performing that very same task that night after we fall asleep. Those dreams may be serving the function of reinforcing the cell connections needed to perform the task even more fluidly and effortlessly in the future, whether we want to or not!

Why are dreams so "fantastic"?

The key to understanding the strange nature of dreams, say many researchers, lies in two different sets of neurons in the primitive brain stem which release two different kinds of chemical signal.

One set releases "adrenergic" chemicals (chemicals which interact with adrenaline and adrenaline-sensitive neural receptors), which keep the mind alert, attentive, and free from stray images. These neurons are active when we're awake, but shut down when we're asleep.

The other set releases "cholinergic" chemicals (which interact with acetylcholine and acetylcholine-sensitive receptors). These chemicals stimulate the body's motor centers, emotional centers, and information-processing centers. While cholinergic neurons are active during the day, they kick into high gear when we fall asleep, sending bursts of impulses from the brain stem up into the brain's higher regions.

When the motor centers are stimulated, we visualize all kinds of movements which we would physically act out if not for the fact that the brain also sends a signal to the spinal cord which paralyzes all our muscles except for our eyes. That's why we don't (normally) thrash out or run around while we dream, and why the dream period of sleep is associated with rapid eye movement (hence the term "REM sleep" for the phase during which we're most likely to dream).

The cholinergic chemicals' stimulation of the brain's emotional regions explains the frequency of anxiety dreams and nightmares, as well as our common dream experiences of eroticism, anger, and uplifting joy.

Why dreams often serve up such valuable insights

Perhaps the most intriguing part is the stimulation of the brain's information-processing centers. This is what accounts for the unique logic and coherence of dreams. Due in part to the suppression of the parts of our brain sensitive to adrenergic chemicals, the content of dreams seems diametrically opposed to the lines of reasoning we follow when alert and focused. As the brain stem releases its bursts of cholinergic chemicals, our stimulated information-processing centers strive to make sense out of the images generated, free of the fetters of focused concentration.

This is also why some of our most creative insights occur to us in dreams, and why scientists and artists so often attain the solution to a vexing problem while dreaming. It's not that we're more or less "smart" while we dream. Our dream intelligence is just different: more associative, more integrative, and less linear. As anyone who has watched the movie *The Last Wave* knows, many cultures believe that we ignore our dreams, and the insights gained in them, to our own peril.

Dreams and madness

That's why dreams hold such fascination for us. They give us insight into what it must be like to be a different kind of person, or even a different kind of animal. They give us glimpses of what the world may be like from the perspective of a creature that is intelligent but bizarrely lacking in self-awareness. They show us, too, how the world may look through the eyes of an insane person. In fact, some schizophrenics have an overabundance of cholinergic neurons, which may explain the hallucinations characteristic of that mental illness.

EXERCISE: Feynman's real-life exercise in dream control

The following account describes one person's successful attempt not only to control the content of his dreams, but to *see* color and *feel* sensation at will. The object of this exercise is to be inspired to try it yourself.

As a young undergraduate at MIT, the physicist Richard Feynman had a real-life waking experience of the sort of thing that runs as an anxiety motif through the dreams of countless college students and former college students. At the end of a year-long philosophy class in which he had failed to understand a single thing the professor had said, he was assigned to write an essay about what the professor had been lecturing about all year. He was at a loss until he remembered that the professor had once mentioned the term "stream of consciousness." So he decided to write about dreams.

Feynman approached the assignment as any good scientist would: not just through introspection, but through observation. The first thing he did was to observe himself during the process of falling asleep. He discovered that his internal monologues and visualizations became utterly illogical as he drifted toward sleep. He had never noticed that before simply because he had never before paid any attention. Of course, the fact of making this observation would wake him back up, so he decided to move on to other things.

Next, with enough practice he learned the trick of observing himself while he dreamed. He found that the "seeing department" of the brain could produce images as lucid and detailed as any visualization involving real external stimuli. He observed himself dreaming in color. (Do you? How do you know?) He learned that if he wanted, he could see each single hair on the head of a woman lying beside him in the dream, and that he could even reproduce the rainbow effect of the sun diffracting off the follicles. (Can you dream that vividly? How do you know?) He learned, by running his dream-finger over a dream-thumbtack, that the "feeling department" of the brain can also re-create vivid tactile sensations despite the lack of any sensory input. Not only that, he learned he could turn off one "department" at will while leaving the other one on — make the thumbtack disappear, but run his finger over the spot where it had been and still feel it.

He found, to his delight, that he could manipulate the content of his dreams at will.

How self-conscious are you?

When asked to rate their own sociability, most people's self-reports are very different from what an observer will report about their behavior in a social situation. When seated in front of a mirror, however, people tend to be much more accurate in their self-reports. In social interactions, people's tendency to view themselves as responsible for what happens during the interaction will also increase if they can see their own reflection in a mirror. When people are provoked to anger, they'll react more aggressively if they are made self-aware by seeing a reflection of themselves.

If you are rejected do you think it must be *your* failure?

Some people seem to view themselves as if a mirror were always present. If they're rejected by someone at a party, they're especially likely to hold themselves responsible for the rejection. If they give a work presentation that isn't well received, they'll consider themselves to have failed rather than viewing the audience as unreceptive. If they're provoked to anger, they'll respond more emotionally than will others who spend less time mulling over their own internal state. These people, high in self-consciousness, go through much of their life as if they were viewing their own reflection in a mirror.

Many theorists have considered what we loosely call self-consciousness to be best broken down into at least two components: private self-consciousness and public self-consciousness. Private self-consciousness is roughly what we might otherwise refer to as self-awareness or introversion: a focusing on one's internal states, moods, and motives. Public self-consciousness has more to do with others' views and evaluations. Private self-consciousness may be a prerequisite for public self-consciousness, but you can be privately self-conscious without being very preoccupied about other people's responses to you. Finally, public self-consciousness may or may not lead to social anxiety: a frequent sense of apprehension about other people's views and reactions to oneself in a social situation.

SELF-TEST: Self-consciousness inventory

Answer the following questions to determine your degrees of public self-consciousness, private self-consciousness and social anxiety. At the end of the "Self-Test," total the points as shown in the "Scoring" box.

1. You're introduced to a young woman at a party. She mentions that she works at a hospital. You ask if she's a nurse. She turns red and responds that she's a doctor. You

(a) *feel very embarrassed about your social blunder (2 pts.)*

(b) *feel amused by the blunder, and/or evaluate the young woman as insecure (0 pts.)*

2. Do you spend a lot of time trying to figure out the reasons you've chosen the career you have, why you give money to some people on the street but not others, and generally what your motives are for acting as you do?

(a) *Yes, very much (2 pts.)*

(b) *Rarely (0 pts.)*

3. When you're buying something at the supermarket, do you like to make small talk with the checker, even if you've never seen him or her before?

(a) *Rarely (2 pts.)*

(b) *Often (0 pts.)*

4. Do you spend a lot of time trying to figure yourself out?

(a) *Yes, very much (2 pts.)*

(b) *No, that's a waste of time (0 pts.)*

5. When you're walking down a commercial street, do you look at your reflection in the plate-glass windows of the shops you pass by?

(a) *Yes, frequently (2 pts.)*

(b) *No (0 pts.)*

(cont'd on next page)

6. Do you think a lot about how you present yourself to others?

(a) Yes (2 pts.)

(b) No, that's not very important to me (0 pts.)

7. Do you spend a lot of time trying to figure out the origins of aspects of your personality or behavior that make you less happy or successful than you otherwise might be?

(a) Yes (2 pts.)

(b) No (0 pts.)

8. Are you often anxious speaking to large groups?

(a) Yes (2 pts.)

(b) No, that's a sign of immaturity (0 pts.)

9. When you're leaving the house, do you take a look in the mirror before walking out the door?

(a) Yes, usually (2 pts.)

(b) Not normally (0 pts.)

10. Do you often worry about making a good impression on others?

(a) Yes (2 pts.)

(b) No (0 pts.)

11. In new situations, are you often shy or inhibited at first?

(a) Yes, and it takes me a while to overcome it (2 pts.)

(b) No, what's the point? (0 pts.)

12. I'm usually aware of changes in my mood.

(a) Yes (2 pts.)

(b) I don't think so (0 pts.)

(cont'd on next page)

Scoring:

For your **private self-consciousness score** add your point totals for questions 2, 4, 7, and 12.

High: 6-8 pts.
Average: 4 pts.
Low: 0-2 pts.

For your **public self-consciousness score** add your points for questions 5, 6, 9, and 10.

High: 6-8 pts.
Average: 4 pts.
Low: 0-2 pts.

For your **social anxiety score** add your points for questions 1, 3, 8, and 11.

High: 6-8 pts.
Average: 4 pts.
Low: 0-2 pts.

If you're immoral and lazy, you may not be able to blame that on your parents

If there were any part of our mind we'd think was all "nurture" as opposed to "nature," it would be whatever part houses morality and social conscience. The next likely candidate for behavior that is learned rather than inborn might be such executive functions as self-monitoring, planning, and manipulation of oneself and others to achieve some desired goal. However, even these vaunted higher human faculties develop by way of an interaction between environment, in particular nurturing styles of the infant's caregiver, and inborn tendencies. Here's one model that explains how it works.

Individual differences in temperament begin to show themselves at a very young age. Even newborns exhibit different levels of distress, and different degrees of frustration and fear as these emotions emerge during the first few months of development. (In fact, one of the five physiological indicators of shyness is evident even before birth: Children who turn out to be shy have a higher-than-average heart rate in the womb.) At about six months of age, infants learn to approach and interact with their environment in a more positive way — they learn so-called approach-related behavior. Shortly thereafter, infants begin to learn to inhibit their approach-related behavior, to control their interaction with things and people around them through effort of will. This learning process continues through much of childhood and, arguably, beyond.

EEG readings show different baseline levels of activation of the "motivating" and "inhibiting" parts of the frontal lobes of the brains of infants, corresponding to differences in the degree to which they are characterized as "inhibited," "shy," or "anxious." Even though all infants enter a period of "behavioral inhibition" at around the same age (seven months), some infants just seem to be more predisposed than others to view their environment with caution.

Are some temperaments "good," and others "bad"?
From one perspective, it's wrong to view temperament in absolute terms. A given temperament may translate into a well or poorly adjusted individual depending on how well matched

that temperament is with the demands and expectations of others — a concept sometimes referred to as "goodness of fit." Different societies place different values on different temperamental profiles, and different occupations or subcultures may reward or punish temperament types at variance with the norms of the dominant culture.

On a developmental level, what this means is that an infant's innate temperamental predisposition will tend to elicit a different response from the mother or caregiver depending on the culture or individual temperament of the mother herself. Distress-prone infants tend to develop different personalities depending on whether their mothers are German or Japanese, since German mothers are more likely to expect their children to deal with emotional challenges on their own.

We can only go so far, however, in our liberal-minded relativism. All humans, regardless of culture, have a negative biological stress-response to the sound of a screeching baby. To a point, this serves a useful purpose, since it elicits attempts to soothe, comfort, and bond. But too much screeching can also cause a mother to avoid or even dislike her baby. Regardless of culture, distress-prone infants whose mothers avoid or dislike them are far more likely to become maladjusted than those whose mothers respond with soothing behavior. The child's future behavior is influenced by the reactions elicited by its inborn temperament, and certain temperaments tend to carry with them inherent risks.

A little anxiety is a good thing...

If a child were somehow unable to learn to inhibit his or her impulses, he or she would have serious problems later in life in almost any culture. While guilt, shame, and anxiety may *seem* to be unhealthy traits in a child, they are in fact helpful in the learning of effortful self-regulation and the acquisition of moral behavior.

If a child has a highly active "anxiety" center in the right frontal lobe, then she may well be quicker to learn this process of self-regulation. She may also, of course, grow up to be a social phobic. It is no coincidence that phobics and obsessive-compulsives tend to be empathetic and highly sensitive to the needs and feelings of others.

On the other hand, if the child has low baseline activation levels of the right-frontal "anxiety" center, and a high threshold for anxiety, guilt, and shame, it seems to be much more difficult for him to develop impulse control, a social conscience, and moral standards of behavior. (The choice of masculine gender for this child, and feminine gender for the overly anxious one, is not arbitrary; boys and girls seem to have a tendency to differ along these lines.)

Again, temperament doesn't determine morality; it just carries with it certain predispositions and risks. A child who is anxious and inhibited by nature won't develop a strong social conscience in the absence of appropriate models in the environment — a caregiver who helps her understand the consequences of her actions, and the reasons why she should or shouldn't do certain things. And even a child with an extraordinarily high threshold for anxiety and guilt can internalize moral standards if the caregiver treats him with patience and understanding, rather than simply punishing, threatening, or ignoring him.

...but too much anxiety is bad

Given the relationship between anxiety or inhibition, and the development not only of morality but also of executive functions of self-regulation, attention, and planning, one might suppose that anxious infants might be more likely to develop into high-achieving adults. It does seem to be true that young children who have a highly developed faculty of effortful self-control perform better scholastically when they get older. On the other hand, children who are *too* anxious may develop an avoidant behavioral style, and may be so preoccupied with monitoring imagined threats that they have difficulty focusing their attention on complex new information.

EXERCISE: Frontal lobe logic

One ability associated with the frontal lobe of the brain is that of holding one option in your mind while you track its sequential entailments. Remembering options is a crucial prerequisite to forecasting the consequences of your actions and planning and manipulating future events.

Part 1.

The CEO of a certain Silicon Valley corporation was faced with a familiar problem of the times: downsizing.

"We have to cut our payroll in half," he explained to his assistant. "But how do I make sure the ones I lay off won't return the favor with an Uzi? There's a lot of that going around, you know."

"No problem," replied the assistant, who knew a thing or two about both logic and human psychology. "Don't lay anyone off. Let them lay themselves off. That way they can't blame you. Just let me handle it."

The assistant invited each employee into her office, one by one. As each employee entered, the assistant explained that she had on her desk two envelopes. One contained a pink slip, while the other contained a contract renewal.

"All you have to do," she would tell each employee with a wink, "is pick the right one."

"How do I know which is which?" the employee would ask.

"Simple. Just read what's written on the envelopes."

The envelopes had the following instructions:

Envelope A

Pick me! I have a contract renewal inside me.

Envelope B

Either I or the other envelope contains a pink slip.

(cont'd on next page)

"Are these instructions true and accurate?" the employee would ask.

"Only one," the assistant would reply.

"Which one?"

"If I told you that," the assistant would answer in an admonishing tone, *"then I would be denying you the opportunity to prove your value to the company. If you can't figure it out on your own, then surely you don't deserve a contract renewal."*

If you were the employee, which envelope would you choose, and why? (See "Hint," p. 56.)

Part 2.

The next day, the CEO was still not satisfied.

"You've given ten employees a shot at your puzzle, and they've all picked the correct envelope. I don't think you're making it hard enough."

So the assistant agreed to crank it up a notch. Now, she explained to each employee that she had two envelopes; both might contain pink slips, or both might contain contract renewals; or one might contain a pink slip and the other a contract renewal. She presented one of the envelopes with her left hand, and one with her right. If the left-hand envelope contained a contract renewal, the instructions on the envelope would be correct, but if it contained a pink slip, the instructions would be wrong. For the right-hand envelope, if a contract renewal was inside, the instructions would be false; if a pink slip was inside, the instructions would be true.

The envelopes had the following instructions:

Left Envelope

It doesn't make any difference which envelope you pick.

Right Envelope

The other envelope has a contract renewal inside.

(cont'd on next page)

If you were the employee, which envelope would you choose, and why?

Part 3.

The third day, the CEO was even more agitated.

"Twenty employees have now had a shot at your puzzle, and they've all passed! This is not helping me solve my payroll problem. You have to make the puzzle harder!"

The assistant thought for a moment.

"The remaining employees are all very smart. I don't know whether I can make the puzzle hard enough. And even if one or two should make a mistake, the payroll won't be cut in half. There is, however, one solution I haven't tried yet."

"By all means then, try it. And if it hasn't worked by the close of tomorrow's stockholders' meeting," the CEO added with a threatening glare, "I know of at least one head that will roll!"

At the next day's meeting, the assistant rose to explain the problem to the assembled major shareholders. She concluded her presentation with the following remarks:

"As yet, our payroll is still twice what it should be. The problem is, all the employees so far have been too smart to pick the pink slip. However, the shareholders will observe," she said, gesturing with a pointer to a piechart she had prepared the night before, "that half the payroll is taken by the salary of a single executive."

The CEO blanched.

"If," she continued, "we could find a legitimate way to rectify this situation, then our payroll problems would be instantly solved. I therefore propose to present the hardest puzzle yet to the one who makes the most money: the CEO!"

The assembled shareholders murmured their approval.

Turning to the CEO, the assistant explained as follows:

"I have here, sir, three envelopes."

(cont'd on next page)

Hint for Part 1: The crucial piece of information is that only one envelope has correct instructions. Given this, only one answer is possible — and it's not the same answer you'd otherwise expect.

"Three envelopes!" exclaimed the CEO. "That's not fair! The others only had to choose between two!"

"True, but you told me to make the puzzle harder. And," the assistant added with a sly wink, "surely you're at least 50% smarter than the rank and file. After all, you earn fifty times as much."

The CEO glared, but held his tongue.

"Of these three envelopes," continued the assistant, "one contains a contract renewal. The others contain pink slips. As usual, each envelope has a statement written on it. No more than one is true. Which envelope do you choose?"

The three envelopes had the following statements:

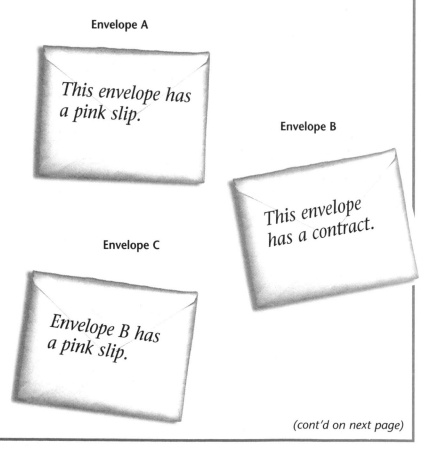

Envelope A

This envelope has a pink slip.

Envelope B

This envelope has a contract.

Envelope C

Envelope B has a pink slip.

(cont'd on next page)

Which envelope would you choose, and why?

Part 4.

By the end of the meeting, the company's payroll problems were solved and the shareholders went home happy.

The final puzzle: Did the CEO choose the right envelope?

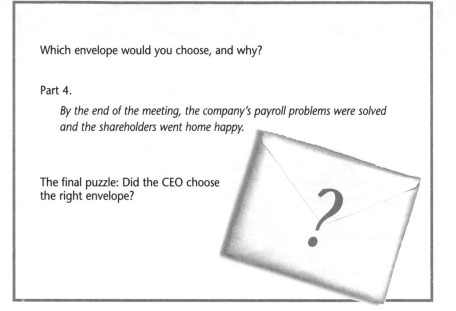

Hint: The shareholders were so pleased with the assistant's solution that they promoted her to the recently vacated CEO position.

EXERCISE: If-then thinking

if...then

Here are five statements:

1. *Only one of these statements is false.*

2. *Only two of these statements are false.*

3. *Only three of these statements are false.*

4. *Only four of these statements are false.*

5. *All five of these statements are false.*

Which, if any, of the statements is true?

"Show me the child at seven and I'll show you the man": a genetic clue to personality

Midwives often claim to be able to predict the temperament of a child as soon as it is out of the birth canal. Those who prefer to believe in the malleability and improvability of human character reject such notions out of hand; personality, they argue, is influenced by environment, not determined by genetics. It turns out that they're both right. New evidence confirms that some aspects of personality — those aspects traditionally referred to as "temperament" — are indeed strongly molded by our genes. Other aspects — what we might call "character" — are more a product of upbringing, environment, and values we choose for ourselves in a self-willed process of emotional maturation. Together, both sets of components contribute to our personality as a whole. (See "If you're immoral and lazy...," p. 51.)

Four inherited "temperaments" and three learned "characters"
One version of this model of personality, developed by Robert Cloninger at Washington University of St. Louis, posits four basic building blocks of temperament, and at least three dimensions of character. The four building blocks of temperament are *novelty seeking, harm avoidance, reward dependence*, and *persistence*. The three character dimensions are *self-directedness, cooperativeness*, and *self-transcendence* (as opposed to self-centeredness). The four temperaments tend to be stable from childhood to adulthood and constant across cultures, while the three character dimensions may change significantly in a manner that appears to be influenced by environmental factors. Overall, based in part on studies of twins, it is estimated that about 50% of what we call personality is genetically determined.

Do you have a "novelty seeking" temperament?
Each of the four temperament variables is associated with different structures in the brain and different brain chemicals. Novelty seeking is

modulated by the neurotransmitter dopamine, which is linked to pleasure-seeking behavior. Patients with Parkinson's disease, which is marked by a depletion of dopamine in the brain's basal ganglia, become rigid, stoic, and uninterested in novelty, but remain otherwise unchanged in temperament. People high in novelty-seeking behavior tend to have a higher-than-average tendency to indulge in alcohol, nicotine, and cocaine, which stimulate dopamine transmission in the brain. Harm avoidance is associated with the neurotransmitter serotonin, while reward dependence is modulated by norepinephrine.

Recent research has even identified specific genes which contribute to novelty-seeking behavior and to harm avoidance. The novelty-seeking gene, which encodes the instructions for one of five dopamine receptors in the brain, tends to be longer in individuals who habitually seek the thrill of adventure. They are impulsive, quick to latch onto new ideas, and equally quick to become bored with them, and are impatient with structure and monotony. The harm-avoidance gene, which is involved in serotonin regulation, also comes in two versions, with the more common version predisposing most of us to chronic but mild anxiety — part of the typical human condition. The less common variant — a "natural Prozac," as it were — contributes to an unusually cheerful and outgoing temperament.

Taken one by one, low or high values for the four different temperament variables correspond to different personality traits. (See "Self-Test" on following pages.) Anyone may have high, low, or average values for each.

Each one of these parameters varies independently of the others, and different combinations yield different behavioral tendencies. Someone high in novelty seeking but low in harm avoidance will have a marked risk of self-destructive behavior such as alcohol abuse. High novelty seeking combined with high harm avoidance may give rise to conflicted or neurotic behavior, such as bulimia (binging and purging). In all cases, though, the contribution of "character" — those aspects of personality most strongly influenced by upbringing and environment — is crucial. For example, someone low in reward dependence — say, a nonconformist personally contemptuous of others' opinions — may still be high in cooperativeness and self-transcendence, and thus act with tolerance, respect, and compassion for others, and have high moral principles. Adolf Hitler didn't have bad temperament; he had bad character. Nobody is born evil.

SELF-TEST: The temperament identifier

High or low levels of the following four different outlooks on life are thought to be built into a person's genes at birth. Most people's temperaments show either high or low tendencies toward more than one of the outlooks. Do you assign the highs and lows to your own temperament the same way someone else does? The description below and charts on the following three pages provide a guide to the high vs. low relationships among the four genetically based temperaments identified by Robert Cloninger.

Novelty Seeking

> *High:* *Thrill-seeking, adventurous, disorderly, intuitive, impatient with structure, impulsive, histrionic, fickle with friendships.*

> *Low:* *Orderly and organized, self-controlled, analytical, detail-oriented, direct, loyal, stoic.*

Harm Avoidance

> *High:* *Anxious, pessimistic, inhibited, given to depression, easily fatigued.*

> *Low:* *Uninhibited, carefree even in the face of imminent risk, confident, optimistic, highly energetic.*

Reward Dependence

> *High:* *Dependent on the emotional support and feedback of others, highly sentimental, sensitive to social cues and the needs of others.*

> *Low:* *Socially detached, content to be alone, nonconformist, cynical, socially insensitive.*

Persistence

> *High:* *Eager, ambitious, determined.*

> *Low:* *Unambitious, uninterested in achievement.*

(cont'd on next page)

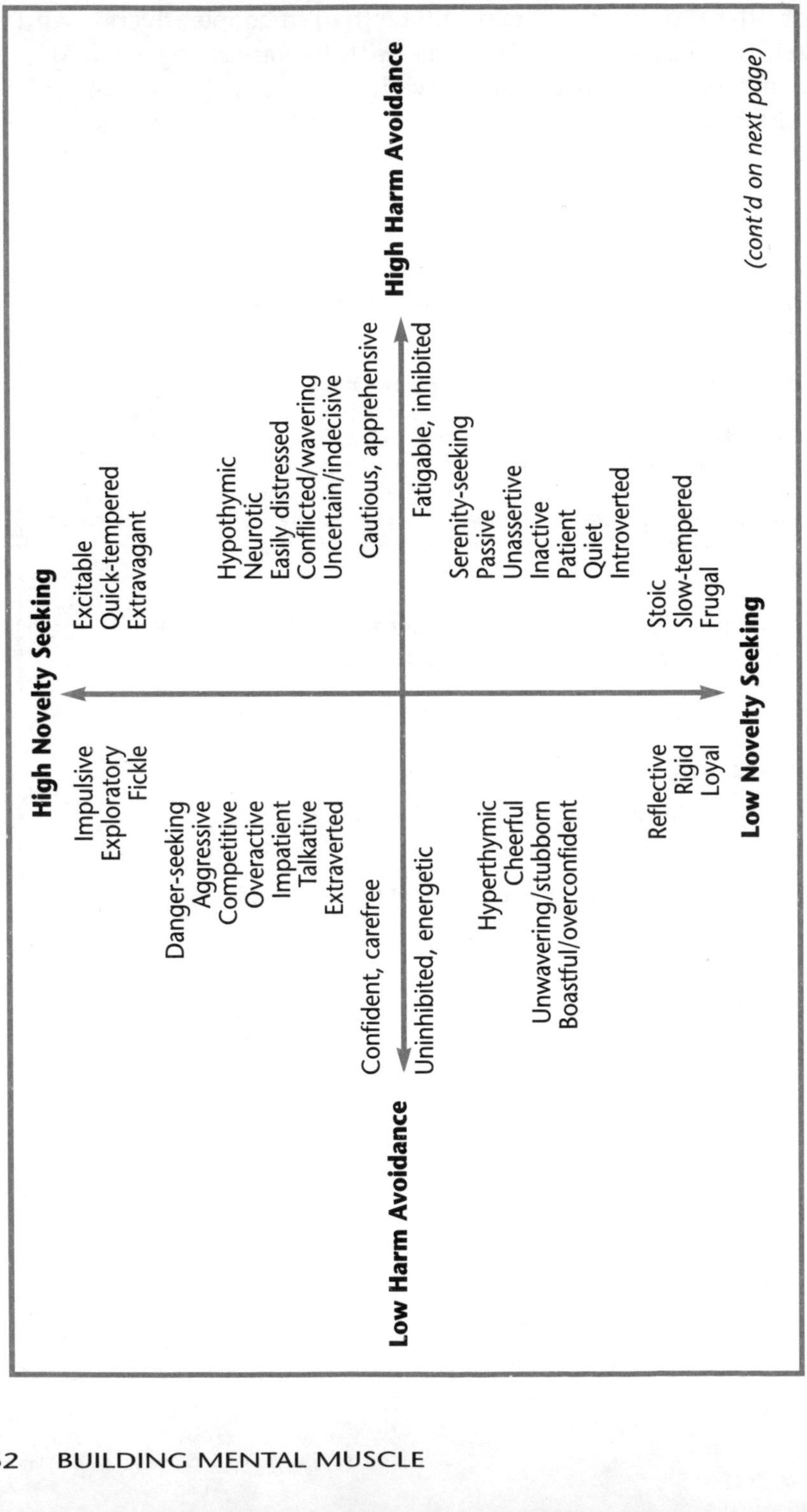

High Novelty Seeking

High Harm Avoidance

Top-left quadrant (High Novelty Seeking / Low Harm Avoidance):
- Impulsive
- Exploratory
- Fickle
- Danger-seeking
- Aggressive
- Competitive
- Overactive
- Impatient
- Talkative
- Extraverted
- Confident, carefree

Top-right quadrant (High Novelty Seeking / High Harm Avoidance):
- Excitable
- Quick-tempered
- Extravagant
- Hypothymic
- Neurotic
- Easily distressed
- Conflicted/wavering
- Uncertain/indecisive
- Cautious, apprehensive
- Fatigable, inhibited

Bottom-left quadrant (Low Novelty Seeking / Low Harm Avoidance):
- Uninhibited, energetic
- Hyperthymic
- Cheerful
- Unwavering/stubborn
- Boastful/overconfident
- Reflective
- Rigid
- Loyal

Bottom-right quadrant (Low Novelty Seeking / High Harm Avoidance):
- Serenity-seeking
- Passive
- Unassertive
- Inactive
- Patient
- Quiet
- Introverted
- Stoic
- Slow-tempered
- Frugal

Low Harm Avoidance

Low Novelty Seeking

(cont'd on next page)

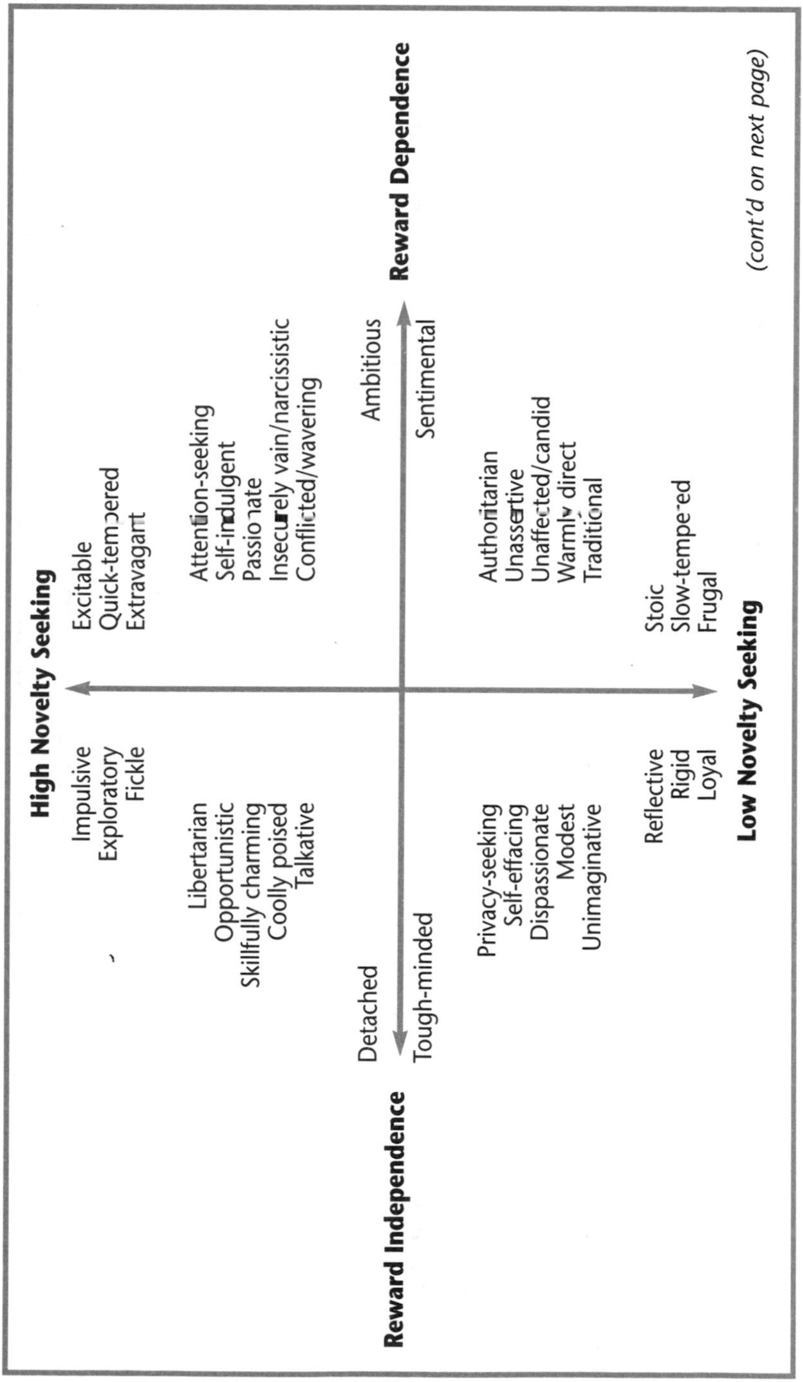

High Novelty Seeking

Reward Dependence

Reward Independence

Ambitious

Sentimental

Detached

Tough-minded

Excitable
Quick-tempered
Extravagant

Attention-seeking
Self-indulgent
Passionate
Insecurely vain/narcissistic
Conflicted/wavering

Authoritarian
Unassertive
Unaffected/candid
Warmly direct
Traditional

Stoic
Slow-tempered
Frugal

Impulsive
Exploratory
Fickle

Libertarian
Opportunistic
Skillfully charming
Coolly poised
Talkative

Privacy-seeking
Self-effacing
Dispassionate
Modest
Unimaginative

Reflective
Rigid
Loyal

Low Novelty Seeking

(cont'd on next page)

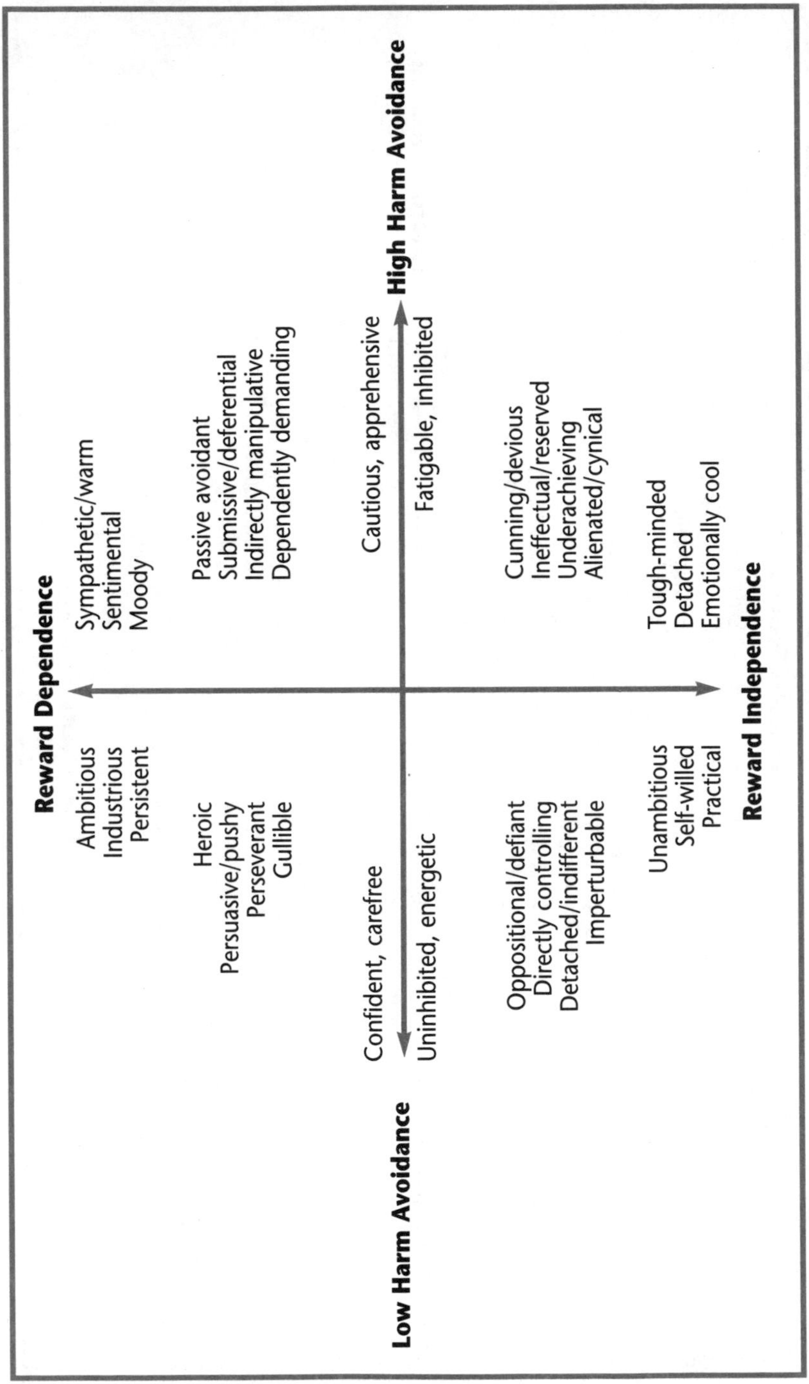

Reward Dependence

High Harm Avoidance

Sympathetic/warm
Sentimental
Moody

Passive avoidant
Submissive/deferential
Indirectly manipulative
Dependently demanding

Cautious, apprehensive

Fatigable, inhibited

Cunning/devious
Ineffectual/reserved
Underachieving
Alienated/cynical

Tough-minded
Detached
Emotionally cool

Reward Independence

Ambitious
Industrious
Persistent

Heroic
Persuasive/pushy
Perseverant
Gullible

Unambitious
Self-willed
Practical

Confident, carefree

Uninhibited, energetic

Oppositional/defiant
Directly controlling
Detached/indifferent
Imperturbable

Low Harm Avoidance

Physical exercise helps the brain grow more effective cells

Studies have shown a correlation between level of physical activity in the elderly and retention of mental function, but it hasn't been clear exactly what's causing what. Is the exercise somehow helping the brain to maintain its neurons in good working order, or does physical activity simply correlate with other factors which interact in some other way with mental function, such as level of education, diet, maintenance of a mentally active lifestyle, and so on?

New evidence points to a direct causal relationship. Physical exercise promotes production of a growth factor which plays a critical role in the function and survival of brain neurons. Experimental studies with rats show that the growth factor, brain-derived neurotrophic factor (BDNF), is not only increased with exercise, but may be selectively increased in parts of the brain associated with memory formation and the translation of cognition into action.

Rats like to run 1-2 K's a day (at their own pace)

In the experiment, rats were provided free access to running wheels; since rats seem inherently to enjoy physical activity, they automatically fell into a pattern of running 1-2 kilometers each night, with each rat choosing and consistently maintaining its own preferred activity level. The BDNF messenger RNA in various brain structures of the rats was measured following 0, 2, 4, and 7 nights of free access to the wheel. After two nights BDNF RNA was found to be significantly increased over control levels (i.e., the level before any exercise), and to remain elevated over the full seven-night period. Also, there was a positive correlation between distance run per night and BDNF RNA levels in the hippocampus and caudal neocortex.

One of the most exciting findings of the study is that the greatest effects of exercise on BDNF occur in precisely those highly "plastic," or changeable, areas implicated in degenerative age-related diseases

Exercise increases BDNF levels in the hippocampus, which in turn transports the growth factor to cholinergic neurons of the forebrain — a locus of Alzheimer's and similar age-related degeneration. The authors of the study from which the information in this article is drawn arrived at a finding with a practical application for everyone over 40 years old: *"Exercise-induced upregulation of BDNF could help increase the brain's resistance to damage and degeneration through BDNF's support of neuronal growth, function, and survival."*

As you age, physical debility is no more inevitable than mental dementia

In addition to increasing BDNF levels, exercises designed to build strength can help prevent premature loss of muscle tissue and can improve muscle strength, size, and endurance at any age. Calisthenics work muscles against resistance, which enables them to grow and maintain their tone. The benefits of such exercise also include improving reaction time, reducing the rate of muscle atrophy, increasing work capacity, and helping prevent back problems and injury.

Apparently an active life *and* attitude are common among humans who have lived to unusual ages

The following is a selective list of people who have lived long. Some of them are known primarily for other achievements. The fact that those people excelled suggests that they pursued the interests from which they took personal satisfaction and that they invested their energies in those interests aggressively and constantly through their lives. For example:

Red Grange, a famous football player and superb athlete, lived to the age of 87.

Pablo Picasso, the Spanish painter and sculptor, worked in his studio up to the age of 91.

Grandma Moses taught herself to paint quite late in life and continued until her death at 101.

Gabriel Erazo claimed to have worked in his garden every day until his death at 130.

Gabriel Sánchez, who farmed for 120 years, died at 135.

Zabo Agah lived more years than any of the above, and for 100 of his years he worked as a porter.

EXERCISE: On the fastest track

The 100-meter run in the Olympics is a thrill to watch. It is over in seconds and requires a young lifetime of unremitting training and constant physical conditioning. Over the last 100 years the time it takes to run 100 meters has steadily decreased by about 20%.

Examine the two columns below. One shows the dates of Olympic 100-meter races. The other shows the winning times, but their order is incorrect. After you have matched the times with the dates — an easy task — you will see that it took 54 years, between 1906 and 1960, to shave one second off the winning time. Assuming that same rate of improvement from the '84 Olympics, which broke ten seconds for the first time, in what year can we expect to see 100 meters run in less than nine seconds?

OLYMPIC YEARS	WINNING TIMES
1. 1896	A. 10.30 Seconds
2. 1906	B. 11.20 Seconds
3. 1920	C. 9.99 Seconds
4. 1932	D. 10.80 Seconds
5. 1960	E. 10.20 Seconds
6. 1984	F. 12.00 Seconds

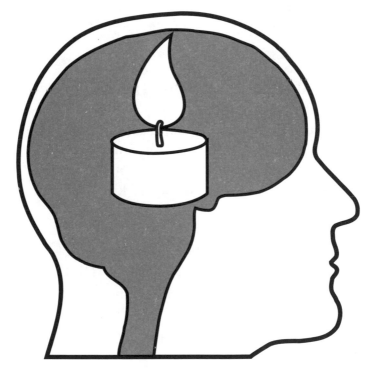

**memory
function**

MEMORY

Memory is a partner in developing all other mental skills. The key to learning is the brain's ability to convert a current experience into code and store it so, later, the experience can be recalled for your benefit. The brain codes some kinds of inputs from the senses permanently with no conscious effort on your part. It can also store other kinds of data because you consciously pass that data through a rehearsal loop repeatedly — which, incidentally, can also take place during sleep.

The brain codes some kinds of experiences indelibly, instantly, and without any conscious effort. It reads that kind of experience as so closely linked to raw survival that your conscious mind has to stand aside so instincts, which trigger emotions, can take over. Other, less crucial data earns permanent storage for its code by passing that experience through a rehearsal loop again and again. There is some evidence that is what dreams do. During sleep, while the cortex isn't busy sorting out data coming in through the senses, it can rehearse bits of recent experience to help them become permanent memories. Remember the multiplication tables?

And so, the more experiences the brain is exposed to, the more its cells send out branches from their axons and dendrites to link those cells with as many other cells as possible to help solve current problems. The more links that are available, the easier the brain can spot similarities between parts of a new experience and old experiences it already knows about. That way, the brain doesn't have to create all new codes to store the new experience — only the unfamiliar parts of it. Apparently it's true that the more you know, the easier it is to learn even more.

But first you must pay attention. If you don't focus your attention on new experiences they can never make it into memory. Fortunately, to life-threatening experiences, the brain pays close attention automatically without our having to focus consciously at all. It pays such close attention that when it thinks it has a crisis on its hands, it ignores anything else going on. That may explain why self-conscious people have difficulty noticing the forest around their own tree, so to speak.

However, when you use your short-term memory system to recall someone's name so you can say "good night" after a party, for example, you have to make an effort. Even when you look up a phone number just to dial it right away, you must concentrate to fix it in immediate memory even if you needn't rehearse it consciously or compare it with other data.

If short-term memory requires manipulation of the retained facts, such as when you have to remember how much something costs and how much money you've given the clerk in order to calculate how much change you should get back, it's called *working memory*. As we age, our ability to remember a phone number long enough to dial it stays about the same, but our working memory usually gets worse. Facts stored in short-term memory are usually forgotten, but they can sometimes be transferred into *long-term memory* for more or less permanent storage.

The new functional MRI scanning technology has given brain researchers studying working memory a tool that shows where in the brain different *kinds* of working memory are active — spatial, objective, verbal, analytic reasoning, etc. The brain reaches into long-term memory for data it needs to reason with by comparing it with other data. (For example, if someone tells you his graduating class and asks whether you were in front of or behind him in school, you pull your own graduating class date out of long-term memory and compare the dates in your working memory.) That work takes place in one of the sections of a band stretching across the front of your brain above your eyebrows. This is the area that is much more developed in humans than in apes. The same general zone is also activated when the Executive/Social intelligence is functioning.

Your "memory" is, in fact, many processes that occur in different parts of the brain

An injury to one part of the brain may affect the conscious recall of facts and events (declarative memory), while leaving intact various forms of unconscious (nondeclarative) memory, including skill and habit learning. It is even possible to show that someone with apparently complete amnesia for pictures shown to him only minutes earlier may nevertheless retain an accurate memory of them, as demonstrated by a tendency to pick out those same pictures from among other ones on a repeat showing. Part of the brain has registered and stored the images, even though another part of the brain can't bring that knowledge to conscious awareness. Recent studies have shown that a structure responsible for retrieving memories is the part of the medial temporal lobe called the hippocampus, which acts to bring together widely distributed sites in the brain in the formation of a conscious memory.

The brain stores the components of a personal experience near the senses that registered the event

Memories themselves — as opposed to the structures that retrieve them — seem often to be localized, with some redundancy, in the very same regions where the sensory perception of the related stimulus first occurred. The neurologist Oliver

When the senses pick up impressions from the outside world those inputs travel along neural pathways from the organ that took in the data to the section of the brain that interprets input from the eyes, or ears or nose or skin. From there the information is normally shunted to the hippocampus for short-term storage — a matter of weeks, usually. If the data seems to be important somehow — often because it is consciously rehearsed — the hippocampus sends code for the various aspects of that memory to the part of the cortex that specializes in each aspect. For example, codes to recognize a face, or to attach a use to a tool, to

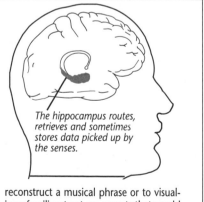

The hippocampus routes, retrieves and sometimes stores data picked up by the senses.

reconstruct a musical phrase or to visualize a familiar street are aspects that would be stored at different spots in the cortex. If that spot is damaged, the ability to recall that aspect is lost.

Sacks describes a painter who suffered neurological damage to the visual cortex, which robbed him not only of the ability to perceive color, but of any memory of color whatsoever.

The distinction between explicit, declarative memory and implicit, nondeclarative memory can also be illustrated with an experience familiar to all of us. We've all had what is called "infantile amnesia" — the inability to recall events that happened before our third year of life. Obviously, we do remember things as infants — we learn to recognize faces and voices, we learn to perform certain tasks — but we somehow can't remember learning these things, nor can we recall any events at all from before about age two. Apparently, events experienced before the development of the brain system supporting declarative memory can't be consciously retrieved even after that system has developed.

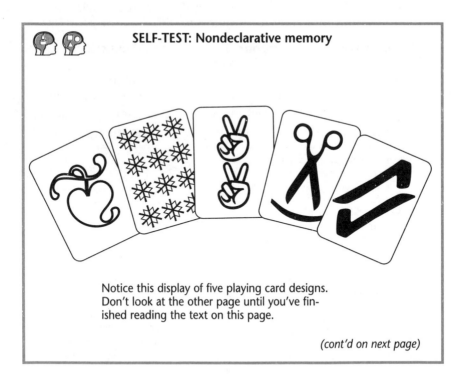

SELF-TEST: Nondeclarative memory

Notice this display of five playing card designs. Don't look at the other page until you've finished reading the text on this page.

(cont'd on next page)

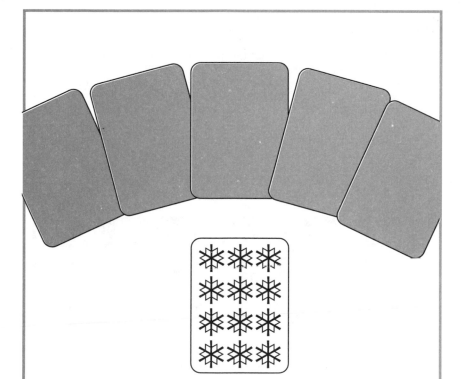

Don't look at the preceding page where these five cards are shown face-up.

Try to remember which of these five cards shown face-down would reveal the same design, if you turned it over, as the one shown below them. Follow your instinct. Very likely you stored a "nondeclarative" memory (which means you know it but cannot say it because you don't know you know it) of the image of those cards face-up when you first saw them on the preceding page.

You may not know why you retain visual memories for a while rather than erase them immediately, but you do. That may be why instinctive trust in the accuracy of the "mind's eye" works in this test. (But not always. The brain can persuade itself that it experienced something it did not if it has a reason to believe the fantasy can better protect the body the brain loyally serves. This can happen, for example, when you unconsciously incorporate a false image into your memory in response to the suggestion of another person in order to avoid invoking their ire.)

EXERCISE: Card senses

Rearrange these 16 playing cards so that no 2 of the same value or the same suit are in the same row either vertically, horizontally or diagonally. The small white boxes in the lower right corner of each space allow you to write in the initials (JH for jack of hearts, QS for queen of spades, etc.). If you prefer, lay out cards the same way as shown below, using your own deck of playing cards.

This exercise uses short-term memory skills and builds concentration because you must hold certain possible locations in memory while testing other possibilities in your mind's eye. About five minutes is a reasonable norm for completing the task. A "Hint" appears below to get you started on the right track, if you need a little help.

Hint: Put these cards in the four corners: ace of spades in the upper left, jack of clubs lower left, king of diamonds upper right, queen of hearts lower right.

Imagine a memory-enhancing drug that would make you remember EVERYTHING the first time it happens. Would you want to take that drug?

While it is an old truism that practice makes perfect — that repeated practice and rehearsal aid in the long-term memory of a skill or knowledge — it is also true that, sometimes, a single salient event is seared permanently into memory because that event has triggered an emotional response. Recent advances in the understanding of the molecular underpinnings of long-term memory shed light on this apparent paradox and even suggest ways we might manipulate our powers of learning through "smart" drugs.

In memory formation, the brain works at two levels, *immediate* recognition of an event, and long-term memory retention. The formation of those long-term memories involves a process of protein synthesis. (See the "Research" box on page 80 for more details on how this affects your ability to learn and retain information you want to remember.)

The fly that at 12:41:06 p.m. passed through the right extreme of your field of vision. This event had no emotional impact. Your brain secreted a chemical that prevented you from remembering that you even saw it, much less what it looked like.

If you think about it, you are subjected to millions of individual data bytes that your senses pick up even in an "uneventful" day. Don't blame your senses. They are just trying to protect you by keeping your eyes, ears, nose, mouth and skin open. But how does your brain decide which of these data bytes are worth remembering, and which aren't?

The reason you can remember some things the first tIme is linked to forgetting everything else

With most events, the brain processes the information, allowing you to cope with that information as it is occurring. If your brain perceives the event as affecting your ability to survive — in whatever ways you have defined survival for yourself, from charging mastodons to your boss's refusal to reply to your cheery "Good morning!" greeting — your brain kicks in with a mechanism that transmits action messages to the rest of your body. Because it sees the situation as a kind of crisis, these *emotion-driven* responses cause the event to be stored for future reference (see "What is the brain so busy doing...," p. 177).

However, if an event like a fly buzzing off packs no danger-wallop, you forget it. Current research suggests that the same mechanism that codes an event as a crisis also erases most other events to prevent overload. But, how can you overrule your brain's decision about what's worth remembering? What if you *want* to learn something that's not emotionally charged?

How can I erase the eraser?

Try repetition. Maybe that can make your brain "change its mind," so to speak. Maybe your brain will say to itself, "This person I am trying to protect seems to be paying a lot of attention to an 'event' that my early programming didn't equip me to recognize as a 'crisis' worth remembering. But I am nothing if I can't adapt to protect the boss, so OK, 2 + 2 = 4. I'll store this event away also since it seems to be so important it keeps coming up."

Do I really want this drug?

Recent experimental work hints at another way we might one day be able to outsmart our brain's gatekeeper. The brain mechanism responsible for preventing events from being encoded in long-term memory can be temporarily switched off by administration of an antiserum. Thus far, this "CREB

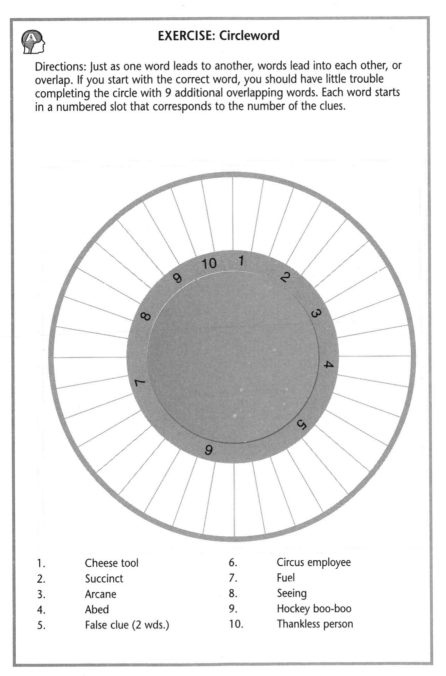

EXERCISE: Circleword

Directions: Just as one word leads to another, words lead into each other, or overlap. If you start with the correct word, you should have little trouble completing the circle with 9 additional overlapping words. Each word starts in a numbered slot that corresponds to the number of the clues.

1.	Cheese tool	6.	Circus employee
2.	Succinct	7.	Fuel
3.	Arcane	8.	Seeing
4.	Abed	9.	Hockey boo-boo
5.	False clue (2 wds.)	10.	Thankless person

Hint: 5: a fish. 9: also goes on a cake.

cocktail" (see the "Research" box below and the diagrams on pp. 81-82) has only been served to white mice and sea slugs. The implications, however, are tantalizing: imagine memorizing any facts you want — quickly, automatically, and without so much as an ounce of self-discipline. On the other hand, think about this: would you really want to take a "smart" drug that wreaks havoc on the brain's tried-and-true system for separating life-essential experiences from inconsequential trivia?

THE RESEARCH — The chemistry of learning

It has been known for some time that the formation of long-term memories requires protein synthesis, perhaps because a permanent alteration in nerve dendrites is involved so that future transmission across a synapse is enhanced. Cyclic AMP (cAMP), a gene regulator within the cells, and a protein called CREB, which responds to cAMP, appear to be involved in the cellular basis of this process. CREB also has a repressor version, which has the opposite effect of the protein-synthesis-stimulator version. Normally, a single training episode releases both the stimulator CREB and its repressor twin; the function of the repressor version of CREB may be to hinder over-memorization of unnecessary details encountered only once.

However, the repressor version deactivates more quickly than the stimulator version, so repeated training or encounters interspersed with rest intervals result in an overall accumulation of stimulator CREB and maximally effective learning. When the repressor version is experimentally blocked by an antiserum, equivalent long-term memory formation occurs after a single training session.

Normally, lasting long-term memories following a single event occur only when that event is particularly emotionally charged. This may occur because the same systems in the brain which mediate the processing of emotional stimuli may also inhibit that repressor version of CREB.

"To store it or ignore it": that is the question that CREB responds to.

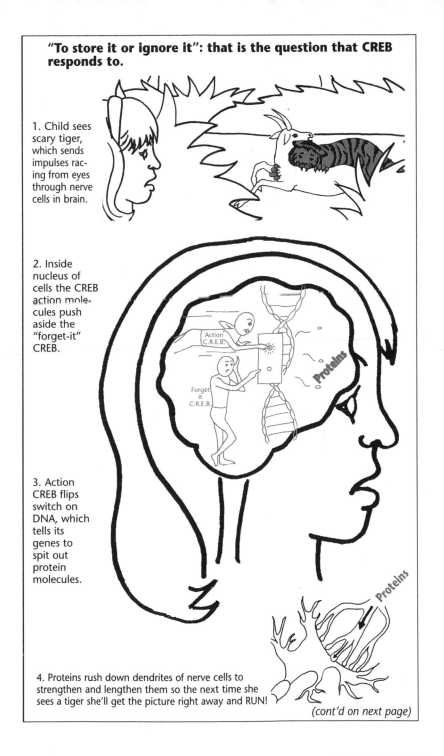

1. Child sees scary tiger, which sends impulses racing from eyes through nerve cells in brain.

2. Inside nucleus of cells the CREB action molecules push aside the "forget-it" CREB.

Action C.R.E.B.

Forget it C.R.E.B.

Proteins

3. Action CREB flips switch on DNA, which tells its genes to spit out protein molecules.

Proteins

4. Proteins rush down dendrites of nerve cells to strengthen and lengthen them so the next time she sees a tiger she'll get the picture right away and RUN!

(cont'd on next page)

However, if the child experiences something not worth noticing, the "forget-it" CREB molecule routinely hits the "OFF" button. No switch, no proteins, the dendrite backs away limp.

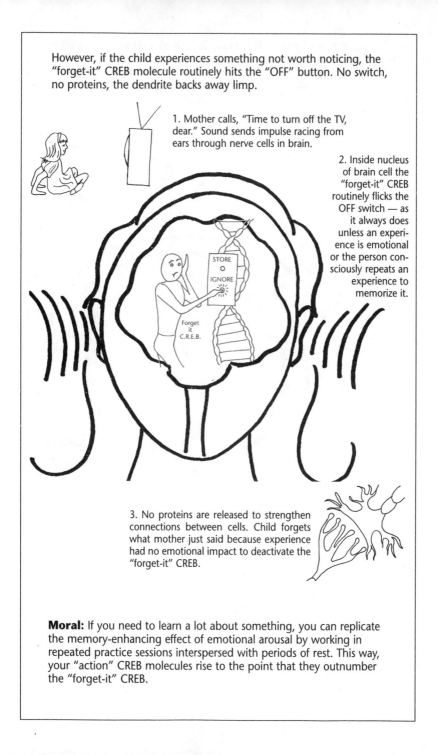

1. Mother calls, "Time to turn off the TV, dear." Sound sends impulse racing from ears through nerve cells in brain.

2. Inside nucleus of brain cell the "forget-it" CREB routinely flicks the OFF switch — as it always does unless an experience is emotional or the person consciously repeats an experience to memorize it.

STORE

IGNORE

Forget it C.R.E.B.

3. No proteins are released to strengthen connections between cells. Child forgets what mother just said because experience had no emotional impact to deactivate the "forget-it" CREB.

Moral: If you need to learn a lot about something, you can replicate the memory-enhancing effect of emotional arousal by working in repeated practice sessions interspersed with periods of rest. This way, your "action" CREB molecules rise to the point that they outnumber the "forget-it" CREB.

You can still use some kinds of knowledge even if you don't know you have them

Imagine the following scenario:

A patient with amnesia is shown a list of words. Within minutes he is unable to remember not only any of the words on the list but even the fact that he has been shown a list at all. And yet, when asked to do an exercise in which his memory is primed — such as filling in blanks with the most appropriate words — an amnesic patient so frequently uses the same words from the earlier list he saw that it is impossible to conclude that he does not somehow remember them.

This kind of experiment shows that the normal, conscious recollection of facts and events — called declarative or explicit memory — is a quite different thing from unconscious, implicit, nondeclarative memory. Explicit memory tasks usually require the participation of implicit memory, but damage to the medial temporal or diencephalic regions of the brain may cause a loss of explicit memory while leaving implicit memory intact.

A similar kind of unconscious memory has been shown to occur in patients exhibiting what has been called "blindsight." Such patients, who have suffered damage to the visual cortex, are blind in the straightforward sense that they are completely unaware of being able to see anything. For example, if shown a bright light in their right visual field, they will report having seen nothing at all. However, when pressed to *guess* where a light *might* have

The Man Who Mistook His Wife for a Hat by Oliver Sacks contains a case history of a patient suffering from an extreme form of prosopagnosia.

been shown, these patients will indicate the correct area with well above chance frequency, and sometimes nearly perfectly.

People who can't recognize familiar faces

Other parallel findings come from the study of patients with prosopagnosia, an impaired ability to recognize familiar faces. When they are shown pictures of faces of famous and unknown people they say they don't recognize any of them. Surprisingly, though, they are just like normal people in coming to a quicker evaluation of whether two simultaneously presented faces are the same or different when the faces are famous compared to when they are not.

Research shows practice and tricks improve explicit memory

All of these pathologies represent extreme forms of the memory lapses everyone suffers from. Even without damage to any part of the brain, we all have different degrees of skill in consciously recording and accessing knowledge and perception. The ability of human brains to consciously retrieve knowledge from memory evolved relatively recently and is still imperfect. But those declarative memory skills — first, the learning of new material, and second, the retrieval of it — appear to be improvable with practice.

 SELF-TEST: Retrieval of implicit knowledge

This simple test will show you just how difficult it can be to retrieve knowledge even if we are intimately familiar with it from daily experience reinforced over many years. Try to answer these questions:

1) On a traffic signal light, which color is at the top, red or green?

2) Try to visualize a telephone keyboard. Sketch the configuration of all the numbers, plus the star and the pound sign.

3) On the spine of a book, is the title rightside up or upside down when the book is laid face-up? (Hint: American and British books have different conventions.)

4) What are the highest and lowest numbers on your oven dial?

5) On a penny, which direction is Abraham Lincoln facing?

6) Of all the former statesmen on the bills between $1 and $100, two are non-presidents. Name them. Next, name all the former presidents on the other bills. (Hint: One was ambassador to France, the other Secretary of the Treasury.)

7) We all know how many stars there are on the U.S. flag. But how many rows are they arranged into, and how many stars are in each row? Next, how many of each of the red and white stripes are there, and which color is the top-most stripe?

SELF-TEST: How to remember people's names

Learning personal names is an ability which appears to vary considerably across individuals, and forgetting names is the most frequent memory complaint among the elderly. Even poor name memorizers, however, can overcome this deficit through the use of simple mnemonic tricks based on an understanding that when information is encoded in a personally meaningful way (which is sometimes referred to as the memorization being more *elaborated*), the memory is more likely to be enhanced.

A. Roundy

C. Bins

A. Miller

J. Richardson

For each of the following face-name pairings:

1) Identify a prominent facial feature.
2) Transform the person's name into a concrete, visually vivid object.
3) Mentally picture the facial feature combined with the transformed name-object.

(Examples: A man with long hair named O'Brien; transform "O'Brien" to "lion," and visualize a lion's mane emerging from his head. A woman with heavy eyebrows named Crocker; transform "Crocker" to "cracker," and visualize a cracker on her eyebrows.) This technique can be further strengthened by performing the final step of making an emotional judgment of the pleasantness or unpleasantness of the image association.

EXERCISE: Memory terms

Work this exercise in the same way as a crossword puzzle. In this case it tests recall of seven key words related to memory. All seven have been used and defined in the preceding article.

ACROSS

3. Inability to recall past events

7. Inability to recognize familiar faces

DOWN

1. Ability of neurologically blind people to correctly identify objects shown to them

2. Adjectival form of "memory"

4. The normal, conscious kind of memory for past events

5. A non-declarative kind of memory one is not aware of having

6. A way to help recall by supplying clues to questions or blanks to fill in

Hint: Seven Across is "prosopagnosia."

A major cause of forgetting

If you've ever been to a movie double feature, you know that you'll have a hard time remembering the plot and details of the first movie immediately after seeing the second. This can't be explained by the greater amount of time since viewing the first — in fact, your memory of the second movie remains stronger a couple of hours later.

This phenomenon is called *retroactive inhibition* or *interference*, and it has been demonstrated to apply to a wide variety of learning and memory tasks, with greater similarity between the first and second task correlating with a greater degree of forgetting. Knowledge of this phenomenon has led to a view of interference of one body of material with previously-learned material as a fundamental cause of forgetting.

Another kind of forgetting that's not your fault either

Interference also works the other way. If, say, two lists of words are memorized in succession, retention of the second list will be worse than if only one list were memorized. This is called *proactive inhibition.*

Retroactive inhibition has one rather bizarre aspect: it actually *fades* with time. Experiments have shown that the apparently extinguished memory of the first of two tasks will undergo a sponta-neous recovery over a 24-hour period. As memory of the first task recovers, it will interfere with mem-ory of the second, and vice-versa, until the amount of forget-ting produced by proactive inhibition will be about as great as that caused by retroactive.

Could these two naturally-occurring causes help explain why people approaching middle-age think their memories are failing when they are only having to deal with greater amounts of data in their work and personal lives?

SELF-TEST: Retroactive inhibition

Study the following word-pairs for five minutes. Then cover them with a piece of paper and look at the list at the bottom of the page, which includes all the first words of the pairs below, arranged in a different order.

Keeping the top list covered, write down each word's matching half from memory as best you can. After writing down as many items as you can remember, uncover the list and note the number correct. Repeat with a fresh piece of paper. Continue until you've memorized all the pairs.

BUG — ONION   BASEBALL — LOCK

WATER — ZEBRA   PAINT — MINT

PAPER — LAMP   GUM — CLOCK

TONGUE — CAR   FAN — CANDLE

HOUSE — SUN   COLLAR — BEE

_____

COLLAR —   FAN —

PAINT —   GUM —

WATER —   PAPER —

BUG —   HOUSE —

TONGUE —   BASEBALL —

(cont'd on next page)

Next, study and memorize this second list of word-pairs. This list matches a different right-hand column of words to the first list's left-hand column. If it takes you longer than it took to learn the first, this is due to proactive inhibition.

BUG — GLOVE   BASEBALL — BELL

WATER — POSTCARD   PAINT — ROCK

PAPER — PHONE   GUM — SHINGLE

TONGUE — BOX   FAN — BEACH

HOUSE — MASK   COLLAR — FIRE

_____

Once you've memorized the second list, re-test yourself on the first list of pairs. If you can't remember those first pairs, what you're experiencing is the effect of retroactive inhibition.

COLLAR —   FAN —

PAINT —   GUM —

WATER —   PAPER —

BUG —   HOUSE —

TONGUE —   BASEBALL —

Finally, wait one day and re-test yourself. If you come up with a mix of the first and second lists' pairs, this is due to a spontaneous recovery of the details of the first memorization task, which will inhibit, but in return be inhibited by, the details of the second. On average, this will result in a wash: you'll forget (or remember) the details of the two lists more or less equally.

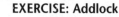

EXERCISE: Addlock

Directions: The numbers in this puzzle are always sums of digits. No digit is used twice in the same number, and zero is not used. For example, 8 Across has five squares, and the clue is "23"; thus you need five different numbers to total 23. Then you have to figure out the correct sequence of those numbers to make it work with the puzzle. We have filled in some of the numbers to give you a start.

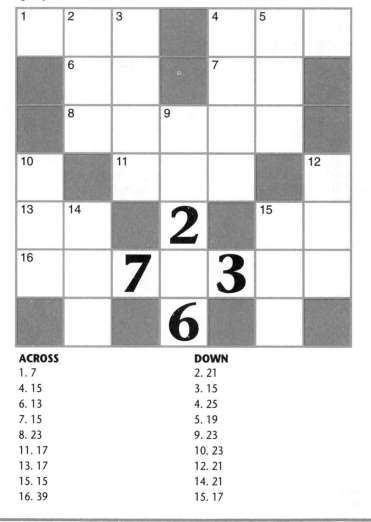

ACROSS	**DOWN**
1. 7	2. 21
4. 15	3. 15
6. 13	4. 25
7. 15	5. 19
8. 23	9. 23
11. 17	10. 23
13. 17	12. 21
15. 15	14. 21
16. 39	15. 17

Hint: The clues are for odd digits, and the answers end in even digits.

If you want to remember complex data, visualize it. Geniuses do

Those rare wizards with incredible memories or prodigious powers of mental calculation have something to tell us about how to use our brains more effectively. Their seemingly super-human skill — acquired through training or compensation for some cognitive disability — may be useless as a practical matter. If we can write things down and if we have access to mechanical calculators and computer databases, why do we need to do all this in our head? Still, such geniuses will always retain a certain fascination even if some of their most remarkable abilities lose their practical value. Who among us wouldn't love to know just how they do what they do — and, perhaps, even learn how to do it ourselves?

Great memorizers often perform their feats by having a special knack — either by gift or hard practice — of translating information into a *visual* mode. British mnemonist Leslie Waugh set up a real-life filing cabinet for all the major sporting events spanning the previous half-century, which he then internalized in his mind's eye. When asked a question about the date of an event or about events that had occurred on a given date, he would picture himself thumbing through the files and then opening one to find the requested information.

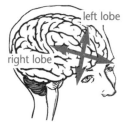

The right and left hemispheres of the brain transmit instructions and process data to and from the opposite sides of the body.

To an extent, Waugh's feat seems within the grasp of most of us. For example, we all presumably have a memory of the layout of our house, and even of a previously lived-in house, which allows us to mentally walk through room by room visually inspecting things as we go. Under the right circumstances — under hypnosis or in a dream perhaps — these recollections are so rich and detailed that we can almost literally touch, smell and stumble over the objects as we perform our mental virtual-reality tour.

In such a case, we've visually internalized information in a manner which almost seems to go beyond memorization. The neurologist Oliver Sacks relates the story of a man with right-hemisphere damage rendering him blind in his left visual field. This affected his visual *memories* just as strongly as his vision: when asked to recall the landmarks in a familiar city square by imagining entering the square from the south end, he could recall nothing on the square's west (left) edge. When asked to imagine entering from the north, his recall of the shops on the west edge returned in full clarity, and it was the east edge that became a complete blank.

The trick is, however, to internalize the sort of information Waugh does at will, in the degree of detail he does, and to recall it whenever we like. This, presumably, is more than just a matter of practice.

"S," a patient of A.R. Luria's, had the keenest memory of all. But the fact that he could not ignore any data often overwhelmed him

"S," the man whose memory the great Russian psychologist A.R. Luria described as "one of the keenest the literature on the subject has ever described," had such overwhelmingly clear and powerful images of visual and auditory stimuli that this almost superhuman ability, which lay at the basis of his seemingly inexhaustible memory, also became something of a handicap. Despite his unsurpassed mnemonic brilliance, he often conveyed the impression of being muddled and dull-witted, since his visual images had nothing to do with the plot or structure of what he was being told, only with individual words or sounds. The result was utter confusion: "No," he would say. "This is too much. Each word calls up images; they collide with one another, and the result is chaos. I can't make anything out of this." S's problem was the opposite of what most of us face: the challenge for him was reining in these images, and learning procedures (such as writing phone numbers down on a piece of paper, which he then burned) for forgetting information he didn't want to retain.

The amazing linguist and calculator Hans Eberstark remembers both words and numbers by the sounds they make

Austrian-born simultaneous interpreter Hans Eberstark has a genius for both languages and numbers, in a manner which makes the two abilities seem intimately related. Once he registers in memory the sound and meaning of any word in any language — that *duk'as* means "abalone" in Kashaya Pomo, for example — he never forgets it.

Eberstark is also a phenomenal mental calculator and number memorizer. A crucial feature of his personal technique is to translate numbers into "words" in a language of his own invention. The words are based on sounds that the numbers' images might suggest — for example, the number seven is an L, since it looks like an L upside-down. Numbers in sequence then become a string of sounds. With this straightforward and completely automatic translation from the domain of numbers into the domain of sound (like dialing a touch-tone phone), combined with his photographic auditory memory, Eberstark is able to memorize pi to over 10,000 places!

Alexander Aitken committed data to memory with incredible speed and accuracy by noticing how new data is somehow related to other data already in memory

The great mathematician, mental calculator, and all-around genius Alexander Craig Aitken also relied on an "auditory-rhythmic memory" of numbers, but in addition had a gift for imbuing even the most arbitrary-seeming data with rich relationships to other facts and patterns in his vast mnemonic store. Thus, he described his associations with the number 7 in terms far richer than a simple visual or auditory image:

> *The line of poetry "They passed the pleiades and the planets seven" — mysteries in the minds of the ancients — Sabbath or the seventh day — religious observance of Sunday — 7 in contrast with 13 and with 3 in superstition — 7 as a recurring decimal .142857 which, multiplied by 123456, gives the same numbers in cyclic order — a poem on numbers by Binyon, seen in a review lately — I could quote from it.* (Hunter 1977:163)

As Ian Hunter put it in a biographical essay:

> *It is clearly misleading to draw a firm line around certain of Aitken's activities, call them "memory," view them as an iso-*

lated "faculty," and attempt to understand them without going outside the circle we have drawn. Aitken's memory was one aspect of an immensely complex, many-sided, highly-integrated system of mutually supporting activities cumulatively developed over the years. (Hunter 1977:159)

Doing what comes naturally

For geniuses such as Eberstark or Aitken, their gifts seem so natural that they believe anyone can accomplish the same feats with a little practice. Of course, this would only be true if we possessed the same sorts of minds such prodigies take for granted. Could you learn to perform mental calculations as quickly and flawlessly as Aitken? For example, could you learn to multiply 2 three-digit numbers — say, 123 by 456 — in two seconds? We return to Aitken's own remarkably self-aware account of his method in a passage from another of Hunter's biographical pieces, and you can decide for yourself:

> *I do this in two moves: I see at once that 123 times 45 is 5535 and that 123 times 6 is 738; I hardly have to think. Then 55350 plus 738 gives 56088. Even at the moment of registering 56088, I have checked it by dividing by 8, so 7011, and this by 9, 779. I recognize 779 as 41 by 19; and 41 by 3 is 123, 19 by 24 is 456. A check you see; and it passes by in about one second.* (Hunter 1978:341)

Strategies for passing the mail carrier exam

Try your hand at the mail carrier exam on the next page. Unless you have a photographic memory, you'd flunk this test without the assistance of some mnemonic technique or other. In fact, people who do well on this invariably avail themselves of tricks of visual association. They devise straightforward methods for translating numbers and meaningless names into familiar concrete images. (See "Hint" on page 96.) In this way, with a little practice, anyone of average intelligence can ace the test.

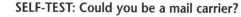

SELF-TEST: Could you be a mail carrier?

Memorizing tricks, useless though they may sometimes seem, do have their practical applications. If you want to become a U.S. Postal Service clerk, carrier, or letter-sorting machine operator, you first have to pass a memorization test, just like the one here. Take a look at it. Try your hand at it if you like. (Good luck!) Once you're feeling nice and humble, read the "Hint" following the exam to see how the people who pass it actually do it.

Directions: Each of the five boxes labeled A-E below has three sets of number sequences associated with street names, and two unnumbered names. You have five minutes to memorize which number sequences and names are associated with which box.

A	B	C	D	E
2900-3299 College	2000-2099 College	6100-7299 College	4100-4899 College	1300-1599 College
Wellmann	Shike	Kaytron	Britt	Farne
8500-9199 Bancroft	3200-3399 Bancroft	9900-9999 Bancroft	2400-2899 Bancroft	4300-4399 Bancroft
Sextor	Dandle	Remy	Funt	Perl
5300-5399 Addison	7200-8499 Addison	6300-6799 Addison	5800-6099 Addison	4500-4799 Addison

After five minutes, cover the boxes. You're not allowed to refer back to them. Working from memory, as quickly and accurately as you can, write the box letter beside each of the addresses below. You have five minutes.

1. 2000-2099 College
2. 7200-8499 Addison
3. Sextor
4. 5800-6099 Addison
5. 4300-4399 Bancroft
6. Funt
7. 2900-3299 College
8. 6300-6799 Addison
9. 8500-9199 Bancroft
10. Kaytron
11. Farne
12. 9900-9999 Bancroft
13. 1300-1599 College
14. 7200-8499 Addison
15. Wellmann
16. 2400-2899 Bancroft
17. Britt
18. 6100-7299 College
19. 6300-6799 Addison
20. Dandle
21. Shike
22. 4100-4899 College
23. 3200-3399 Bancroft
24. 4300-4399 Bancroft
25. 5300-5399 Addison
26. Remy
27. Perl
28. 1300-1599 College
29. Farne
30. 2900-3299 College
31. 2400-2899 Bancroft
32. Wellmann
33. 1300-1599 College
34. 9900-9999 Bancroft
35. Dandle
36. 6300-6799 Addison

(cont'd on next page)

37. 7200-8499 Addison
38. 1300-1599 College
39. 6100-7299 College
40. 3200-3399 Bancroft
41. Shike
42. 4500-4799 Addison
43. 5800-6099 Addison
44. Perl

45. Kaytron
46. Sextor
47. 2900-3299 College
48. 4300-4399 Bancroft
49. 2400-2899 Bancroft
50. 1300-1599 College
51. 9900-9999 Bancroft
52. 7200-8499 Addison

53. Wellmann
54. Remy
55. 4100-4899 College
56. 8500-9199 Bancroft
57. Funt
58. 4500-4799 Addison
59. 4300-4399 Bancroft

Hint: Try visualization tricks like these. Note first that no number sequence is re-used for more than one street or lettered box, so you don't have to bother with memorizing the end of a number sequence or the numbered street names at all.

Let's take the first item in box "A" in the preceding page. "2900-3299 College." The trick is to translate the number into sound, and then into an image. Let the sound corresponding to an initial 2 be "t" (the first sound in the name of the number) and the sound corresponding to a following 9 be "ine." This gives you "tine," which is logically visualized as a fork. To remember that the number sequence beginning "29 — " is in box "A," combine the fork with an easily-visualized object beginning with that letter. A fork stuck in an apple works perfectly well.

The next item in the box is "Wellmann." Picture a welt on an apple, or for that matter an apple in a well — it makes no difference as long as the image is clear and easily remembered — and you've got it. This may seem cumbersome, but such is the nature of mnemonic techniques which rely on visualization. The more you practice the number associations, the more automatically the image comes into your mind when you see any two-digit number. In other words, you quickly enough learn to bypass the compositional step, even though you can always fall back on it if you need to. In this way, you can learn the same sorts of visualization techniques that come automatically to mnemonic geniuses such as Luria's "S."

SELF-TEST: Test yourself against the best

You will need a timer.

A) How long would it take you to memorize the entire table to the far right? Luria's "S" needed just three minutes of study for perfect recall. (As usual, he then retained perfect recall of it, along with thousands of other such tables and number and nonsense-syllable sequences, for the rest of his life.) "V.P.," the mnemonic genius studied by Hunt and Love (1972), took six and a half minutes.

6	6	8	0
5	4	3	2
1	6	8	4
7	9	3	5
4	2	3	7
3	8	9	1
1	0	0	2
3	4	5	1
2	7	6	8
1	9	2	6
2	9	6	7
5	5	2	0
x	0	1	x

B) The table to the right took "V.P." four minutes and six seconds:

1	6	4	3	5	9
2	6	6	5	5	9
4	1	3	2	6	4
9	6	2	4	0	4
0	3	7	4	2	8
5	1	9	7	2	3
5	4	8	4	6	5
6	5	1	3	0	0

C) How many trials would it take you to memorize this list of 25 words? When he had the entire list read aloud to him at a rate of one word per second, Aitken required four trials; the first trial, he got 12 correct, the second trial 14 correct, the third trial 23 correct, and the fourth trial all correct.

HEAD, GREEN, WATER, SING, DEAD, LONG, SHIP, MAKE, WOMAN, FRIENDLY, BAKE, ASK, COLD, STALK, DANCE, VILLAGE, POND, SICK, PRIDE, BRING, INK, ANGRY, NEEDLE, SWIM, GO.

(Aitken, by the way, never used the standard mnemonist's trick of associating each word with a visual image in a story. He simply proceeded by "sound.")

D) How many trials would it take you to memorize a list of 16 three-digit numbers? When the following list was read aloud to him at a rate of one word every two seconds, Aitken needed four trials. In the first trial, he got 6 correct, the second trial 10 correct, the third trial 14 correct, the fourth trial all correct.

194, 503, 876, 327, 714, 961, 583, 259, 487, 364, 950, 613, 294, 437, 182, 659.

EXERCISE: Divvy digit

Directions: Divide the 5 X 5 grid below into five equal sections, each of which has the same numerical value, and also has no two digits alike.

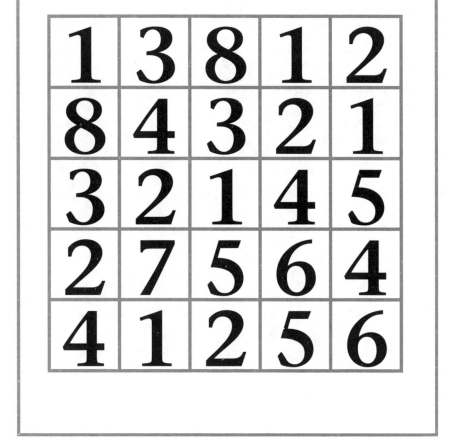

1	3	8	1	2
8	4	3	2	1
3	2	1	4	5
2	7	5	6	4
4	1	2	5	6

Hint: The entire fifth column is one of the five equal sections. The others are all unevenly shaped.

Background noises, including talk, affect your ability to recall

Experiments show that different levels of background noise, ranging from "white noise" (a soothing sound like a low hiss that is almost inaudible) to conversation, affect performance of a variety of tasks involving short-term and long-term memory. Tests varied by sex, time of day and type of noise.

We see that even semi-interesting sounds interfere with tasks that require memory. The brain's job is to protect the body. It can't tell whether the background sounds are more important to survival than the task at hand. That's why the brain has a hard time concentrating sufficiently if there are distracting sounds. Machines that generate white noise in the background improve ability to work with data because the persistence of white noise dominates other distracting sounds.

Are you aged 30-40? Have you been talking with someone at a noisy bar or at a cocktail party recently?

Experiments with divided attention tasks show that the ability to filter out distractions and juggle competing demands on our attention is one of the most fragile kinds of skill we possess. Divided attention tasks require subjects to monitor two or three different information sources simultaneously. For example, the subject may be asked to listen to three pairs of digits in sequence. Each time a number is presented to one ear, another is presented simultaneously to the other. Afterward, the subject must report the digits he or she has heard.

The ability to cope with this kind of task typically begins to decline between ages 30 and 40. Does this represent age-related memory loss? Yes and no. Information processing and retrieval strategies are certainly important for memorization, but in a straightforward sense it isn't memory *as such* which is being affected here. A decline in the ability to recall a single sequence of numbers presented to one ear — a task which isolates short-term memory more neatly — fails to occur until *much* later in life.

EXERCISE: Numberlockers

Working through these two exercises requires concentration — an essential component of memory. For that reason distracting noises or other events must be ignored while you are holding the possible solutions to each clue in memory before writing it down. Directions on the next page apply to both.

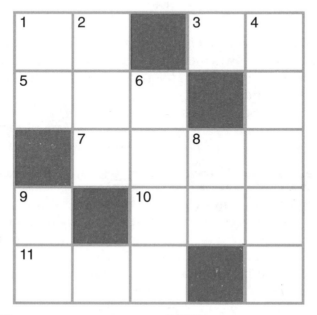

ACROSS

1. The square of an odd number which itself is a square.

3. The square of an even number which itself is a cube.

5. The cube of a prime number.

7. Digits descend evenly.

10. A square followed by its root.

11. Cube the root of 3 Across.

DOWN

1. The sum of its digits are 11.

2. A square.

4. The number composed of the third and fourth digits is 1/3 of the number composed of the first two digits and 3 times the last digit.

6. The first two and last two digits are multiples of the sum of the two digits in 1 Down.

8. The square of a prime number.

9. The same as the first two digits of 4 Down.

Hint: Clue 6 Down is 3322. A "prime" number is divisible only by itself and one. The "square" of a number is the number you get when you multiply a number by itself.

Directions: The digits 1 through 9 are used; there are no zeros. Only one digit may be placed in each box, and a digit may be used more than once in a combination. Where it appears that more than one combination of digits is possible, look for additional clues in interlocking numbers.

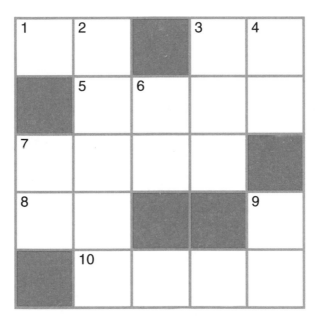

ACROSS

1. Square of the warning cry in golf.
3. Black Thursday, depression day.
5. The year of 3 Across.
7. Year of the Second Continental Congress.
8. Trick-or-treat day.
10. The first 3 digits are the square of 9 Down, and the 4th is like the 3rd.

DOWN

2. A palindrome.
3. A multiple of 9 Down.
4. The square of a prime number.
6. A multiple of 3 Across.
7. The day after Columbus Day.
9. The square of a prime number (different from 4 Down).

Hint: A "prime" number is divisible only by itself and one. The "square" of a number is the number you get when you multiply a number by itself. A palindrome reads the same forward *and* backward.

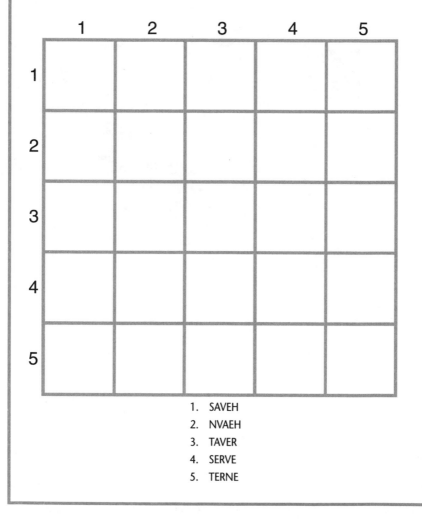

EXERCISE: Analock

This exercise requires concentration that may be difficult to maintain in the presence of distracting background noise.

Rearrange the letters in the anagram clues below to form a word (or a different word). The object is to compose words that, when written into the rows and columns corresponding to their numbered clue, read the same across as they do down.

1. SAVEH
2. NVAEH
3. TAVER
4. SERVE
5. TERNE

Hint: The correct anagram word for clue word 3 is "avert."

Why are stories easier to recall than lists?

With the exception of some idiot savants, or those rare individuals endowed with a photographic memory, most of us will memorize information much better if we can tack that information to something we already know. Any story, for example, will be much easier to recall if we can match it to what are called *schemata* or *scripts:* generic structured outlines of familiar events or routines.

A simple example will illustrate: Anyone familiar with the general rules and structure of chess will find it much easier to remember an account of the details of a particular match than will someone who has never learned how to play the game. According to one point of view, many people with good memories owe their ability simply to the fact that they have such a large store of knowledge that they can rely on it to contextualize new information and make it personally meaningful. That explains why they find it easier to organize and manage new facts.

Your mind tries so hard to fit new data into the patterns it already knows that it may substitute what "probably" happened for what really happened

Our urge to integrate new information into a prior knowledge base — to go beyond the simple objective facts themselves and, as it were, turn mere stimuli into knowledge — is so strong, and so automatic, that it may sometimes lead us to err in our understanding or recollection of events. If we hear a story in which a friend hands over his credit card to the waiter and then asks for the check, we are very likely, when prompted to repeat the story, to unconsciously "correct" the sequence to fit the familiar restaurant script. And the fact that the reference to a "restaurant script" in the previous sentence is sensible rather than confusing to you, the reader, results from your *assumption* that someone asking a waiter for a check has just finished a meal in a restaurant — even though that was never mentioned.

Consider, too, the following mini-story:

A man and his young son were struck by a hit-and-run driver while crossing the street. The father was killed instantly, and the son critically injured. The boy was taken to the hospital and rushed immediately into the emergency room, where the doctor exclaimed, "I can't operate on my own son!"

The confusing effect of this story relies crucially on an *assumption* we make about the doctor being a man, rather than a woman and therefore the boy's mother. Most people will cling to this assumption so tenaciously that they will go to great lengths to make sense of the story without questioning their image of the male doctor — and yet, nowhere is it stated that the doctor is in fact a man.

Why stereotypes come in handy

Even though we are often criticized for maintaining stereotypes of this sort, they are just one of many types of generalization without which we could surely never function effectively in the world. Using strict logic it is unjustified to assume that, just because we got burned once by putting our finger in a flame, the same thing would happen should we do it again — but imagine how quickly an organism would die if it failed to make this sort of inductive leap. No such logical organism would ever get the chance to pass on its genes.

Our need to turn mere stimuli into coherent knowledge is so strong that true non-sequiturs — conversational contributions that simply have *nothing* to do with the previous comment (literally "don't follow") — are rarely interpreted as such. The listeners try their darnedest to find something in their past experience that makes the comment relate *somehow*. Imagine that a young woman has applied for a job with your computer software company, and you contact her previous employer to verify her qualifications. When you ask about her ability as a programmer, her former boss replies, "Ms. Widget always came to work on time and dressed appropriately." You will naturally interpret this as a tactful indictment of her skills — "damning with faint praise," as the saying goes — and you won't hire her. Perhaps, though, the poor woman's former employer was simply saying whatever came into his mind without really trying to respond to your question. Sometimes, as even Freud had to admit, a cigar is just a cigar.

The worst part of your memory to lose is your ability to relate a new experience to old ones

In the field of clinical memory rehabilitation, one of the most difficult kinds of amnesia to overcome involves the inability of the patient to integrate new information into previously-acquired knowledge. Laird Cermak and colleagues describe a severely amnesic patient who, though able to learn a few memory aids, is absolutely unable to profit from them. When he memorizes facts at all, he does so in a parrot-like manner, with little or no understanding of them. Without the ability to give meaning to mere stimuli by bringing to bear a rich knowledge base, this patient has lost a much more fundamentally human ability than memory alone.

SELF-TEST: Memorizing meaningful vs. random patterns

Memorization skill relies on the integration of data into familiar patterns. When presented with a configuration of 28 chess pieces from an actual match (below left), grandmaster-level players are able to memorize about 16 pieces after only five seconds, while beginners memorize only about four. When presented with a board featuring the same pieces arranged randomly (below right), experts and beginners perform the same. If you know the rules of chess, study the board on the left for one minute and memorize as many of the positions as possible. Next, try the same thing with the board on the right.

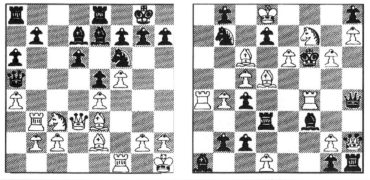

SELF-TEST: Memorizing lists as stories

A typical trick for memorizing arbitrary lists is to connect the items in a meaningful way, by stringing them together into a story. For example, take the following list of apparently unrelated items:

airplane	*ball*
hyena	*grease*
cream cheese	*monument*
moon	*mailman*
volcano	*lunch*

Most people, when presented with such a list, would find its memorization to be a tedious or even daunting task. However, consider an alternative mode of presentation (based on Bower and Clark 1969; Higbee 1977; and Crovitz 1979):

The first word is airplane. Just remember that however you like. The next word is hyena, because all the passengers sitting in the seats are hyenas. The next word is cream cheese, because each of the hyenas is taking bites out of a cream cheese sandwich. The next word is moon, because the moon is really made out of cream cheese. The next word is volcano, because there is a volcano on the moon. The next word is ball, because when the volcano on the moon erupts, it spews out balls. The next word is grease, because the balls are covered with grease. The next word is monument, because the balls have so much grease on them it flows all the way to the Washington Monument. The next word is mailman, because a group of mailmen is touring the Washington Monument. The last word is lunch, because when the mailmen finish their tour they go have lunch.

After being presented this mini-story, most people can recall the ten words embedded in it in both forward and backward order. This sort of mnemonic method, which promotes what is nowadays referred to as "elaborate" encoding of the material, can be traced back two and a half thousand years to the Greek poet Simonides.

(cont'd on next page)

A mnemonic technique which does *not* work well for memorizing arbitrary lists involves what is sometimes called "first-letter mnemonics." For example:

hammer

slipper

peach

trunk

leopard

By taking the first letter of each word and filling in vowels where needed, you can form a word such as "HOSPITAL." An effective trick for coding and retrieval? No. This sort of mnemonic technique is only useful for memorizing the *order* of otherwise known items, as in the use of the phrase "Richard of York Gave Battle in Vain" for memorizing the order of the colors of the rainbow.

 SELF-TEST: The effect of context on memory

Not only are stories much easier to remember than lists, but the easiest kind of story to remember is one that is made meaningful by contextualization. Knowing ahead of time what a story is going to be about makes its details much easier to recollect after the telling.

Consider the following story:

A hundred happy faces dreamed of friends and lovers waiting to the north. Deep within, a container of the stuff we breathe sparked to life, burst, burned. Out of life came death. All choked within the darkening cocoon. The nether world of scaled creatures rushed to greet them, and mud filled their eyes. A nation reeled in shock. The friends and lovers watched lit boxes and cried.

After reading the story, how much of it can you remember? Chances are, not much. Now, consider that the story is about a disaster in the Florida Everglades in which a jetliner full of passengers crashed into the reptile-infested swamps. Now read it through once more. How much can you remember this time?

EXERCISE: Memory path

Start at any "Kn" box and move as a knight moves in chess (an L-shaped move: over one square and down two or over two and down one) in any direction. You may move only to another dot, and you may pass over dots. You may not land on the same dot twice nor retrace your path as you find your way to the bottom. Your last move must land exactly on a star. To make this more difficult, you can cut a dime-sized hole in the center of a piece of paper (about 3" X 5") and lay it over the puzzle so you can see only a few dots at a time as you move it along looking for the correct route. A "Hint" appears at the bottom of the page if you get stuck.

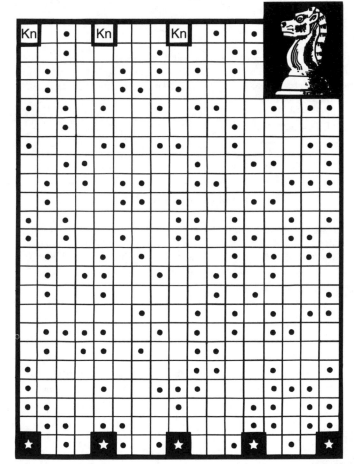

Hint: One path involving 26 moves starts in the far right "Kn" box, weaves straight toward the star below it, then darts to the left and finishes at the lower left star.

A little stress helps memory but too much destroys it

Recent work on the neurological underpinnings of cognitive deficits in the elderly bolsters yet another piece of traditional wisdom: *too much stress makes you old before your time!*

Memory, as we now know, is anything but a passive capacity. Many factors can influence whether we form a long-term memory of a specific fact or event. One such factor is our emotional state: an emotionally-charged, stressful event will much more likely be remembered than one that occurs in the absence of emotional arousal.

Why memory improves after a meal...

While there are various theories about exactly why or how this occurs (see "Imagine a memory-enhancing drug," p. 77), one recent proposal runs as follows: Physical and psychological stress provoke the release of certain neurotransmitters such as epinephrine by the sympathetic nervous system. These neurotransmitters increase the brain's utilization of glucose, and — while research reports differ as to *why* glucose has this effect — it has been shown conclusively that glucose enhances memory, even in Alzheimer's patients. This is why memory formation is better after a meal.

...but stress interferes with memory

Stress also releases a second, slower-acting wave of hormones called glucocorticoids. In low levels, such as those that occur naturally during the day, glucocorticoids enhance long-term memory formation. In higher, stress-induced concentrations, however, they have an inhibiting effect on memory and a toxic effect on neurons. (See "Cortisol," p. 209.)

Once all the details of the role of glucocorticoids in neuron loss are worked out, the hope is that drugs which manipulate the levels of these hormones will help slow the effects of aging and, in particular, forestall the decline in powers of memory. In the meantime, follow your mother's advice and *relax* already.

THE RESEARCH

There are two types of glucocorticoid receptor cells in the hippocampus (a part of the brain crucially involved in some kinds of memory — see "Your 'memory' is, in fact, many processes," p. 73). One type, which stimulates increased memory function, is activated by low levels of the hormone. Once these receptors are saturated, higher levels will activate a different type of receptor cell which has an opposite, inhibiting effect on memory. (Imagine how few women would want to experience a second childbirth if this didn't happen!) One possible way that this second set of cells may inhibit memory function is by interfering with glucose transport and uptake.

If glucocorticoids are kept at stress-induced levels for periods up to a few weeks, they will cause atrophy of the dendritic branches of hippocampal neurons. (Dendrites are the branching structures that convey signals toward the cell body of a neuron.) This damage is, however, reversible.

If, on the other hand, stress levels of glucocorticoids are maintained for a period of months, irreversible loss of hippocampal neurons occurs. In experiments with rats, the effects of this kind of loss mimic the effects of aging at a rapidly accelerated rate. In addition, the older the animal, the more vulnerable it is.

SELF-TEST: Emotion-enhanced memory formation

Here's an experiment you can run to test the claim that emotional arousal enhances memory formation. On the following pages are two stories, equal in length and complexity, but different in the emotional arousal they evoke. The experiment doesn't take long, but you'll need a few willing participants.

To avoid interference effects, choose a different person for each story, rather than presenting them both to the same person or group of people.

Don't reveal ahead of time that the participant will be asked about the details of the story. On the pretext of wanting to find out what kinds of emotions the story evokes, read the neutral version to a friend while he follows along with the accompanying illustrations. Try the same thing on a different friend with the emotion-arousing version.

(cont'd on next page)

1. A grandmother and her young grandson are leaving home in the morning.

2. She is taking him to the bus stop, where he will catch a bus to visit his mother at work.

3. His mother works in a big chemical research lab in the suburbs.

4. They walk to the bus stop.

5. While the grandmother is studying the bus schedule, a bus pulls up to the stop.

6. Two women get out of the bus.

7. One greets the boy and pats him on the head.

8. When the grandmother asks the woman if this is the right bus to the chemical research lab, she says yes.

9. The woman walks away and the grandmother puts the boy on the bus.

10. The bus takes the boy to the suburbs.

11. When the boy gets out, he is in a pretty area with lots of trees and birds.

12. The bus driver calls down to the boy that if he wants his mother to pick him up, he should call her from a pay phone.

13. He finds a pay phone near the bus stop and calls her.

14. She picks him up, and takes him to her workplace.

(cont'd on next page)

1. *A grandmother and her young grandson are leaving home in the morning.*

2. *She is taking him to the bus stop, where he will catch a bus to visit his mother at work.*

3. *His mother works in a big chemical research lab in the suburbs.*

4. *They walk to the bus stop.*

5. *While the grandmother is studying the bus schedule, a car pulls up to the bus stop.*

6. *Two men jump out of the car.*

7. *One man grabs the boy and knocks him unconscious.*

8. *When the grandmother begins to scream, the other man shoots her.*

9. *The two men jump back in the car with the boy and drive off, leaving the grand-mother bleeding on the sidewalk.*

10. *They take the boy to their hide-out.*

11. *When the boy wakes up, he is in a dark basement with lots of rats and cobwebs.*

12. *One of the kidnappers call down to the boy that if he doesn't want the two men to hurt him, he must call his mother and tell her to bring them ten thousand dollars.*

13. *They give him a phone, and he calls her.*

14. *She pays the ransom, and the boy is returned to his mother.*

(cont'd on next page)

You'll have to wait about a week before asking each of the subjects an open-ended question about what details he or she recalls from the story. As an additional check, ask the following multiple-choice questions:

TEST FOR THOSE WHO HEARD THE NEUTRAL VERSION

Question #1 [refer to Picture #1]: <u>Who are these two people?</u>
A) a mother and her son   **B)** a nanny and a little boy   **C)** an aunt and her nephew   **D)** a grandmother and her grandson

Question #2 [refer to Picture #2]: <u>What is one woman asking the other?</u>
A) what time the bus comes   **B)** whether she knows the boy's mother
C) where the bus came from   **D)** where the bus is going

Question #3 [refer to Picture #3]: <u>What is the driver saying to the boy?</u>
A) that the boy should call his mother from a pay phone and she will pick him up   **B)** that the boy forgot to pay his fare   **C)** that he should wait by the tree for his mother   **D)** that he hopes he has a nice day

TEST FOR THOSE WHO HEARD THE EMOTION-AROUSING VERSION

Question #1 [refer to Picture #1]: <u>Who are these two people?</u>
A) a mother and her son   **B)** a nanny and a little boy   **C)** an aunt and her nephew   **D)** a grandmother and her grandson

Question #2 [refer to Picture #2]: <u>Why is the man shooting the woman?</u>
A) because she tried to grab the boy   **B)** because she started screaming
C) because he wants no witnesses   **D)** because she said she would call the police

Question #3 [refer to Picture #3]: <u>What is the man saying to the boy?</u>
A) that he should stop yelling   **B)** that he will never see his mother again
C) that he should call his mother for the ransom money
D) that he will be killed if he says anything to the police

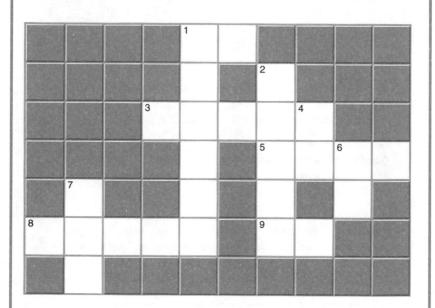

EXERCISE: Alphabetics

"Alphabetics" exercises are similar to crossword puzzles. Use each letter of the alphabet once but only once. (If you want to make this exercise difficult cover the clues.)

Don't try to read the text printed upside-down at the bottom of the page until after you have filled in the solution as best you can. Then cover the grid and clues with a piece of paper. Jot down the two or three clues and solution-words you remember most easily. Do those have an emotional meaning for you that the other, more easily forgettable, words do not?

ACROSS
1. Movie rating
3. Riding whip
5. Kiln
8. Lewd
9. Unit of frequency (elec.)

DOWN
1. Spunky
2. Freshman
4. Kind of dinner
6. Former, as spouse
7. Preserve

Hint: The solution to 3 Across is "Quirt." Have you covered the exercise and clues with a piece of blank paper and written down the first three clues and answers that come to mind?

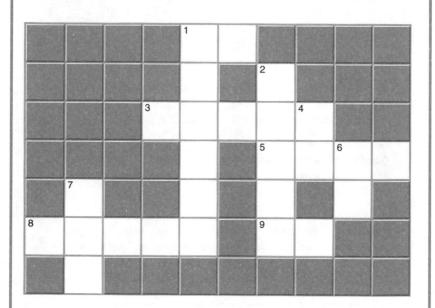

"Now, where did I put my Prozac?"

We all know that failing memory goes hand-in-hand with aging. While forgetfulness may be forestalled to some degree, we generally accept that older people won't be quite as sharp memory-wise as children or young adults. Right?

Yes and no. A growing body of evidence shows that in many cases, a decline in the power of memory may be due not simply to inevitable age-related neurological changes, but — at least in part — to psychological depression. Depression appears to correlate with an increased risk for developing Alzheimer's disease and other senile dementias — along with a poor prognosis for recovery from stroke or heart attack.

Of course, the complexity of the interaction between mood and memory shouldn't be underestimated. Gifted memorizers, as discussed elsewhere (see "Why are stories easier to recall than lists?" p. 103), are often individuals who apply such a formidable body of interests to their environment in general that new information is readily encoded in a personally meaningful and "elaborated" way. This kind of active *engagement* with the world is almost by definition the very opposite of psychological depression. Standard symptoms of depression, according to the diagnostic manuals, include apathy and a lack of interest in usually enjoyable hobbies or activities.

Depression destroys memory faster than age

Conversely, withdrawal from participation in challenging mental activity may lead to depression. This is why depression often follows hard on the heels of retirement.

The lesson to be drawn from this is simple. Since happiness and mental acuity are if anything faster friends than forgetfulness and aging, the best way to be happy is to keep yourself on your toes whether you think you want to or not. Of course, if the things that challenge you intellectually are the things that you love doing, so much the better. And the best way to keep your mind sharp is to keep yourself surrounded with what psychologists call an "enriched environment" — challenging activities and interesting acquaintances — which will in turn make you a happier person.

SELF-TEST: Geographics

Here are seven Middle Eastern nations in the news. Their boundary conflicts can be quickly resolved by drawing only three straight lines from any side of the box to any other without touching any nation. When you are through, each nation must be completely enclosed in its own area. Write the name of each of the seven nations next to one of the numbers in the box below the map. Then write that number in the circle next to that nation's shape.

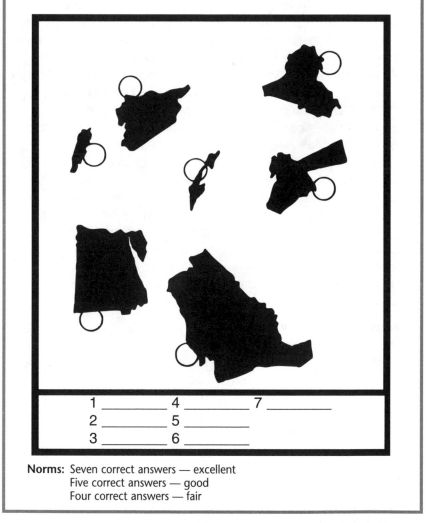

1 _____ 4 _____ 7 _____
2 _____ 5 _____
3 _____ 6 _____

Norms: Seven correct answers — excellent
Five correct answers — good
Four correct answers — fair

Hint: Lebanon, the small one on the far left, and Israel, the small one in the center, are each enclosed by a different small triangle. The first line you draw should divide Saudi Arabia and Egypt and fence Syria off from Iraq.

Can challenging mental activity throughout life forestall age-related cognitive decline?

In a study of cognitive ability and aging in university professors, older professors showed the usual declines in reaction time and some aspects of memory, but no decline at all in the acquisition and organization of conceptual knowledge. This indicates that the pursuit of demanding intellectual activity throughout life may counteract the usual age-related decrement in planning, organizing, and manipulating information.

Younger (age 30-44), middle-aged (45-59) and older (60-71) professors at the University of California at Berkeley were shown prose passages and tested for their recall of the content. Unlike older subjects in the general population, older professors recalled the facts as well as their younger peers. (See "As they age...," p. 123.)

Working memory

In a test of this short-term memory process involved in on-line monitoring or control of information, older professors showed no effects of "proactive inhibition" — the interference of the details of one learning task with performance on a second similar one. Generally, older individuals show a marked decrease in their ability to exclude extraneous details from their minds while performing this kind of task. The older professors, however, appeared to have use of strategies to overcome or prevent this.

SELF-TEST: Why testimony may be inaccurate but not a lie

Read this list to a friend and have him repeat back to you every one of the words he remembers:

bed, slumber, dream, drowsy, pillow, tired, nap, yawn, doze, snore

Chances are, your friend will not only remember some of the words on the actual list, but will also falsely recall the one obvious word you didn't say: *sleep.*

In experiments using lists like this, PET scans show that the auditory cortex is activated every time a previously-recited word is recalled, but not when a word is incorrectly recalled.

Don't read the italic type below or on the opposite page. If possible, have a friend read one of the passages to you. The reading should not be rushed, but no long pauses are permitted and nothing may be repeated. After hearing the entire passage, you should re-tell the story as accurately as you can remember it. Be as specific as possible. Include all details, not just the general outline or plot. Your friend should keep track of how many of the facts you remember as you re-tell the passage you just heard him or her read to you. When you have finished, check your score against the norms shown at the bottom of page 119.

This self-test can also be done unassisted if you have a timer. Read the unsegmented passage (below) once through at normal reading speed; do not take longer than 30 seconds. Next, write down the story from memory to the best of your recollection, and assign yourself points with reference to the segmented passage (opposite).

Jimmy Johnson, a track star from West Los Angeles, was buying clothes one day in Beverly Hills. A 15-year-old from the suburbs mugged a 70-year-old woman five feet in front of him. Jimmy chased the mugger five blocks, caught him and returned the woman's 10 dollars. The old woman told him that she needed the money for her grandson's Bar Mitvah. She gave him a 15-cent reward.

Neurons are the functional units of the nervous system. They transmit signals from one part of the body to another. Neurons have a relatively large cell body, and two kinds of what are called "processes": one type, which convey signals toward the cell body, are called dendrites; the other type, which carry signals away from the cell body, are called axons. An axon is often branched, and at the end of each branch are synaptic knobs, which convey signals across a synapse to other cells by releasing chemicals called neurotransmitters.

(cont'd on next page)

Segmented Versions:

Jimmy Johnson/, a track star/ from West/ Los Angeles/, was buying/ clothes/ one day in Beverly Hills/. A 15-year-old/ from the suburbs/ mugged/ a 70-year-old/ woman/ five feet/ in front of him/. Jimmy chased the mugger/ five blocks/, caught him/ and returned/ the woman's 10 dollars/. The old woman told him/ that she needed the money/ for her grandson's/ Bar Mitvah/. She gave him/ a 15-cent reward/.

Neurons/ are the functional units/ of the nervous system/. They transmit signals/ from one part of the body to another/. Neurons have a relatively large/ cell body/, and two kinds/ of what are called processes/: one type, which convey signals/ toward/ the cell body/, are called dendrites/; the other type, which carry signals away from/ the cell body/, are called axons/. An axon is often branched/, and at the end/ of each branch are synaptic knobs/, which convey signals/ across a synapse/ to other cells/ by releasing/ chemicals/ called neurotransmitters/.

Scoring: Each passage is divided into 25 "facts" or significant details, as indicated in the segmented version (in which the phrases that contain a fact are separated by slashes). Each such fact must be correctly remembered in order for maximal points to be obtained. If you recall all 25 facts, then your score is 25/25, or 100%. Fifteen remembered facts would yield a score of 15/25, or 60%.

Norms (when the passage is read aloud to the subject): For the first passage, the norm for younger subjects is 15 correct, or 60%; for older subjects, 11 correct or 44%.

The second passage, which is more technical, would have somewhat lower norms. (But at least you can learn something interesting.)

EXERCISE: Neuron and off

ACROSS

1. Neuron signal conveyance process
5. Whatnot case
9. Sash
12. Pierre's dream
13. Wallet contents
14. Tommy follower
15. German river
16. No ifs — or buts
17. Palindromic conjunction
18. Unchangeable computer memory
20. Nervous system functional units
22. Ribbed
25. Meadow
26. Unit of work
27. Ascertain
32. Enzymes
34. — King Cole
35. Pet
36. Examined again
39. — Cat (winter vehicle)
40. Cruelest mo.
41. Abase
43. French white wine
47. Describing 43 Across
48. Black dog

(cont'd on next page)

49. Story about a duo
51. Castro's realm
54. Sleeve resident
55. Greek cheese
56. Bone up on in a hurry
57. Washington crossed it (abbr.)
58. Several Peters were one
59. Before plane or drome

DOWN

1. "All the things you —"
2. Deleted
3. Surpluses
4. Fiddler and pianist
5. Greek letter
6. Volunteer state, for short
7. Not removed
8. Creator of a bond
9. Cookie
10. — Free
11. Residential suffix
19. Pre — courses
21. Bulls
22. Rip
23. Gaelic
24. Neuron signal conveyance processes toward the cell

28. Mai —
29. Anxious
30. Ship of 1492
31. Collar or jacket
33. Pierce
37. Kind of bra
38. — Plaines
42. Hadj target
43. Apparelled
44. "He does" in Madrid
45. Cain's victim
46. Bristle
50. Deface
52. Pub
53. Latin I word

EXERCISE: Personal pairs

Make the 10 most logical pairs out of these 20 different items. Use each picture only once and don't leave any picture out. Pair them so all 10 are the *most likely* combinations of similarities. There is no "correct" answer. This exercise requires that you keep specific images in short-term "working" memory while you work through the 10 parings without writing notes as you go. Two possible sets of 10 pairs are shown in the "Solutions" section.

For fun, try this with a friend, and see if you can match the items in the same way you think your friend would. Score two points for each pair of yours that matches your friend's answer and one point for each pair not matching his or her answer. If you have to leave any picture out, subtract one point for each.

After completing this exercise try the matching exercises on pages 124-127. Even if you have already done those exercises once, you may be surprised to find that proactive inhibition interferes with your ability to match those pairs of faces, words or symbols correctly without restudying them.

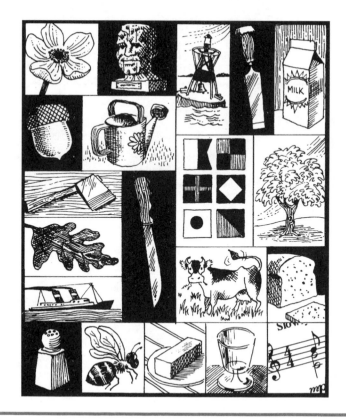

As they age, most people tend to notice problems with their "working" memory

Working memory is the type of short-term memory system the brain uses when it is necessary to retain data only long enough to monitor or manipulate it "on-line." Older people's use of working memory tends to fail because the data they learn temporarily for doing one thing interferes with new data they try to put into their working memory to tackle the next thing. This phenomenon is called "proactive inhibition" — the interference of the details of one learning task with performance on a second, similar one (see "Forgetting," p. 87).

As people move into their 60's their short-term "working" memory normally begins to fail. For example, a phone number just looked up may be confused with another number recently memorized.

Generally, older individuals show a marked decrease in their ability to exclude extraneous details from their minds while performing the kinds of tasks shown in the following tests of "paired associate learning." (Similarly, many older people also notice that it becomes more difficult to concentrate on a conversation when other people are talking in the background.)

However, older college professors often avoid this problem

A very recent study of professors of all ages at the University of California showed that the older professors appeared to have use of strategies to overcome or prevent the effects of proactive inhibition as well as the younger ones could. These results suggest that individuals whose minds have been kept active into old age (60-71 years of age in the study) do not show this type of "normal" decrease in mental ability.

Almost any diagnostic test, cognitive or otherwise, can easily slide over into revealing something other than the narrow task it was designed for. The tests below are designed to reveal the effect of proactive inhibition (see "Can challenging mental activity...," p. 117). If any of the names or faces in them trigger an emotional response, the score may improve because that data may be stored as a more permanent memory.

SELF-TEST: Proactive inhibition (pictorial)

You will need a timer. Your task is to remember which female face goes with which male face. Before looking at the next page study the six pairs of faces on this page for 4 seconds each (24 seconds total); then read the instructions below.

Next, look at the box of six male faces on the next page. Match each male face to one of the female faces in the box below, following the pairings on this page to the best of your recollection. Don't spend longer than a minute. (On these quick timed tasks, ask a friend to time you so you're not preoccupied with the stopwatch.) Repeat the task twice, observing the same time limits.

(cont'd on next page)

Norms:

First trial: two correct for older subjects (60-71 years), three correct for younger subjects (18-23 years)

Second trial: two correct for older subjects, four correct for younger subjects

Third trial: three correct for older subjects, five correct for younger subjects

1___

2___

3___

4___

5___

6___

SELF-TEST: Proactive inhibition (verbal)

Wanda — Norman	Lois — Lester	Colleen — Joe	Janice — Craig
Phyllis — Stanley	Rachel — Henry	Christine — David	Penny — Max
	Susan — Vince	Karen — Mike	

Study each of the 10 pairs of names above for four seconds. Your task is to remember which goes with which. Use a timer so you don't spend more than 40 seconds all told. Then cover up the list with a piece of paper. Next, look at the list of 10 female names below. Match each to one of the male names listed on the right, following the pairings on the above list to the best of your recollection. Don't spend longer than a minute trying to match them. Repeat the same procedure twice, observing the same time limits. Compare your score with age-norms below.

Susan —	Henry
Janice —	Norman
Lois —	Craig
Wanda —	Vince
Karen —	Stanley
Christine —	Mike
Colleen —	David
Penny —	Lester
Phyllis —	Joe
Rachel —	Max

Norms:

First trial: two to three correct for older subjects, six correct for younger subjects

Second trial: four to five correct for older, eight to nine for younger

Third trial: five correct for older; nine correct for younger

SELF-TEST: Proactive inhibition (graphic)

Below are two grids of 36 boxes, with a pattern in each box. Some patterns appear in more than one box. Your task is to work rapidly through the first grid, marking each pattern *once* the first time it appears. To prevent looking back at previous rows, cover upper rows with a piece of paper as you progress down. By the time you reach the bottom right, you should have marked each pattern once and only once. You have one minute to complete the task.

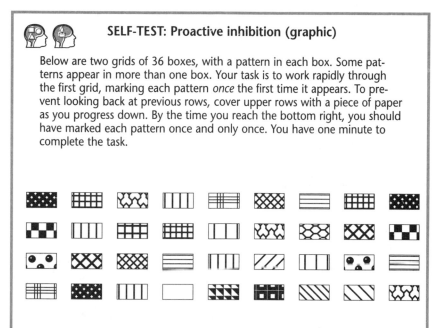

After completing one trial, add up your errors and repeat on the second grid.

On this task, older subjects generally do worse on the second trial than on the first. The increased errors made by the average older subject on the second trial is due to proactive inhibition — the interference of an earlier task with performance on a subsequent task of the same type. In general, older people have a harder time with this phenomenon and with filtering out extraneous information on tasks like this.

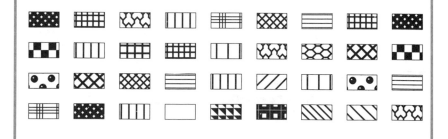

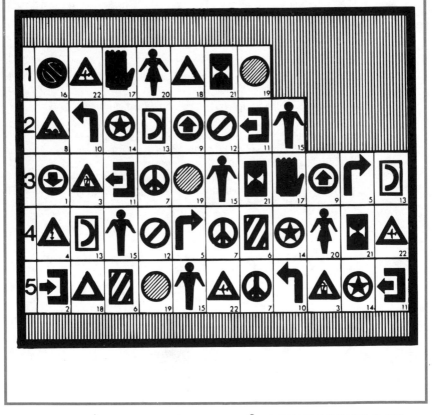

EXERCISE: A mental trick

This exercise requires two people. It works on two levels. One level is to figure out how the trick works. The trick is that you appear to be able to read someone else's mind by telling her which of these symbols she is thinking of. Ask the other person to choose any symbol and tell you only in which rows (numbers 1, 2, 3, 4 and 5) it appears. If, for example, you are told, "It appears in rows 2, 4 and 5," you concentrate on the chart for a few moments and then, with an air of great mystery and wisdom, you announce, "You selected the star in the circle." On another level, this exercise tests the ability to hold the row numbers in working memory long enough to come up with the correct answer. A "Hint" on how this trick works appears at the bottom of this page.

Hint: Have you noticed the small numbers in each symbol? The ones at the end of the rows nearest the large row numbers are the most important.

Normal decline of very short-term memory shows up in some tests of older people

The brain produces a chemical called acetylcholine to carry messages between cells that are involved in recall and strategy-making. The availability of such neurotransmitter chemicals appears to increase in brains which are frequently used to meet problem-solving challenges. This may account, at least in part, for the fact that some older people do not lose these abilities as much as others as they age. Neuropsychologists use variations of the exercise shown on pages 130-131 to measure such changes.

The ability to find the most efficient strategy changes too

In a study of correlations between age and problem-solving strategies for the exercise on the following pages, older people (60 years and older) were shown to be much less likely to use the optimal strategy than were younger people (14-35 years). Also, among a group of 64 participants divided evenly into young and old, only the older group members ever used the least efficient strategy. For a related study see the articles beginning on pages 117 and 123.

A self-test similar to the age-related memory research

For this exercise, you need a playing partner. The two extra grids printed on page 131 allow you to experiment with different strategies. However, you may want to photocopy the grids so you can play this brain game again with the same or other partners. You can then keep track of the difference in the target square the "examiner" had in mind.

In some ways this is similar to the game called "Battleship." For each grid, an "examiner" must select one square without telling the "examinee" which square has been chosen. (Numbers and letters have been written along the edges for easy reference and identification.) The examinee's task is to find the chosen square by asking a series of yes/no questions. The fewer the number of questions asked, the higher the score.

To solve a problem like this, there are essentially three possible types of strategy

The simplest but least efficient strategy is to ask, for each square in turn, "Is this the right square?" This strategy is not too bad for very small grids, but quickly becomes hopelessly inefficient for larger ones. For example, for a 2 X 2 grid, you'd always get the right answer after no more than three questions, but for an 8 X 8 grid you might have to ask as many as 63; and for a 100 X 100 grid, you may need 9,999 questions before hitting the chosen square.

Of course, with the least efficient strategy you might get lucky and hit the right square on the first question. For a really large grid, this would be as likely as winning the lottery. With the optimal strategy, you'll never get the right square on the first question. But on average, for any grid 2 X 2 or larger, you'll be better off with the optimal strategy. A "Hint" appears below. A description of the most efficient, optimal strategy appears in the "Solutions" section.

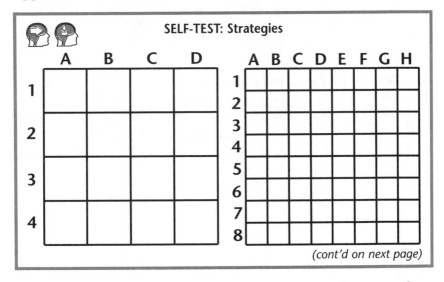

SELF-TEST: Strategies

(cont'd on next page)

Hint: A somewhat more efficient strategy is to proceed row by row and then, once the right row is found, square by square until the correct one is reached. For a small, 2 X 2 grid, this works as well as any strategy (maximum number of questions = 2), while for a larger, 8 X 8 grid the maximum possible number of questions required will be 14. For a 100 X 100 grid, you'll need up to but never more than 198 questions.

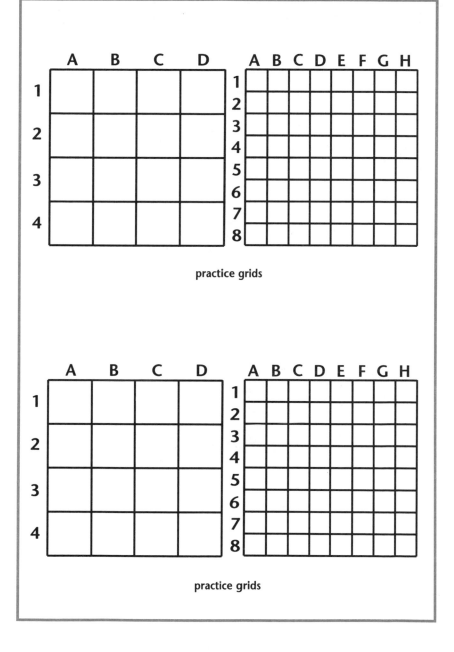

practice grids

practice grids

EXERCISE: Eliminating possibilities

Here are three boxes of fruit, one containing one dozen bananas, one with a dozen lemons, and a third with six bananas and six lemons. But all the covers have been switched. Now imagine that you can select one box. Shut your eyes, open the box, take out only the first fruit you touch. Don't feel around inside the box. Close the cover. When you see what fruit you have, can you tell which fruits, or combination of fruits, are in each box?

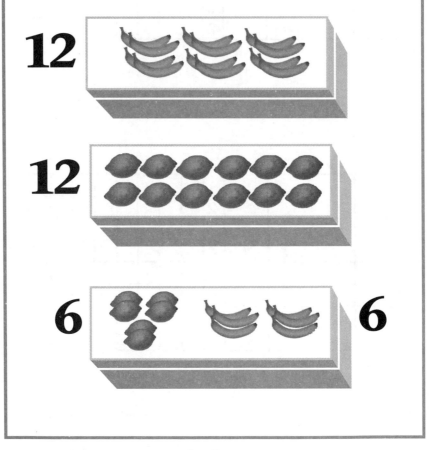

Hint: Start with the box whose cover gives you the most information.

New hope for those at risk for Alzheimer's: Estrogen replacement therapy

In what a leading researcher calls "the most promising thing that's happened so far in Alzheimer's disease," new evidence indicates that supplements of the hormone estrogen may prevent and perhaps even reverse the most common form of senile dementia in women. Support for this conclusion comes from population studies that show a reduced incidence of Alzheimer's and other dementias among women undergoing estrogen replacement therapy (ERT) and less severe symptoms among Alzheimer's patients who happen also to be on ERT. In addition, animal studies demonstrate that estrogen may stimulate the growth of neurons in brain regions affected by Alzheimer's.

ERT has been used by millions of women since the 1940's to counteract some of the effects or risks of menopause

In the 1950's, it was common for women to take estrogen for relatively benign symptoms such as hot flashes and vaginal dryness. Recent research indicates that ERT may be effective as well in counteracting the increased post-menopausal risk of osteoporosis and heart disease.

Medical opinion about this practice has fluctuated over the decades, as initial enthusiasm became tempered in the 70's by research that showed a 5- to 15-times increase in the risk of uterine cancer by women taking estrogen supplements. This led to the use of the hormone progesterone together with estrogen, which appears to lower the incidence of uterine cancer while sparing estrogen's heart-disease-fighting capability.

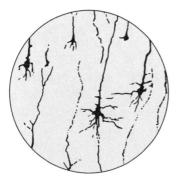

Compare this picture of brain cells called neurons with the one on the next page. The difference is not the number of cells — they both show about seven — but the number and length of the dendrites that branch off of them. The more dendrites that branch out to touch other cells, the better they can combine forces to recall information or solve problems fast.

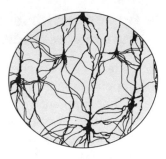

This pictures healthy active neurons. The adult human brain has billions of them, and each has thousands of contacts with other neurons. Estrogen may cause brain cells to expand these contacts. Also, a brain that is kept busy grows more dendrites than an idle one.

One of the questions still to be answered is whether the possible benefits of estrogen in combatting Alzheimer's outweigh any remaining potential risks of cancer

It is also uncertain at this point whether progesterone, which appears to negate the cancer-causing effect of estrogen by inhibiting the stimulation of cell growth in the uterus and breasts, might also inhibit estrogen's ability to stimulate nerve growth in the brain. In rodents, a rise in estrogen is associated with an increase of synaptic density and neural dendrites in the brain, while increased levels of progesterone are associated with a loss of synapses and dendrites.

Recent research raises hope that one chemical component of a common estrogen replacement drug may grow brain cells without also encouraging growth of cancer cells

One of the most encouraging facets of this new research is the prospect of isolating a subcomponent of the most commonly prescribed ERT drug. That subcomponent has the specific effect of stimulating brain neuron growth but *not* the growth of breast and uterine cells. Success in this area would bypass the need for progesterone supplements accompanying ERT. There are already reports that the isolation of such a hormonal molecule may be imminent.

Another as-yet unanswered question is whether ERT would be effective in forestalling Alzheimer's in women who are inherently at greatest risk for developing the disease, carriers of the "Alzheimer's gene," ApoE4. If estrogen is effective in preventing dementia in this high-risk subgroup, there is little doubt that its benefits would outweigh its risks for them at least.

Where the neurons first begin to degenerate in Alzheimer's dementia

Inability to recall recent events is the first sign of the progressive deterioration of brain function accompanied by a buildup of a pattern of protein amyloid "plaques." It starts in the cortex along the inner side of the temporal lobe, typically in the hippocampus. It then spreads to other circuits including memory of events in the distant past. The ability to come up with words for common objects begins to fail, followed by not recognizing familiar people and places or even knowing what things such as a coffee cup are used for.

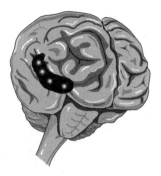

The buildup of a pattern of protein amyloid "plaques"— typically in the hippocampus — accompanies the beginnings of memory loss for recent events.

Women who keep their minds active into old age are less likely to suffer. However, "early-onset" Alzheimer's, which typically shows up in the early 50's, is a genetically inherited condition that cannot be lessened or delayed by keeping one's mind active.

 EXERCISE: Singles only please

The point of the exercise on the following page is to stretch your short-term memory slightly. There are two of almost all the objects. What makes it interesting is the "almost." It should not take you more than four minutes to count how many objects there are only *one* of.

Try to find the solution by keeping track of the images in your mind's eye only — without making marks on the page or taking notes. When you have the answer you may write down the names of the single objects, if you like, before you check the hint at the bottom of the page or the answer in the Solutions section. Before you start get a timer ready and allow yourself four minutes.

(cont'd on next page)

Hint: Look for warm-blooded animals and the tea that is most pleasing to the palate.

emotional
function

EMOTIONAL

Neuroscience is revealing the loci in the brain of our emotional faculties, and the neural pathways linking emotion to the "intellectual" functions of the mind. Emotion is intimately linked to cognition, and to the maintenance of the health of our brain cells as well as our body's immune system.

By a traditional view familiar to all of us, our brain and our emotions are two quite different things, often even in competition with each other. While we may no longer subscribe to the ancient Western notion of moods and humors deriving from our bodily organs' fluids, we still preserve a folk theory of love as housed in the heart. Perhaps it is partly a holdover of this tradition that modern neuroscience has focused more on the brain's role in cognitive processes such as memory than on emotion.

All that is changing. We now know that emotion — dependent on structures in the brain itself — plays a crucial role in memory formation. There's a neural pathway directly linking the brain's emotion and memory centers. The cortex — housing "higher," more complex and conscious faculties — may join in the act of interpreting or evaluating a threatening stimulus, but only after the emotionally-charged experience has been seared into memory. In fact, emotional memories are very hard to extinguish, even though some particularly traumatic ones may be banished from the conscious mind, only to reappear years later in times of stress.

And mood and temperament fluctuate with levels of neurotransmitters, chemicals involved in the transmission of messages between brain cells. Some of the most philosophically challenging medical research of the last decade has centered on the manipulation of mood through the pharmacological manipulation of the brain's levels of neurotransmitters such as serotonin and norepinephrine. For the first time in human history, changing your emotional profile and, in a real sense, your personality seems as safe and easy as taking an aspirin.

We're also learning more, at a rapid clip, about the complex interactions between emotion and health, including the function of the immune system. Depression is linked to heart disease and reduced immunity, while laughter boosts your T-cell count. One of the most exciting recent discoveries is that stress, through the release of the hormone cortisol, can destroy brain cells and may lead to Alzheimer's. The more we know about this, the better our prospects for controlling our stress-response, counteracting the cognitively destructive effects of stress, and keeping both our body and mind healthy.

Here is a trick you can make your body play on your emotions. The way you arrange your facial muscles and posture can change your feelings. If you don't believe that, next time you are feeling blue stand up straight, walk with a spring in your step and compose your facial muscles into a smile with your eyes wide. You will begin feeling better. The reverse is also true. In fact if a mood-altering drug this effective were discovered it would probably be illegal to sell without a doctor's prescription.

It's cheaper than gin

 What would you think of someone who could control his or her emotional state with the same ease with which you comb your hair or stick out your tongue? You'd probably think they had a special gift, or an unusual power of the sort only attainable through years of practice or training. It turns out that the trick of manipulating your emotions is probably far simpler and more obvious than you'd ever imagined — so obvious, in fact, that it's been staring you in the face your whole life and you've never even noticed.

You have more control of your emotions than you think

We typically think of emotions as things that "happen" to us, that exist independently of us, that rise up inside us (and sometimes come out of us) whether we like it or not, or that come from outside and involve us in an event in which we're a purely passive participant. Consider the way we talk about emotions: we are "overcome by anger," "paralyzed by fear," "thrown into a state of confusion," or "overflowing with joy." A University of California researcher has accumulated an impressive body of evidence over the last several years that challenges this view. Among other things, he's shown that by consciously manipulating your facial muscles, you can actively generate whatever emotion you like — anger, fear, disgust, sadness, or pure, sweet joy.

You can change your mood by changing facial expressions

 Paul Ekman, in collaboration with colleagues in the psychology and psychiatry departments at U.C. San Francisco, U.C. Berkeley, the University of Wisconsin at Madison and elsewhere, has per-

formed experiments showing that subjects who simply manipulate their facial muscles according to his instructions frequently show many or all of the physiological correlates — increased heart rate, higher finger temperature, etc. — of the emotions associated with those facial expressions. EEG measures, too, show that manipulation of the facial muscles associated with happiness results in the same left-frontal brain activity known to correlate with spontaneous joy. And for all expressions, subjects report subjective feelings of emotion corresponding to the expression they're making.

Facial expressions and emotions are biologically linked
This fits well with Ekman's independent findings of the universality of facial expressions of emotion. In fieldwork with preliterate, isolated cultures of New Guinea, he found that members of those cultures matched descriptions of emotions to photographs of facial expressions just as Western subjects would match them.

This sort of evidence indicates that there are hard-wired, innate links between certain facial muscle movements and autonomic motor activity (heart rate, skin conductance, etc.) and brain activity. This in itself is controversial, but not shocking. What *is* astounding in its implications for our ability to control our quality of life is the finding that the direction of this connection can run from facial expression, which we usually think of as a mere *signal* of emotion, to the emotion *itself*.

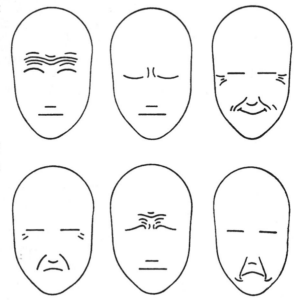

How distracting thoughts destroy effective mood control

Almost all of us have some degree of ability to control our own mood. Typical commonsense strategies include reminiscing about happy or sad memories (actors do this in order to cry on cue), paying selective attention to good or bad thoughts (deliberately focusing on just good or bad thoughts or events), and engaging in activities that support the way we want to feel.

All these strategies may be defeated by competing cognitive tasks, stress, or time pressure. The "ironic process" theory of mental control has the following story to tell about why this happens.

Your unconscious tries to help set your mood by whatever you are consciously thinking

Successful mental control works simultaneously by way of two cooperative processes. One intentionally searches for thoughts and stimuli that promote the desired mental state. The other, less conscious and more automatic, "ironic" process monitors mental contents for signals of a failure to reach the desired state. If it determines that the desired state hasn't been attained, then the conscious process responds with renewed effort. The ironic process is like a shadow of the intentional one: less noticeable, not directly manipulable, but always there.

Problems may occur if some other task interferes

Stray thoughts can derail the deliberate, effortful attempt to attain a desired state. Conscious attempts at mental control are easily distracted by other conscious and effortful activities. The unconscious ironic process, on the other hand, continues to run, monitoring our mental contents for failure. In this way, the ironic process may increase the accessibility of undesired contents to consciousness. The shadow assumes a life of its own, and the result is exactly the opposite of what we want to accomplish.

SELF-TEST: Mood control

This provides a brief illustration of an "ironic" effect: Attempts to suppress a thought may make that thought more accessible.

Consider for a moment the following word: HOUSE. Now, you are to eliminate this word from your thoughts for the rest of the exercise.

For each of the words in the following list, provide a related word, as illustrated with the first two items on the list. Work quickly — don't spend longer than two seconds on each item.

envelope — letter   needle — _____

gift — present   curtain — _____

flower — _____   bottle — _____

collie — _____   street — _____

oil — _____   shop — _____

clock — _____   home — _____

Next, consider the following word: HOP. This time, you are to concentrate on the word rather than eliminate it from your thoughts.

For each of the words in the following list, provide a related word, as illustrated with the first two items on the list. Work quickly — don't spend longer than two seconds on each item.

hamburger — bun   door — _____

litter — trash   grass — _____

monkey — _____   faucet — _____

bath — _____   honk — _____

pan — _____   string — _____

wash — _____   jump — _____

Most people are more likely to supply the word *house* as a match for *home* in the first list than they are to supply *hop* as a match for *jump* in the second — despite the fact that they're trying to suppress *house*, and concentrate on *hop*.

SELF-TEST: Ironic processes in mood control

Step 1.

First, search your memory for a particularly sad event in your past. Take however long you need to think. When you've thought of one, proceed to the next paragraph.

Try to imagine the sad event as vividly as you can — without actually letting yourself feel sad. Picture the event as it happened. Recall as many details as you can. Who else was involved? What objects were present? What sounds did you hear? Try as hard as you can to re-create the sad event in your mind, including all your thoughts at the time, but without actually feeling sad.

Step 2.

Here's a seven-digit number that you must now memorize: 7834562. Whatever else you do, you have to memorize this number, so take whatever time you need to commit it to memory. At the end, you'll have to show that you still remember the number in order for the results to be meaningful, and you won't be allowed to look back at it. Proceed to the next step when you feel confident you won't forget the number.

Step 3.

Next, think back again to that sad event you were thinking about in Step 1. Again, think about it without letting yourself feel sad. And don't forget that number!

Step 4.

Next, spend a few minutes writing down whatever thoughts come into your mind. Just start with whatever thought you like, and then jot down whatever thoughts, feelings, fantasies, ideas, and memories come into your head. Don't worry about structure or grammar — this is supposed to be nothing more than a stream-of-consciousness report. While you're writing, be sure not to forget the seven-digit number you were told to memorize. After about seven minutes, proceed to the next step.

(cont'd on next page)

Step 5.

Finally, take a look at the following list of adjectives. Rate your present mood according to the adjectives, on a seven-point scale, with seven being highest/strongest and one the lowest/weakest.

Happy

Nervous

Depressed

Worried

Serene

Inspired

Uncomfortable

Calm

Gloomy

Cheerful

Step 6.

Without looking back at the number you memorized, write it down here:

_____

Results:

The memorization task in Step 2 generally has the effect of making it harder to control your mood in the way you want — in this case, it interferes with your attempt to suppress feelings of sadness. This means that your self-ratings on the list of 10 adjectives in Step 5 will indicate a sadder mood than if the memorization task in Step 2 were left out. You can test this by trying the exercise again sometime without the number-memorization step.

Self-illusions are good for you

Common sense has it that an accurate self-perception is essential to good mental health. By this view, "normal" people have a realistic understanding of who they are, what they are capable of, and what will happen in the future. People who lack such a balanced understanding, by contrast, may be unwell or, in extreme cases, insane.

The facts show that the opposite may be true. The healthiest and happiest people, it seems, are the ones who have unrealistically positive illusions about their own good qualities, their control of chance events, and their future prospects. The realistic ones have a tendency to suffer from some degree of depression.

Do you view yourself as happier, healthier, luckier, more virtuous, and more skilled than others?

People who score low on inventories of depression tend to exaggerate their own positive qualities. They'll rank themselves as having a stronger sense of ethics than most others, as being more creative, imaginative, and intelligent. On an individual basis, this kind of self-evaluation may or may not be realistic. But when 80% of the population opine that they are better drivers than most others, it just doesn't add up: 80 out of 100 people just can't all be better than 51 out of 100. Those remaining people who fail to consider their driving better than average — who, on average, are more realistic — tend to be at least somewhat depressed.

Do you think your good qualities are unique, and your flaws common?

Well-adjusted people tend not to focus on negative aspects of themselves to begin with. But pressed to acknowledge their flaws, they dismiss them as unimportant, often because "everybody's like that." Positive aspects, on the other hand — abilities, talents, and virtues — are perceived as rare and distinctive. Depressed people tend to have a more even-handed view of themselves and others.

Do you think your future will be better than your past?
Most people characterize themselves as more oriented toward the future than the past, and most people believe the future will be better than the past. There's really no way to know beforehand whether such beliefs will turn out to be justified or realistic. But some things point clearly to the fact that most of us are simply not facing reality.

Why is life insurance such a hard sell? Because most of us cultivate comforting illusions about our mortality. Far fewer people believe that they'll ever be in a serious automobile accident, or be a victim of violent crime, than statistics indicate is realistic. Why would otherwise happy and intelligent people indulge in life-threatening activities — cigarette smoking or tailgating at 80 miles per hour — if they were being realistic about the risk involved? Happy and optimistic people aren't realistic — they think *other* people will get lung cancer or die in a car accident.

People with mild depression and low self-esteem tend to have views of their prospects more in line with statistics and hindsight, and tend to be more sober and analytical about their future. It's a telling comment on the pervasiveness of unrealistic optimism that the sober realists are often accused of being pessimists. It is, in fact, *depressing* to be realistic, and indulgence in realism about the future is even considered socially unacceptable. And woe betide any politician who admits that the future might not be better than the past.

Do you indulge in magical thinking?
It appears to be a good sign for your mental well-being if you have an exaggerated view of your control of events and people around you. "Normal" people indulge in this kind of thinking much of the time. In games involving pure chance, we imagine we can somehow influence the outcome even though we can't — by rolling the dice softly if we want low numbers and hard if we want high numbers, for example.

Many people select lottery tickets with personally meaningful numbers — birthdates, anniversary dates, and the like — rather than buying a randomly generated "quick-pick" ticket. Rationally, this makes no sense. First, there's no way that a personally meaningful number sequence will stand a greater chance of winning in a random drawing. Second, "quick picks," while admittedly not more likely to win, are likely to result in a greater prize if they do win: certain date-based numbers (1 through 31) tend to be picked by people who take that approach, thus increasing the chances of having to share a prize with like-minded others. We may speculate that it might  be possible to identify those at risk for mild depression by the fact that they choose the rational approach, rather than the irrational "magical" one. On the other hand, given that your chances of winning the lottery are probably less than those of finding buried treasure in your back yard, the very fact of buying the occasional lottery ticket may be indicative of a healthy temperament.

Illusions aren't just comforting — they improve performance

People like to have the illusion of control. Businesses have recognized this for many years: Employees are less likely to resist change if they're informed beforehand of what's happening and included in the decision-making process — even if they're given no real authority to change the ultimate outcome.

But there's more to it than just this. Having an unrealistically positive self-image and an exaggerated sense of control over events may be construed as a sort of egocentricity. Memory is organized egocentrically: The more personally meaningful something is, or the more self-relevant it is, the easier it is to remember. Therefore, positive self-illusions may have cognitive benefits for memory.

Even more important, positive illusions feed back into performance. People with unrealistically high self-perceptions, belief in personal control, and optimism about their future are often more motivated and persistent, and may perform better because of this.

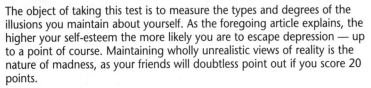

The object of taking this test is to measure the types and degrees of the illusions you maintain about yourself. As the foregoing article explains, the higher your self-esteem the more likely you are to escape depression — up to a point of course. Maintaining wholly unrealistic views of reality is the nature of madness, as your friends will doubtless point out if you score 20 points.

At the end of this self-test you will find a scoring legend based on the number of points you have earned by totaling those allocated to each answer to the questions that follow.

Do you think you're more honest than others?

(a) Yes, very much so (2 pts.)

(b) Maybe a little (1 pt.)

(c) No (0 pts.)

You and a friend each buy a quick-pick lottery ticket. You ask him to hold your ticket while you tie your shoe, and you later realize the tickets must have been jumbled: the one you have is not the same as the one you originally had. Does this bother you?

(a) Yes, very much so (2 pts.)

(b) Maybe a little (1 pt.)

(c) No, it makes no difference (0 pts.)

Of all your talents and abilities, which one do you think is best or most important? _____

What percentage of other people in the country do you think share your level of skill in this ability?

(a) 0-30% (2 pts.)

(b) 30-70% (1 pt.)

(c) 70-100% (0 pts.)

(cont'd on next page)

Do you think you're a better driver than other people?

(a) No doubt about it (2 pts.)

(b) Better than average, but not dramatically (1 pt.)

(c) No (0 pts.)

Do you think that the success you've had in life is due more to hard work than just being in the right place at the right time?

(a) Very much (2 pts.)

(b) Somewhat (1 pt.)

(c) No (0 pts.)

Of all your flaws, which one do you think is worst or most significant?

_____

What percentage of other people in the country do you think also have this flaw?

(a) 70-100% (2 pts.)

(b) 30-70% (1 pt.)

(c) 0-30% (0 pts.)

Do you think you're more sincere than others?

(a) Very much so (2 pts.)

(b) Somewhat (1 pt.)

(c) No (0 pts.)

How true do you think the following is?

Most people act out of self-interest, but I try to help people rather than hurt them.

(a) Very true (2 pts.)

(b) Somewhat true (1 pt.)

(c) Not true (0 pts.)

(cont'd on next page)

Do you think that good things happen to people who do good, and bad things to people who do bad?

(a) Definitely (2 pts.)

(b) To some degree (1 pt.)

(c) No (0 pts.)

Do you think that people who get in automobile accidents are bad drivers?

(a) Almost all of the time (2 pts.)

(b) Only occasionally (1 pt.)

(c) No, it's basically random (0 pts.)

Scoring:
Add up your point total.

15-20 pts. =
You probably have very strong happiness-enhancing illusions.

8-14 pts. =
You have moderate happiness-enhancing illusions.

0-7 pts. =
You're a sober realist, and quite possibly at greater risk for mild depression.

How the brain recognizes fear

Evidence has just come to light that a brain structure called the amygdala, about the size and shape of an almond and buried deep in the temporal lobe, has the highly specialized role of perceiving emotions displayed in human facial expressions.

People whose amygdala has been damaged due to disease or invasive treatment of epilepsy lose the ability to discern fear in another's face, and are unable to match pictures of facial expressions with names of emotions or with other pictures of faces displaying the

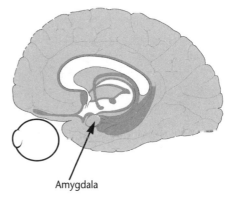

Amygdala

same emotions. The ability to identify the direction of another person's gaze also seems to be affected. These patients, however, have no difficulty recognizing the *identity* of a familiar person's face.

These new studies corroborate previous experimental evidence of the amygdala's role in social communication. Experiments with cats in the 1950's monitored the neurons in their amygdalas while they were interacting with each other or with humans. The amygdala neurons fired while the cats were miaowing and flank-rubbing, but did not fire when social interaction stopped. Experiments in the 1970's also implicated the amygdala in various aspects of social behavior in monkeys, including discrimination of the direction of another monkey's gaze.

Organic damage to the amygdala, it is speculated, may explain certain mental illnesses, including those involving a paranoid delusional state: if you're unable to ascertain a person's emotions by examining their facial expressions, then paranoia about their intentions may follow.

EXERCISE: Martha and George Washington

Most emotional responses start from a point of view. Please make a judgment about what is going on emotionally in the drawing below.

No question, right?

Turn the page upside down. Now what is going on? Hidden expressions — and the sharp eye that reads them — are in the eyes of the beholder of the moment.

Right?

Hint: Before you make an emotional commitment to a person take a full-face photo. Use any excuse. Blow up the photo. Lay a piece of white paper along the midline from hair to chin; bisecting the nose. Make a judgment about the character of that half-person you see there. Now switch the white sheet of paper to mask the other side. Make a judgment about that person you see. Can you live with a mix of both? If one side is a revelation, read this article again. Dominance counts.

SELF-TEST: Facial expressions and emotions

There is good evidence that there are six basic emotions that correlate universally with facial expressions, regardless of culture. These emotions are happiness, sadness, anger, fear, surprise, and disgust. Even though much finer-grained emotions may be recognized on a culturally specific or language-specific basis (e.g., German Schadenfreude, *"the feeling of pleasure you derive from someone else's misfortune"), these six basic emotions are recognized in every culture and universally recognizable from facial expression.*

Match these six words for emotions with the expressions in the six illustrations:

Sadness	**Disgust**	**Anger**
Surprise	**Fear**	**Happiness**

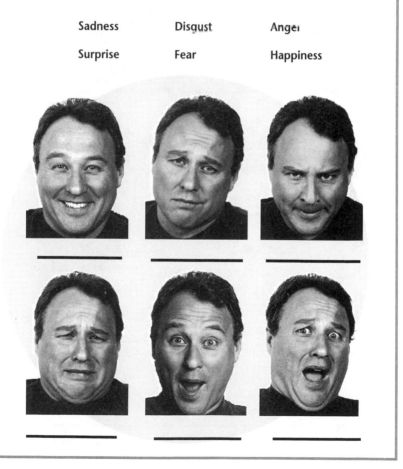

EXERCISE: Emotions

ACROSS

1. Brain part that perceives emotion in another's facial expression

3. Be offensive to

5. Be afraid of

6. Emotional response to the unexpected

7. A state of well-being and contentment

DOWN

2. Rage

4. Grief or unhappiness

Hint: 1 Across is amygdala.

"Watch two Marx Brothers movies and call me in the morning"

Science is finally catching up to what we knew all along: Laughter is good for you. Or, as Proverbs 17:22 puts it, "A cheerful heart is a good medicine."

Laughter improves your blood circulation, exercises your abdominal muscles, increases your heart rate, expels stale air from your lungs, aids digestion, and releases muscle tension. After a bout of laughter, your blood pressure drops to a lower, healthier level. According to laugh researcher William F. Fry, one hundred laughs provide the same cardiovascular benefit as ten minutes of rowing.

Why *Duck Soup* may be better than chicken soup

In addition, researchers working in the new field of psychoneuroimmunology — the study of the effects of psychological status on immune function — have determined that laughter has a beneficial effect on the immune system. While stressful emotions trigger the release of cortisol and aldosterone, which may reduce immunity by lowering your T-cell count, laughter does just the opposite. It also activates virus-fighting killer cells and interferon-gamma, lowers your levels of the stress-related neurotransmitter epinephrine (a.k.a. adrenaline), raises your levels of immunoglobins, and increases the production of natural pain-reducing neuropeptides such as endorphin. Now *that's* a gut laugh!

What happens when you laugh?

Psychologist Peter Derks, using EEG readings, has done more than anyone to improve our understanding of the neurological underpinnings of laughter. When you're presented with a joke, your left hemisphere's language centers begin the task of processing the words. Within milliseconds, "emotional" regions of the frontal lobe kick in, followed instantaneously by regions of the right hemisphere responsible for posing the juxtaposition or finding the incongruity involved in getting the point of a joke. (Stroke patients who have lost the

function of this region will be unable to get the point of a joke or story, or will laugh inappropriately at any non-sequitur.) This is followed within milliseconds by the participation of the sensory-processing region of the occipital area, and finally — still only a fraction of a second, typically, after hearing the punch line — negatively charged delta waves wash over your entire cerebral cortex as you "get" the joke and commence to laugh. Some have speculated that the creativity-jogging potential of humor comes precisely from its activation of so many regions of the brain in this marvelously complex and integrated effort.

Women tend to laugh more often during conversation

All humans in all cultures have the capacity to laugh. Human babies universally begin to laugh at around two to three months, and primate researchers tell us that chimpanzees respond with breathy, pant-like laughter when tickled or chased. Even anacephalic infants, born with nothing but a brain stem, will appear to laugh when tickled. Laughter is, then, an automatic and innate behavior. However, there are also some interesting cultural variations.

In our culture, the number of laughs per day peaks at around age six, and then declines as we move into adulthood. This is a culturally specific fact. Also specific to our culture is the fact that, when a man is talking to another man, speaker and listener tend to laugh roughly equally. When a woman talks to another woman, the speaker tends to laugh more frequently than the listener. This effect is much stronger when a woman is talking to a man. But when a man is talking to a woman, the listener will laugh more frequently than the speaker.

It's an open question, however, whether this sort of polite social laughter produces the same physiological and psychological benefits as a laugh of abandoned joy. And is derisive laughter as salubrious as mirthful laughter? Apparently not. What about laughter at another's expense? Perhaps initially, but subsequent guilt or other negative repercussions may outweigh any initial stress-reducing effect. True mirthful laughter is surprisingly difficult to fake. It is not simply the physical act, but also the emotional state underlying it that is important.

There do exist largely innate (see "Show me the child at seven...," p. 59) individual differences in temperament which predispose some people to laughter more than others. But the humorous insight underlying mirthful laughter is more a matter of perspective than biological determination. Anyone can develop this perspective, and sometimes all it takes is allowing oneself the indulgence of a moment's irreverence for a stressful event to release itself in a cathartic appreciation of life's absurdity. Shakespeare exploited this in his alternation of serious scenes with humorous ones. For Goethe, humor was one means of releasing emotional blockages that could harm both mind and body, just as in oriental medicine certain physical or emotional states may block flow of life's energy, or Chi.

EXERCISE: Pick the punch line

Read the story below and pick what you think would be the funniest punch line. There is no correct answer. However, absence of an ability to detect humor is often linked to the right hemisphere of the brain, where the components of poetry and music are also synthesized.

A politician campaigning yet again for reelection arranged to speak at a full-care retirement facility seeking the senior vote. When he rose to start his speech he asked his audience, "Do you know who I am?"

After a brief silence a quavering old voice spoke from the audience:

1. "No, but we won't remember later anyway."

2. "Yes, that's why those of us who came are all sitting near the door."

3. "No, but if you go to the front desk they'll tell you."

Are you phlegmatic or bilious? Do you suffer from choler? Would you choose to be more sanguine if it were as easy as taking an aspirin?

If mood were determined purely by identifiable events in our life — good news from the boss or bad news from the IRS — then we could view our emotional life as a canvas upon which our environment paints a picture of anxiety, depression, ela-

Melencolia I by Albrecht Dürer, 1514. (See Exercise on page 164.)

tion, or optimism. But this is clearly the wrong way to look at it. Our moods seem to fluctuate from hour to hour and day to day in a way that can't be reduced to external events. And some people just appear to have a dour or melancholy outlook, while others are naturally optimistic. If the painter metaphor is at all appropriate, then it seems to be our inner mood which is coloring our environment, not vice versa.

In medieval European medicine, fluctuations and individual differences of temperament were attributed to the effects of various bodily *humors* (literally, "moistures" or "fluids"): blood (associated with optimism, hence "sanguine"); phlegm (apathy — hence "phlegmatic"); bile (melancholy or irascibility — hence "bilious"); and yellow bile or choler (anger — hence "choleric"). An imbalance of phlegm, then, would cause apathy, and to cure this all you had to do was bring the phlegm into proper balance with the other fluids. A person with just the right balance of each was said to be in "good humor."

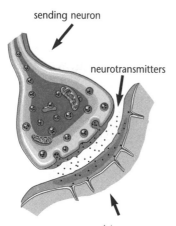

sending neuron

neurotransmitters

receiving neuron

The traditional approach captures the idea that mood is an internal state that may fluctuate independently of external circumstances. Current wisdom differs from the "humor" theory, however, in the substances viewed as responsible for this state.

Mood is in the brain, not the spleen

The dominant theory at the moment is that the locus of mood is in the brain, and the precise substances implicated in mood fluctuation, as well as in states of chronic depression and mania, are chemicals called biogenic amines — otherwise known as neurotransmitters.

The way it works is this:

The cellular basis of mood lies in the transmission of messages across the synapses of certain brain neurons. Chemicals that facilitate this kind of transmission are called neurotransmitters. One important member of their class is called amines, a group of chemicals with a structure resembling that of ammonia.

When amines are released by a nerve cell into the synapse, a message is conveyed to an adjacent cell. (A particular nerve cell will produce just one kind of amine neurotransmitter, and hence send just one kind of message; however, any given nerve cell may have receptors for more than one neurotransmitter, and hence receive more than one kind of message.) This process is terminated when the amines are reabsorbed into the transmitting cell and deactivated by "janitorial" enzymes.

An excess of amines is considered to cause mania, and a deficiency, depression. One way of treating chronically depressed individuals, then — those who once would have been considered to suffer from an excess of bile or phlegm — would be to increase the level of amines either by slowing their reabsorption back into the nerve cell or blocking the janitorial enzyme that deactivates them. This is, in fact, precisely how most antidepressants work, such as imipramine, iproniazid, Elavil, Norpramin, and Prozac.

Like the "humor" theory that preceded it, the biogenic-amine theory is far from perfect. One problem is that, while imipramine blocks the reuptake of amines within a matter of minutes or hours, it takes weeks before a patient actually begins to *feel* less depressed. Second, some effective antidepressants have no direct interaction with amines, and others actually decrease the level of amines in the brain. Clearly, then, the facts are somewhat more complex than the amine theory would indicate.

Should we interfere with nature?
One reason it's risky to treat mood disorders with drugs like these is that the interactions of brain chemicals are so complex that it's hard to isolate and treat just one problem without causing other problems elsewhere. In this respect, the environment of brain structure and chemistry is not unlike the external ecosystem. For example, a class of monoamine-oxidase inhibitors (MAOIs), still in common use in Great Britain, work by blocking the amine-digesting janitorial

enzymes. But some amines raise blood pressure, and these same amines are present in foods such as aged cheeses, some wines, ripe figs, and other foods. So when a patient on MAOIs eats these foods, blood pressure may shoot up to dangerous and sometimes life-threatening levels.

Antidepressants such as Prozac are considered by many physicians to be superior to other amine regulators precisely because they're so specific in their effects: they interact with just one single amine — serotonin — by blocking its reuptake into the nerve cell. This results in elevated serotonin levels — ideally resulting in greater self-confidence, lessened anxiety, improved optimism, and enhanced energy and mental clarity — but few other side effects, and with none of the distortions of perception or mood crashes caused by alcohol or cocaine. True, Prozac is not quite as "clean" a drug as one could imag ine. Serotonin has at least fifteen different kinds of receptors in the brain, only some of which have to do with mood; others regulate different functions such as digestion and sexu al appetite. Prozac, in inhibiting the general reuptake of sero tonin rather than in stimulating or blocking serotonin- sensitive sites, affects all of these receptors. Clinical trials of a new generation of "cleaner" antidepressants — ones which target specific receptors rather than raising neurotransmitter levels throughout the brain — are in fact already under way in both Europe and the United States. (The French, by the way, consume more antidepressants than Americans per capita; so much for the myth of the low-stress Mediterranean lifestyle.)

Prozac even appears to have beneficial effects on the mood and temperament of many individuals who fail to meet the criteria for true clinical depression — people who tradi tionally might have been viewed as having levels of depres sion or anxiety well within the "normal" range, or as suffering from extremely mild personality disorders. This has given rise to the uniquely modern dilemma of "cosmetic" psychophar macology: Is it right to take a drug that has the sole effect of making you more like the kind of self-confident, outgoing, optimistic, energetic person you always wished you could be, or should you simply accept your inborn temperamental con stitution as the hand that nature dealt you?

EXERCISE: "Melencolia I"

Albrecht Dürer's engraving on page 160 is based on the writings of Marsillo Ficino, who claimed that anyone who excels in the arts is a "melancholic." He distinguished between "black bile" and "white (or yellow) bile" melancholy, with black being mania and white being brilliancy.

Architects, artisans, and artists (all of whom used mathematics as a tool) were inclined toward the "imaginative" melancholic temperament as depicted in the engraving. Clearly, the medieval meaning of the word *melancholy* was not sadness, as it means now, but an enlightened frustration over the attempt to understand and design a meaningful order from observation of the chaos and contradictions of nature.

Without looking back at page 160, list as many of the objects in the engraving as you can that relate to art, architecture, the artisans' crafts, and mathematics. This is an exercise in observation, memory, and imagination.

ACROSS

1. Humor identified with an apathetic temperament
5. Adjective describing temperament formerly associated with blood
8. Antidepressant that blocks serotonin from being reabsorbed into a cell
9. Emotional condition caused by insufficiency of amines
10. Class of neurotransmitter having chemical structure similar to ammonia

DOWN

2. Blocks enzyme that digests amines
3. Humor identified with melancholia
4. Emotional condition caused by excess of amines
6. Humor identified with an angry temperament
7. In medieval medicine, fluids in the body that determine temperament

Hint: 9 across is depression.

SELF-INVENTORY: Neuroticism, extraversion, openness, agreeableness, and conscientiousness

One of the most widely used tools for categorizing individuals according to basic personality traits is called the NEO-Personality Inventory, short for Neuroticism, Extraversion, and Openness to experience; a more recent revised version adds Agreeableness and Conscientiousness.

It's easy to be judgmental about someone's "definition" with respect to these traits. For example, nobody would want to characterize himself or herself as basically moralistic and uncomfortable with complexities, as opposed to introspective, creative, and open to new experiences. It's therefore always necessary to find a less direct way of eliciting such information, either by interviewing friends or family members or by asking the person how he or she would think, feel, or act in a given situation, without ever mentioning the loaded adjectives themselves.

It's also important to realize that high or low values in any of the dimensions don't necessarily mean the person has a "good" or "bad" personality, or is well or poorly adjusted, successful or unsuccessful, and so on. Fighter pilots are high in Extraversion, but low in Agreeableness. Modesty and tender-mindedness may be good qualities in some walks of life, but certainly don't represent the "right stuff" when it comes to flying an F-14. It may well be that there has been evolutionary selection for a wide range of personality traits in different individuals, since different kinds of people with different modes of action and interaction may enhance the survival prospects of the social group as a whole.

There is persuasive evidence, by the way, that some of these variables are strongly determined by birth order. Oldest siblings may tend to rate higher in Conscientiousness than youngest siblings, while the youngest tend to rank higher in Openness. Whether you think a high Conscientiousness ranking is "good" or "bad" — whether it means the person is ethical and responsible or simply a moralistic goody-goody — may well depend on whether you yourself are a youngest or oldest sibling.

See where you rate by answering the following questions and adding up points in each section. There is a key at the end to give an idea of what personality traits you most likely have.

(cont'd on next page)

A.

1. When you travel on vacation, do you like to plan an itinerary in advance and make reservations for each night's stay, or do you prefer to leave your options open?

a) plan an itinerary (1 pt.)

b) leave options open (2 pts.)

2. When you go to a new restaurant and get a dish that you really like, will you order that dish again on a repeat visit, or will you try something different?

a) order dish again (1 pt.)

b) try something different (2 pts.)

3. Ralph Waldo Emerson once wrote that "a foolish consistency is the hobgoblin of little minds." Do you think that people tend to adhere to consistency too uncritically, or do you feel we'd all be better off if consistency were more highly valued?

a) consistency should be highly valued (1 pt.)

b) people adhere too uncritically to consistency (2 pts.)

4. If you see a child displaying acrobatic skills on his bike in the middle of a busy sidewalk, would you be more likely to be angry at him for endangering others or to admire him for his skill?

a) angry (1 pt.)

b) admire (2 pts.)

5. If your child were to ask to put an unusual condiment or topping on her food — say, parmesan cheese on her breakfast cereal or jam on her spaghetti — would you be inclined to let her try it, or would you forbid it outright?

a) forbid it (1 pt.)

b) let her try it (2 pts.)

(cont'd on next page)

B.

1. If a coworker made a clearly phony excuse to stay home sick one morning, would you be irritated at her duplicity or concerned that she might have some problem that she feels she has to hide?

a) irritated (1 pt.)

b) concerned (2 pts.)

2. Imagine you order a dish at a restaurant and find it to be overcooked and oversalted. When the waiter comes by and asks, "How is everything today?" would you be more likely to tell him what you don't like about the dish or to say, "Fine, thank you"?

a) tell him (1 pt.)

b) say, "Fine" (2 pts.)

3. Which would you say better characterizes your attitude toward friendship?

a) it is good to push your friends to their limits, and to make them question their satisfaction with themselves and their own performance or behavior, in order that they achieve more in life (1 pt.)

b) it is important to show friends that you like and support them, and to avoid making them feel insecure or hurting their feelings (2 pts.)

4. If someone you're talking to uses or pronounces a word incorrectly, would you be more likely to correct them or to ignore the error?

a) correct them (1 pt.)

b) ignore the error (2 pts.)

5. When you're driving on the freeway and someone pulls in front of you, do you automatically slow down to make room between you and him, or do you ever stay on his tail for a while or pass him to show your irritation?

a) stay on his tail or pass him (1 pt.)

b) slow down (2 pts.)

(cont'd on next page)

C.

1. If a close friend were to tell you that she's concerned about you because you seem to be depressed, would you feel upset or flattered that she cares enough about you to tell you?

a) flattered (1 pt.)

b) upset (2 pts.)

2. If you were to meet a graphologist (handwriting analyst) at a party, do you think it would be fun to show him a sample of your handwriting, or would you be anxious or self-conscious about the conclusions he might draw about you?

a) fun (1 pt.)

b) anxious (2 pts.)

3. When you express anger or irritation with someone, do you usually later feel that you did the right thing, or do you sometimes feel guilty or worry that you might have overreacted?

a) feel I did the right thing (1 pt.)

b) feel guilty (2 pts.)

4. Do you think that a stranger would be able to tell much about you after a single encounter, or do you feel that your projected personality changes enough from one setting to another that any such evaluation would probably be incorrect?

a) would be able to tell (1 pt.)

b) evaluation would probably be incorrect (2 pts.)

5. Do you ever have the experience of feeling guilty or mortified about something you've said in the past, or are you more likely to have the attitude that everyone makes mistakes and that all you can do is learn from them and try to avoid making the same mistakes in the future?

a) everyone makes mistakes (1 pt.)

b) feel mortified (2 pts.)

(cont'd on next page)

D.

1. When arriving at or departing from a dinner party given by close friends, do you prefer to hug or shake hands?

a) shake hands (1 pt.)

b) hug (2 pts.)

2. If given a choice between cooperating on a project with a group of others, or finishing a task on your own, which would you usually choose?

a) finish on my own (1 pt.)

b) work with others (2 pts.)

3. When you buy something that turns out to be defective, does it bother you to go back to exchange it, or do you think it's silly to feel shy about it?

a) bothers me (1 pt.)

b) silly to feel shy (2 pts.)

4. If someone wants to take your picture at a party, do you usually feel that they should just go ahead and take it without making a fuss, or do you think it's fine for them to interrupt what you're doing and ask you to pose and smile?

a) just go ahead (1 pt.)

b) OK to interrupt (2 pts.)

5. Orson Welles, in a certain wine commercial which aired in the 1970's, once said he liked to "cast" parties the way he casts a play. Would you like to attend such a party, or would you resent the host's manipulative expectations and prefer to stay home?

a) prefer to stay home (1 pt.)

b) like to attend (2 pts.)

(cont'd on next page)

E.

1. Let's say a package arrives on December 10 addressed to you and your spouse. You open it, and find dozens of cunningly crafted Swiss chocolates in red and green Christmas foil. Would you go ahead and taste one, or feel compelled to save them all until Christmas?

a) go ahead and taste one (1 pt.)

b) wait until Christmas (2 pts.)

2. While waiting in line at an automated bank teller, you step on a small brown paper bag, pick it up, and find $500 in 20-dollar bills inside. There's no name or identification of any kind. Would you keep it, or go inside the bank and give it to the teller with your name and telephone number in case nobody claims it?

u) keep it (1 pt.)

b) give it to the teller (2 pts.)

3. Would you be more inclined to agree with those who opine that a neat desk is the sign of a sick mind, or that a messy desk betrays a lazy nature?

a) a neat desk is the sign of a sick mind (1 pt.)

b) a messy desk betrays a lazy nature (2 pts.)

4. Do you think that laws should always be obeyed by everyone, or that rules are made to be broken?

a) rules are made to be broken (1 pt.)

b) laws should always be obeyed (2 pts.)

5. If you're halfway through a book, do you usually finish it even if your interest flags, or do you see no point in finishing it if you're no longer interested?

a) no point in finishing (1 pt.)

b) finish it even if no longer interested (2 pts.)

(cont'd on next page)

Key:

A: 10 pts. = *Rebellious, nonconforming, imaginative, liberal-minded:*
    high in Openness to experience

5 pts. = *Conventional, conservative:*
    low in Openness

B: 10 pts. = *Sympathetic, compassionate, compliant:*
    high in Agreeableness

5 pts. = *Suspicious, critical, antagonistic:*
    low in Agreeableness

C: 10 pts. = *Temperamental, self-pitying, thin-skinned, vulnerable:*
    high in Neuroticism

5 pts. = *Calm, self-assured, objective:*
    low in Neuroticism

D: 10 pts. = *Gregarious, assertive, socially poised:*
    high in Extraversion

5 pts. = *Quiet, reserved, most comfortable alone:*
    low in Extraversion

E: 10 pts. = *Well-organized, dependable, ethical, dutiful:*
    high in Conscientiousness

5 pts. = *Disorganized, self-indulgent, capricious:*
    low in Conscientiousness

Why are women more affected by seasonal fluctuations in day length?

When lengthening shadows send the squirrels scurrying to hoard nuts for the winter nights ahead, your own brain chemistry is adjusting to the waning daylight hours in a way that may explain seasonal affective disorder (SAD) — at least, if you're a female of the species.

SAD, also known as winter depression, is a kind of depression that typically occurs during the winter months of temperate or high-latitude climates, and affects far more women than men. Perhaps this is because women are much more sensitive than men in their hormonal responses to the seasons.

Women respond to melatonin more than men do

As the summer solstice comes and goes and the nights begin to lengthen, women experience a proportional increase in their levels of melatonin, a hormone secreted by the brain's pineal gland. (Melatonin is involved in the regulation of the body's biological clock; that's why it's taken in pill form by frequent flyers who have difficulty adjusting to time-zone changes. It's also an increase in melatonin production, in response to the lengthening nights, that prompts squirrels to gather nuts for the winter.) Other hormones adjust to the shortening days as well; prolactin, which induces a sense of well-being during what nature intended to be a long night of rest, experiences a lengthened nightly surge.

If left to follow their internal adjustments to the seasonal rhythms, most women would presumably fall quite naturally into a winter pattern of long nightly slumbers. As it is, in our modern world, they must instead force their bodies to adhere to what is in effect a year-round summer pattern of long days and short nights.

Men, on the other hand, appear relatively immune to seasonal changes, permitting their bodies to be convinced by artificial light that summer never ends. In order to experience the sort of hormonal fluctuation that women do, they must be isolated at night from the yellow glow of the electric bulb and the shifting blue light of the television set.

Is there a cure for SAD?

Some researchers have found that light therapy — exposure to intense artificial light at a phototherapy clinic or from a commercially available personal "light-box" — has such a beneficial effect on wintertime depression that it has been dubbed a "natural Prozac." This would come as no surprise to the ancient Greeks, who recognized the therapeutic potential

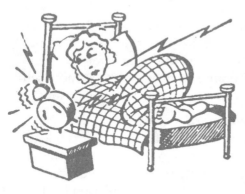

of light, or to early twentieth-century physicians who advocated the use of "solariums" for the treatment of both physical and psychological ailments.

Experiments have shown that the therapeutic effect of light works through the eyes, not the skin. People who are naked but blindfolded show no antidepressant response to light therapy, while people wrapped like mummies except for their eyes respond well.

Is it necessary to expose oneself to UV light in order to cure winter depression? Maybe not. The problem with relying on typical artificial light sources for your wintertime needs may be quantity, not quality. A well-lit home or office typically has only 300 to 600 lux (a standard unit of brightness roughly equivalent to a candle flame), while a sunny summer day outdoors may provide over 100,000 lux. In any case, personal light-boxes, which typically provide about 10,000 lux, are available in both UV and UV-shielded versions.

How sleep patterns change in the winter months

When humans — of both the XX and XY persuasion — are left undisturbed to the high-latitude seasonal fluctuations of nature, this is what happens:

During long nights of winter darkness, we lie quietly for far longer than the demands of modern life would normally permit. Twelve hours seems about average, with four or five hours of deep sleep, followed by several hours of quiet, wakeful but meditative resting, followed by another four or five hours of REM (or dream) sleep.

One reason for the nonanxious, meditative character of the period of quiet wakefulness between the two sleep periods is that release of the hormone prolactin is sustained during the entire 12 hours. This is the same hormone that keeps animals from getting restless when tending the den or nest. During shorter summer nights, melatonin secretion drops dramatically, and prolactin is released in a relatively brief burst.

Perhaps what those who meditate today are seeking is a state that our ancestors would have considered their birthright, a nightly occurrence. Given, however, that the boss and kids probably won't permit 12-hour slumbers ... prolactin pills, anyone?

EXERCISE: How not to be SAD

If you're curious about wintertime sleep the way we're "really" supposed to experience it, try the following simple experiment.

Choose a night without any conflicting obligations, hang a "do not disturb" sign on the bedroom door, cover the bedroom window so no light comes in, unplug the phone, and settle in at six or seven o'clock for a long night's slumber. Don't worry if you don't fall asleep immediately — you probably won't, but that's perfectly natural. After perhaps a couple hours of lying still and thinking, you'll probably drift off to sleep.

You probably won't sleep through the entire night, but that's OK too. If you wake up at one or two o'clock, don't feel obligated to get up and do anything — just lie still, letting your thoughts run however they like, and you'll drift back to sleep again within an hour or two. You'll probably awaken naturally at seven o'clock or so, without need of an alarm clock. Pull back the drapes and feel how wonderful, how refreshing, how calming a really good night's sleep is.

This experiment works best in the wintertime, in which case (assuming your latitude is high enough), you won't even need to shut out any unwanted natural light — just go to bed at sunset, and awaken at sunrise.

GENDER DIFFERENCES IN THE BRAIN

Many studies have shown gender differences in the brain, but the results are difficult to evaluate and easy to misinterpret. For one thing, there is almost always a huge amount of gender overlap, so that the differences only emerge in large sample sizes. Any given man's brain may fit the generalizations made about women's brains, and vice versa. In this respect, the biological differences observed in the brain mirror what is found with gender differences in cognitive abilities. Men generally perform slightly better on certain tests of spatial ability (visually rotating three-dimensional objects), while women tend to perform a bit better on certain verbal tasks — but any given woman may be a genius at visually-oriented math or physics, and any given man may be a brilliant linguist or wordsmith. Another problem is that the absolute size of a brain region, or of the brain as a whole, does not necessarily translate into a given level of intelligence. Neural density, rather than size alone, may be a more meaningful indication of mental ability.

Still, these studies can be fascinating and provocative. A recent report published in the journal *Science* indicates that, in a resting state, men have more activity in the temporal-limbic region and women have more activity in the cingulate region. The temporal-limbic region is a "primitive," action-oriented part of the limbic system, a brain structure that regulates emotions. The cingulate is also part of the limbic system but evolved more recently. It plays a role in symbolic representations of actions rather than the actions themselves.

Another study in *Science* reports that women have a greater density of neurons in the cortex of the planum temporale within the Sylvian fissure, a region involved in auditory association and part of the neural substrate of language function, especially intonation.

What is the brain so busy doing, and not doing, while we sleep?

Everyone from Plato to Freud, it seems, has had his own pet theory about why we dream. Now it's the turn of scientists with PET technology: positron-emission tomography, that is, the new high-tech method of obtaining a visual map of the brain in action.

When we dream, the PET image shows that many regions of the brain are, well, asleep: dark as the arctic on a winter solstice eve. A vast section of the prefrontal cortex, for example — a part of the brain cru-

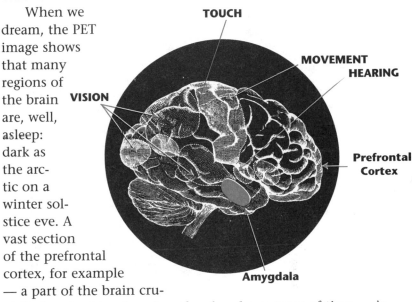

TOUCH

MOVEMENT
HEARING

VISION

Prefrontal
Cortex

Amygdala

cially involved in planning ahead and our sense of time — is completely deactivated; this may explain the curious temporal distortions we experience in our dreams. One area that lights up like a Christmas tree, though, is the amygdala — the emotional control center of the brain. (See "How the brain recognizes fear," p. 153, and diagram on pages 180-181.)

What's the connection between emotions and dreams?

Evidence is accumulating that a major function of dreaming is to reinforce lessons learned during the day. (See "The night a middle-aged man tackled his bureau in his sleep," p. 43.) When we're challenged to learn complex material, the proportion of REM sleep — the "rapid eye movement" phase, during which we dream — increases. And when REM sleep is disrupted or suppressed one or even several nights after our learning a complex logic task, we're much more likely to forget what we've learned — even if the rest of our sleep cycle is permitted to proceed undisturbed. (It's easy to try this at home, since you can suppress your REM cycle by drinking alcohol before bed.)

Next, consider the fact that emotionally charged experiences tend strongly to be seared into permanent long-term memory (see page 180). Since the amygdala is the prime locus of emotion it must somehow be responsible for getting past the gatekeeper that prevents the details of everyday life from being remembered forever (see "Imagine a memory-enhancing drug...," p. 77.) As we dream the amygdala is performing its otherwise familiar role of mediating memory formation.

How can I trick my amygdala into helping me learn faster?

In addition to the basics — get enough sleep, don't drink too much in the evening — sleep scientists have discovered a simple but effective way to enhance memory formation. In an experiment with undergraduate psychology students, they first played a tape of a clicking sound (not too disruptive, but loud enough to be heard) while the students applied themselves to learning a difficult logic task. They then played the tape that same night as the students slept. When those students were retested on the task a week later, their performance was 23% better than that of a control group. This shows that you can use background noise as a nighttime cue to aid in the processing and memorization of learning tasks.

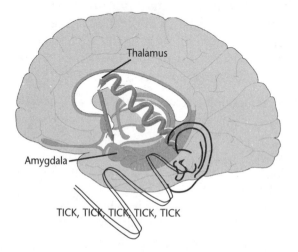

Thalamus

Amygdala

TICK, TICK, TICK, TICK, TICK

The goal of picturing brain activity without surgery is to locate damage or to identify where the brain processes different tasks, or fails to.

X-rays (1920's) showed only rough structure since they couldn't image the soft tissues such as the cortex.

The electroencephalograph, or EEG (1920's), was found to measure changes in electrical activity in the brain correlating with different kinds of mental activity.

CAT, computerized axial tomography (late 1960's), could take "snapshot" images of detailed structures, so CAT scans could be used diagnostically to locate tumors, lesions, or blood clots in the brain.

Modern PET, positron emission tomography, MRI, magnetic resonance imaging, and MEG, magnetoencephalography, provide information about activity in different areas of the brain in response to specific stimuli — such as attempting to describe a scene, looking at a disgusting picture, reading a dull list of words or a love story, etc.

With PET scans, a volunteer is injected with a mildly radioactive solution or inhales a radioactive gas and places his head in a ring of gamma-ray detectors. The parts of the brain that are working hardest receive the most radiation-tainted oxygenated blood, and those parts show up as bright reds and yellows in a computer-generated photograph.

Magnetic resonance images of a female (left) and male (right) brain. Note that the female's corpus callosum (in the center of the brain image) is thicker towards the rear than the male's. The corpus callosum stops growing at puberty; since males reach puberty earlier, a man's corpus callosum — which connects the left and right hemispheres of the brain — is thinner than a woman's. This may account for a tendency towards more "integrative" thinking among women than men.

THE FAST TRACK:
Why the amygdala shortcuts conscious thought

When Louis Armstrong was asked once to define jazz he responded: *Man, if you gotta ask, you'll never know.* The amygdala never asks. It punches the panic button the instant the brain senses trouble. It stores the life-threatening experiences such as the heat of flame, shape of snake, or approach of an abusive parent.

Its partner, the thalamus, routes data coming in through the senses to the part of the cortex that decides how to use the information — *unless* the data appears life-threatening. Then the thalamus sends the message directly to the amygdala at the same time. In the example shown here the visual cortex can take its time considering whether this tiger is an endangered species or stuffed with kapok. Then it can override the amygdala's instantaneous reaction to the possibility that it could be lunch.

One reason adults have difficulty understanding or changing their responses to abuse experienced as children is that they have learned and stored such serious threats in this subconscious system of the primitive brain. That brain system was designed to keep us alive. It depends on emotional responses that can't afford the luxury of critical reasoning.

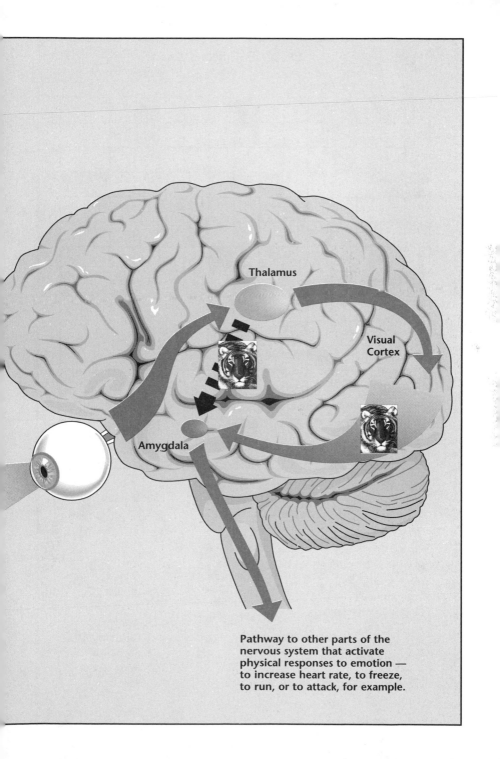

Thalamus

Visual
Cortex

Amygdala

Pathway to other parts of the
nervous system that activate
physical responses to emotion —
to increase heart rate, to freeze,
to run, or to attack, for example.

EXERCISE: Thinking ahead

1	2	3	■	4	5	6	■	7	8	9	■	10	11	12
13			■	14			■	15			■	16		
17			■	18		19			■	20				
■		21	22			■	23					■		
24	25				■	26			■	27		28	29
30			■	31			■	32					
33			34			■	35					
■		36			■	37			■		
38	39	40			■	41				42	43	44
45			■	46			■	47			
48			■	49			■	50			
■		51	52			■	53			■
54	55			■	56			■	57	58	59
60		■	61			62			■	63		
64		■	65			66			■	67		

ACROSS

1. Ship deserter
4. Boston's transit sys.
7. TV program abbr.
10. Socialite
13. — I saw Elba
14. — Lingus
15. — and a bone
16. Hematite, for one
17. After Feb.
18. Cape location
21. Pierre's state, for short
23. All — (conductor's cry)
24. Beer glass
26. Tribe
27. St. —'s fire
30. Chums
31. Cloy
32. "No man has a hope who has not had —"
33. Brain part that interprets data and signals action
35. Scans a sentence
36. Hockey great and family
37. Bullring star
38. Gazes fixedly
41. Kind of guidance
45. Trace of color
46. Part of TLC
47. Gait
48. Opposer
49. London gallery
50. Shore birds
51. Recorded
53. Paper raw material
54. Certain islander
57. Horse morsel
60. Pig's home

(cont'd on next page)

61. Movie dog's first name
62. Madrid wife
63. Presidential initials
64. The piper's son
65. Past due
66. Brain activity scanning technology
67. Defeat at bridge

DOWN

1. Kind of sleep during dreaming
2. Altar in the sky
3. Succinctly
4. Naval historian
5. Ship-building wood
6. Kennedy letters
7. Clannish
8. Breakfast food
9. Near Eastern title
10. Draws, in a way
11. Sin
12. Wager
19. Half a Washington city
20. Section of the cortex that monitors social consequences
22. Giving up, as profits
24. Watering place
25. Scottish cap
26. Coolidge and Peete
28. West of early movies
29. Hosp. units

31. Golfer's aims
32. Berne's river
34. Dreary, to a Scot
35. Skin opening
37. Weight allowance
38. RR stop
39. Wedding anniversary
40. Opposite
41. Father, to an Etonian
42. Camera supports
43. Web company initials
44. Certain linemen
46. Chicago gangster
49. Long-nosed mammal
50. Attack
52. Pielet
53. Peel
54. Kennedy visitor
55. Simpson's judge
56. Clairvoyance, for short
58. Summer cooler
59. Asian holiday

Hint: 54 Across is *Singaporean* and 18 Across is *Harwichport*.

EXERCISE: Terms test

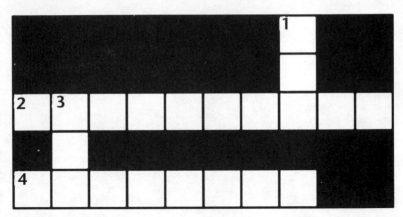

ACROSS

2. The section of the cortex that judges time, monitors the social consequences of actions, and projects sequences of events into future time

4. Part of brain which interprets and signals action on data which seems life threatening or emotionally powerful

DOWN

1. A scanning technology able to observe areas of activity in the brain

3. A phase of sleep associated with rehearsing newly learned material

Hint: 1 Down is *PET*.

Verbalizing unpleasant experiences helps physical health

Mounting evidence indicates that the degree to which you express negative emotions may put you at risk for a range of diseases from high blood pressure to cancer. And, contrary to what you might think, if you insist on getting your own way, and complain if you don't, you're probably better off than if you always strive to maintain a cheerful front.

Are you an internalizer or an externalizer?

When confronted with an emotion-evoking stimulus (say, an unpleasant story or picture), internalizers show little overt response, while externalizers react more openly. Those who show little outward response, however, tend to react with greater internal stress, as measured by heart rate and skin conductance. Also, when asked to talk into a tape recorder about their most traumatic personal experiences, those who are willing to disclose the most personal and stressful details show lower skin conductance (lower stress) than those whose stories are less personal and upsetting.

These experiments suggest that when unpleasant experiences are suppressed, they have a more severe effect on the autonomic nervous system than if those experiences are expressed either nonverbally or verbally.

It makes a difference *why* you're inexpressive

Some infants are simply born with low expressivity. As early as the second day after birth, differences in facial animation emerge quite clearly, and these differences tend to be stable as the infant grows older. It seems, then, that emotional expressivity is at least to  some extent innate. People who are naturally inexpressive probably experience little in the way of conflict or health problems as a result. Those adults who are inexpressive because they have learned to suppress their emotions, however (a learning process that has been shown to begin as early as one to two years of age), may be at higher risk.

Forgive me, Father, for I have sinned

What are the consequences of internalizing unpleasant feelings? Research shows that many health problems are associated with inhibiting negative emotions; conversely, talking or writing about personal trauma has been shown to have a therapeutic effect and to yield improvements in health.

In one study, college students and corporate employees were asked to indicate on a questionnaire which of several categories of personal trauma (e.g., death or divorce of parents, sexual abuse) they had experienced at any time in their life. They were also asked to rate the degree to which they had talked with others about their traumas. A correlation emerged between failure to talk about a traumatic experience and diagnosis with cancer, high blood pressure, ulcers, and other health problems.

Writing may work as well as talking

Other studies have shown that writing about extremely traumatic events brings about an improvement in resistance to
infection and disease, according to blood-sample measures of
immune function.

But what about nonverbal communication?

Language — whether oral or written — is just one of many
forms of communication we have. Other ways of giving someone else a glimpse of one's feelings are gestures made on purpose or unconsciously. Obvious examples of this are the way
one composes his or her facial features or through "body language" movements and attitudes such as a leg crossed toward
or away from the person one is speaking with. The moods and
attitudes of artists express themselves through painting and
music as powerfully, at least, as through words. Can the
expression of emotion through these other symbolic systems
have a beneficial effect as well? Although the evidence is less
conclusive, it appears that it might.

For one thing, externalizers don't just talk about their feelings; they tend to display them on their faces. In experiments
in which test subjects are shown pleasant and unpleasant pictures, judges can easily guess the nature of the pictures just by
watching the facial reactions of externalizers. Judgments are
less accurate with internalizers.

The inhibition of facial response has the same kind of
effect on the body as the inhibition of verbal response. In a
recent study, a group of normal people were given some secret
"guilty knowledge" and were told to hide from the others by
masking their facial expressions. They were told this "knowledge" was part of the experiment. Even so, their skin conductance levels increased just as they do when people lie or suppress their emotions in conversations or answering questions.

Art therapy — the resolution of internal psychological
pain or conflict through nonverbal means such as drawing or
painting — is often used with patients who have severe difficulty with verbal communication, such as autistic or abused
children. It's possible that regular nonverbal artistic expression
would have a beneficial effect on the nervous and immune
systems of others as well.

SELF-TEST: Ink blot personality test

The Swiss psychiatrist Herman Rorschach felt that people's responses to a random image betray factors affecting their personality. Rorschach showed his test subjects ten different ink blots, some colored and some black and white, and asked the subjects to relate images and ideas evoked by each blot. With tests such as these there is no "right" or "wrong" answer, but the results may help to provide clues to a person's personality traits or temporary state of mind.

Examine the three Rorschach images below. Find a shape that reminds you of a personally unpleasant experience from your past. Describe to another person what happened and what you saw in the shape you chose that reminded you of the experience. Ask the person to whom you just opened up the window of your experience to pick a shape and do the same.

Why are you not surprised that your immune responses and brain are linked together?

The immune system has evolved as a tool for coping with threats to the body that originate both inside and outside it — much like a sixth sense. (The other five, incidentally, are sight, smell, touch, taste, and hearing.) However, the interactions of the immune system with other systems of the body (nervous/behavioral and endocrine/hormonal) make it seem less like a single organ and more like one part of a complex system encompassing many physical sites around the body.

They even respond to each other's chemical transmitters

For example, neurotransmitters are the chemicals by which nerve cells (including neurons in the brain) communicate with one another. Cytokines are their counterpart in the cells of the immune system. While it used to be believed that the two systems worked independently, it is now known that both types of system produce and respond to *both* types of chemical. In fact, they are both parts of a single, integrated defense mechanism. The new name created for the study of the interaction between psychological states and the immune system is *psychoneuroimmunology*.

Left-handers are more susceptible to autoimmune disease

Given the acceptance of the neural basis of emotion, it shouldn't come as a shock that emotion and the immune system are linked too. The reason is that it has long been known that injury to neurons in the brain may lead to immune system problems.

Injury to the brain may increase or decrease immune system response, depending on the part of the brain injured. In mice, a lesion in the left hemisphere suppresses the activity of T-cells (the "attack troops" of the immune system), but a lesion in the right hemisphere enhances T-cell function. Perhaps this kind of asymmetry explains why left-handedness, which has been theorized to develop in response to some sort of disease or injury to the left hemisphere, has a greater-than-chance correlation with dyslexia and autoimmune disease.

How do you die from grief?

People have always known that certain stressful experiences appear to increase the risk for infection, disease, and even death. After the death of their spouse, for example, mortality among bereaved men rises. Sometimes people do, in fact, "die from grief."

This has even been known to occur in nonhuman primates. Jane Goodall observed one juvenile chimpanzee who had never fully weaned himself from an unusually intimate relationship with his mother when she died. Although fully capable of feeding and caring for himself (he was eight years old, which is well past childhood for a chimp), he never recovered psychologically from her death, and  became increasingly listless and apathetic. Within a month, he died. Goodall concluded that "psychological and physiological disturbances associated with loss made him more vulnerable to disease."

How stress and depression lower your resistance to disease

On a cellular level, clinical depression is associated with a lower level of the body's natural defenses against bacterial and viral infections and disease, including T cells and so-called natural killer cells. This may mean that viruses which are always around us (including perhaps those for Parkinson's disease, various cancers, and even warts) may breach our body's defenses during periods of depression, chronic anxiety, or other kinds of stress.

Some viruses which may be present but inactive in our body may become reactivated during times of stress. This is why college students are more likely to have herpes outbreaks during exam time, for example.

Relatives of Alzheimer's patients have impaired lymphocyte reactivity (a measure of immune-system health). So did people living near Three Mile Island after the accident at the nuclear power plant there. Animals, too, are more susceptible to immune deficiencies and illness when subjected to conditions of overcrowding.

Relief from stress, on the other hand, may have the opposite effect. In one study, gay men experienced a doubling of lymphocyte reactivity within a week of being told they were HIV-negative.

Pleasant experiences may have a more lasting effect than unpleasant ones

A recent study shows that pleasant experiences, such as enjoyable social activities, games, or sports, may help the immune system for two days. The immune-system-suppressing effects of routine unpleasant events, on the other hand, such as irritating or frustrating encounters with an employer or coworker, are typically gone within a day. This study had volunteers fill out daily evaluations of their ups and downs. Samples of their saliva showed how effectively their immune systems produced anitbodies to a rabbit protein pill they took each day.

The same study shows that an *absence* of pleasant events predicts susceptibility to a cold more accurately than the *presence* of mildly stressful events. In other words, it's not simply the case that stress can reduce your immunity; enjoyable experiences can actually have a *protective* effect against illness.

Psychological depression may also cause heart disease

For years, evidence has accumulated that depression and heart disease are linked, with researchers uncertain about whether the heart disease causes the depression or vice versa.

New evidence indicates that it's the depression that may be the prime culprit. How does it work? People in a state of depression secrete higher levels of potentially harmful stress hormones, including cortisol and noradrenaline. These hormones have the effect of accelerating the heart rate, disturbing sleep, raising blood pressure, increasing blood clotting, raising the blood's proportion of "bad" cholesterol, and disturbing the heart's rhythm. Cortisol can even increase the potentially life-threatening bouts of erratic heartbeats called arrhythmias. When the depression is treated, the body's biochemistry returns to normal and, often, so do erratic heart rhythms.

How can I help my mood — and my physical health?

One lesson to draw from this research is that a stressful schedule must be punctuated with fun and enjoyable activities.

Obvious as this may sound, many hard-driving overachievers seem to think that recreation, adequate sleep, and a good diet are unaffordable luxuries — and pay for it, in many cases, by developing autoimmune disease or chronic fatigue syndrome.

Sometimes, feeling happier is a lot harder than following traditional commonsense wisdom — ask anybody who suffers from dysthymia (literally "ill spirit," roughly translatable as low-level depression), let alone from severe clinical depression. There is one neurotransmitter in particular — serotonin — that has been shown to have the potential to combat depression, anxiety, low self-esteem, social inhibition, and a host of other unpleasant or culturally undesirable facets of personality. Serotonin levels may be raised in many ways. Sunshine helps, as do physical exercise and adequate sleep. Since all neurotransmitters including serotonin are manufactured from amino acids that are supplied by the food we eat, it's essential to get enough amino acids. A good source is animal protein. (One theory holds that the widespread nature of dysthymia and other depressive mood disorders stems from our under-consumption of lean animal protein compared to our neolithic forebears.) During the last decade, many people have found that selective serotonin reuptake inhibitors (SSRIs), such as Prozac, can have a dramatic effect on depression. This in turn reduces the chronic overproduction of stress hormones, and lowers the risk of heart disease and, possibly, immune-system-related ailments.

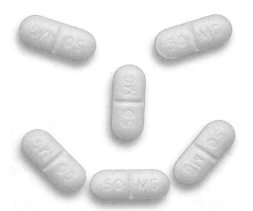

language
function

LANGUAGE

Our acquisition of language in infancy is so instinctual and automatic that we sometimes take it for granted. Recent evidence shows us that a life-long willingness to push the envelope of our linguistic abilities helps keep our brain cell's dendritic branches from atrophying, and may even help prevent Alzheimer's.

The human language faculty is complex and mysterious. We know that we are built to acquire language in infancy, and even to create linguistic structure out of relatively unstructured or chaotic raw material. Infants are not blank slates upon which caretakers write the rules of grammar, but highly active language *creators*. It takes extraordinarily rare circumstances to prevent these little language artists from achieving their goal of constructing a complete mental grammar within the first few years of life.

So language is a natural faculty uniting all humans, yielding an impressively subtle and complex set of internal mental rules acquired with no formal instruction or education. At the same time, there are important individual differences among us.

Older people tend to have larger vocabularies than their younger counterparts. Vocabulary growth is a result of the general accumulation of experience we associate with aging, and is not crucially dependent on the sort of mental agility that allows 20-year-olds to beat their parents in games of rapid calculation. And we all know that some people have larger vocabularies than their age-mates. While vocabulary size may not depend on mental agility, it tends to correlate with other measures of intelligence, such as the ability to manipulate numbers, rotate 3-dimensional objects in the mind's eye, and perform logical operations.

Cause and effect runs both ways here. A large vocabulary results from an interest in reading and learning about challenging new information. Think of how much more effort and self-discipline it takes to read a work of non-fiction in the *New Yorker,* or an article in the *Wall Street Journal*, than it takes to digest one of the potato chips in a supermarket tabloid.

A growing body of evidence also supports the idea that a willingness to challenge yourself linguistically helps to maintain your brain cells. In the so-called "nun study," it was found that those nuns who used a relatively complex writing style as young novitiates were much less likely to develop Alzheimer's later in life than those nuns who wrote in a style marked by simpler, shorter sentences. So a life-long willingness to challenge yourself to grapple with complex linguistic structures may have a preventive effect against Alzheimer's.

As we age, we tend to have an increasingly difficult time manipulating complex sentence structures. This probably results from an erosion of short-term working memory. So it becomes harder to analyze sentences such as *Despite having finished her pie, Henry nevertheless refused to deny Laura the opportunity to offer him a piece of cake*. It also becomes harder to "get" the acceptable reading of "garden path" sentences such as *The dog walked through the park barked*. ("Garden path" sentences are ones that "lead you down a garden path" in your linear word-by-word parsing. When you get to the end of the sentence, you're left with nonsense, prompting the realization that you must have analyzed the sentence incorrectly, and leading you to re-parse it to obtain better results. All this places a burden on your working memory.)

This ability, just like other abilities resting on working memory, is subject to the "use it or lose it" principle. Even as teenagers, we'll lose our facility with mental calculations if we rely on mechanical calculators rather than our brains. Your brain cells can grow new dendrites throughout life, so don't despair. But the longer you wait to rectify the situation, the harder it will be.

Injuries help to map the brain's language regions

Aphasia — a disturbance in the comprehension and production of language caused by disease or injury to some part of the brain — has provided over a century's worth of invaluable insight into the localization of language centers. If some specific part of the brain is damaged by a blow to the head or a stroke and a particular kind of language function is lost, then we may infer that that language function is localized in that part of the brain.

Two of the "classic" types of aphasia are Broca's aphasia and Wernicke's aphasia, named after the pioneering 19th-century neurologists who first identified the parts of the brain associated with these two kinds of language dysfunction. The parts of the brain, in turn, are called Broca's area (the inferior left frontal gyrus) and Wernicke's area (the posterior section of the left auditory-association cortex). Both are in the left hemisphere, and the identification of the role of these areas in language was an important contribution to the understanding of the left brain's specialization for linguistic tasks.

Are you beginning to make silly mistakes in grammar?

Broca's aphasics suffer from a drastic loss of fluency; their speech is labored and delivered in a monotone, often with appropriately-selected nouns but inappropriate use of verbs and grammatical morphemes (such as tense and agreement suffixes) — a condition known as *agrammatism*. Their comprehension is quite good, even though they may not be able to repeat an utterance spoken by someone else.

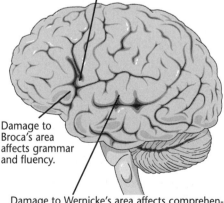

Damage to the Insula, hidden deep inside, causes "apraxia," the inability to organize the component sounds and rhythms to say words correctly.

Damage to Broca's area affects grammar and fluency.

Damage to Wernicke's area affects comprehension of word meaning, not fluency of speech.

Wernicke's aphasics speak rapidly and melodically, although their speech is often unintelligible because they're frequently unable to think of the right word to express the meaning they want to convey. When faced with this situation, Wernicke's patients may do any of several things. One is to omit the word altogether. Instead of saying "The lamp is on the table," they may say, "The table is under, let's assume that." A second option is to substitute another word for the desired one, a behavior know as *paraphasia*. A common strategy is to substitute a word that is related in meaning, such as "hole" for "doughnut," "dog" for "bear," "Mickey" for "mouse," or "biting" for "eating." Another option, known as *circumlocution*, is to paraphrase the desired word, as in saying "water is coming through his eyes" instead of "he's crying." Other options may be to substitute a garbled version of the intended word, as in "hipidomateous" for "hippopotamus," or a novel coinage such as "headman" for "president." Sometimes, only a single specific class of words is lost, such as concrete as opposed to abstract nouns, living versus inanimate objects, fruits and vegetables, body parts, or colors.

Do you resort to saying "thing" or "gizmo" because you can't come up with the right word?

While it is generally accepted that Wernicke's patients tend to have more difficulty with nouns and Broca's patients more difficulty with verbs, there is no clear-cut dichotomy: Wernicke's patients often have difficulty retrieving verbs as well. For both Broca's and Wernicke's aphasics, verb-retrieval problems are usually more disruptive than difficulties with accessing nouns, since generic nouns, such as "stuff" or "thing," or pronouns may always be used in place of a noun they can't think of.

Wernicke's patients, unlike Broca's patients, often have difficulty comprehending others' utterances, and may therefore become anxious or paranoid. Broca's patients, however, are more aware of their disability and have a stronger tendency to become frustrated and depressed.

Some language skills are right-brain — getting the point, for example

Even though all the "classic" aphasias are associated with left-hemisphere damage, there is evidence that the right hemisphere is crucially involved in language ability of a different kind. Right-hemisphere damage may lead to an impairment of discourse-related functions — getting the point of a story or joke, or organizing a narrative into a well-structured and coherent whole.

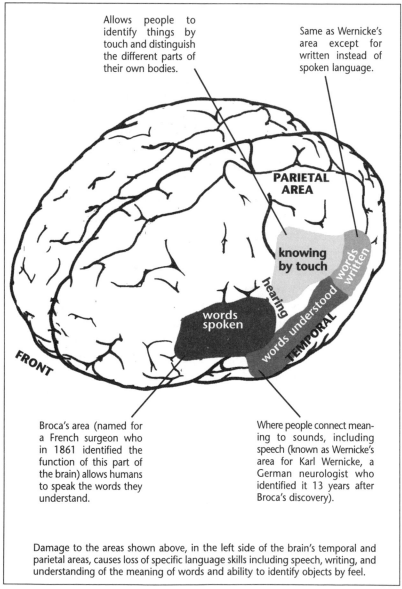

Allows people to identify things by touch and distinguish the different parts of their own bodies.

Same as Wernicke's area except for written instead of spoken language.

PARIETAL AREA

knowing by touch

words written

hearing

words understood

TEMPORAL

words spoken

FRONT

Broca's area (named for a French surgeon who in 1861 identified the function of this part of the brain) allows humans to speak the words they understand.

Where people connect meaning to sounds, including speech (known as Wernicke's area for Karl Wernicke, a German neurologist who identified it 13 years after Broca's discovery).

Damage to the areas shown above, in the left side of the brain's temporal and parietal areas, causes loss of specific language skills including speech, writing, and understanding of the meaning of words and ability to identify objects by feel.

A new language area

The areas Broca and Wernicke determined over one hundred years ago to be crucial to language are located along the left hemisphere's sylvian fissure — the cleft dividing the temporal lobe from the rest of the cortex. Ever since, neurologists have assumed that all the brain's critical language areas — with the exception of the discourse-related functions just mentioned — must be in this same region of the brain.

New research performed with the help of computerized axial tomography and magnetic resonance imagery has uncovered an entirely new structure in the brain responsible for speech articulation. The region, called the *insula*, lies beneath the temporal and frontal lobes in the left cortex. While previously identified, the insula had been considered responsible primarily for the processing of tastes, smells, sights, and sounds in humans and monkeys.

When a specific part of the insula is damaged, the result is a problem known as *apraxia*. Apraxics have difficulty manipulating the musculature of speech in the appropriate order and with the appropriate timing. They will grope for just the right sequence of sounds, sometimes even getting it right once but then failing on a repeat effort.

Apraxia is easy to confuse with Broca's aphasia because both pathologies show themselves in slow and labored speech, articulatory errors, and a monotonous delivery. However, apraxia has none of the agrammatic (that is, non-grammatic) features of Broca's aphasia. Apraxia might be thought to resemble Wernicke's aphasia, which may also involve the garbling of the sounds of words. Unlike Wernicke's aphasia, however, apraxics have no difficulty with accessing the right word or with word perception or comprehension. Rather, apraxics' recognition of word and speech sounds remains perfectly normal and they're fully aware of their own faulty articulation — a source of considerable frustration.

EXERCISE: Confused speech

The 3 italic paragraphs labeled "A," "B," and "C" below contain transcriptions of recorded answers of four patients, each of whom suffered from damage to a different part of their brain. Try to match those paragraphs with the following three descriptions of the damaged areas and abilities.

"Apraxia": One of the paragraphs below is a transcript of speech by a subject who suffers from apraxia resulting from damage to the insula, an area very near the motor centers across the middle of the cortex involved in the manipulation of muscles used in speech.

"Wernicke's": Another paragraph transcribes the speech of subjects with damage to an area closer to the back of the brain. They come up with words easily and speak freely but stumble along with inappropriate words.

"Broca's": Another paragraph reconstructs recorded speech of a subject with damage to an area nearer the frontal cortex. The person understands the meaning of words but has trouble putting a meaningful idea together using verbs and grammar. Broca's aphasics speak slowly, without inflection, and in a worried, guarded way. Unlike Wernicke's aphasics, they are aware of their disability.

A *The subject was shown a drawing of a kitchen scene in which a woman didn't notice two boys stealing her cookies. Asked to describe the scene the subject said: "Mother is away here working her work to get her better, but when she's looking the two boys looking the other part. She's working another time."*

B *When the subject was asked why he returned to the hospital he said: "Yes...ah...Monday...ah...Dad and Peter Hogan, and Dad... ah... Hospital...and ah...Wednesday...Wednesday, nine o'clock and ah Thursday...ten o'clock ah doctors... two...two...an doctors and...ah...teeth...yah, And a doctor...an girl...and gums, and I."*

C *The subject, who was asked to say the word "cushion," responded: "oh, uh, uh...chookun...uh, uh, uh...dook...I know what it's called, it's c-u, uh, no, it's, it's...chook...chookun...no." When asked to repeat "catastrophe" five times, the subject said: "catastrophe, patastrophee, t, catastrophe, catasrifrobee, aw sh..., ka, kata, sh..., sh..., I don't know."*

Hint: Typically, people with damage to the area nearest the frontal lobe can select the correct words for things but their speech is broken because they have trouble linking the words grammatically.

EXERCISE: Language areas

Crosswords, like many other puzzle formats, allow a correct answer to help recall or selection of another element of the puzzle. Since figuring out the meanings of words requires recall, the memory and language functions are closely allied cognitive tools. Can you still recall the answers to 41 Across and 3 and 42 Down from the exercise on pages 182-183, for example?

(cont'd on next page)

ACROSS

1. Statutes
5. Landed
9. Alphabet run
12. Locale
13. North or south
14. Cry of discovery
15. Balkan
16. Part for Olivier
17. Arrest
18. Compo ser Rorem
20. Counts
22. Church features
25. Coffee alternative
26. Joan of —
27. Aquatic sport
32. — ten (rest)
34. — Maria
35. Chemical compound
36. Most odoriferous
39. Confederate commander
40. Roman hearth god
41. Jostling weapons
43. Condition describing loss of language skills
47. — -Magnon
48. Mme. in Madrid
49. Rabbit's tail
51. Approval
54. Like a — of bricks
55. Merit
56. Grant
57. Total
58. Blind part
59. Elvis's middle name

DOWN

1. — Vegas
2. Form of to be
3. Discoverer of brain area for processing spoken language
4. — -toothed tiger
5. IRS month
6. Appear suddenly
7. Uncomfortable
8. Seesaw
9. Suffix meaning poison
10. Sear
11. Small amounts
19. Morning moisture
21. Record
22. Student tests
23. British buggy
24. Sardonic
28. Cravat
29. Viewer
30. Name in the theater
31. Cries in the bullring
33. Queen of scat
37. Scottish girls
38. Function of an RN
42. Discoverer of brain area controlling word meaning
43. Movie dog
44. Urge
45. Applause
46. Halo
50. Explosive initials
52. Much — About Nothing
53. Itch

Hint: 36 across is "smelliest."

EXERCISE: Damaged language

Rearrange the letters of each word in the left column to create a synonym for the word opposite it in the center column. Write it in the spaces in the right. In the numbered spaces at the bottom write in the first letter of each new word to form a phrase (without word spaces) related to a preceding article.

SCION	=	IMAGES	=	1. _ _ _ _ _
KNEAD	=	DEFOLIATED	=	2. _ _ _ _ _
JANES	=	DURABLE PANTS	=	3. _ _ _ _ _
RUSES	=	MANIPULATORS	=	4. _ _ _ _ _
LAGER	=	SUITABLE FOR A KING	=	5. _ _ _ _ _
FINER	=	DEDUCE	=	6. _ _ _ _ _
SITED	=	CUTS AND REARRANGES	=	7. _ _ _ _ _
SNAIL	=	MURDERED	=	8. _ _ _ _ _
CHARM	=	GREGORIAN 3RD MONTH	=	9. _ _ _ _ _
TACOS	=	NECK SCARF	=	10. _ _ _ _ _
GRAPE	=	BEEPER	=	11. _ _ _ _ _
BRAIL	=	ZODIAC'S SEVENTH	=	12. _ _ _ _ _
SONAR	=	BAD LIGHT	=	13. _ _ _ _ _
NERVE	=	NOT AT ALL	=	14. _ _ _ _ _
SARGE	=	TOOTHED WHEELS	=	15. _ _ _ _ _
SURGE	=	ENTREATS	=	16. _ _ _ _ _
LATER	=	TO CHANGE	=	17. _ _ _ _ _
LUGER	=	THIN PORRIDGE	=	18. _ _ _ _ _
SPICE	=	OVERSIZED NARRATIVES	=	19. _ _ _ _ _
IDEAL	=	SUFFERED	=	20. _ _ _ _ _
DIRGE	=	RAISED GROUND	=	21. _ _ _ _ _
LEASE	=	ART SUPPORT	=	22. _ _ _ _ _
WAKES	=	OUT OF LINE	=	23. _ _ _ _ _
CURBS	=	BACKUP PLAYER	=	24. _ _ _ _ _
CANOE	=	ATLANTIC OR PACIFIC	=	25. _ _ _ _ _
RIFLE	=	ADVERTISING CIRCULAR	=	26. _ _ _ _ _
GABLE	=	CEMENT DOUGHNUT	=	27. _ _ _ _ _
SPORE	=	LASSOES	=	28. _ _ _ _ _
BLAME	=	SAUNTER	=	29. _ _ _ _ _
TRINE	=	INACTIVE	=	30. _ _ _ _ _
STONE	=	MARGINALIA	=	31. _ _ _ _ _

1_	2_	3_	4_	5_	6_	7_	8_	9_	
10_	11_	12_	13_	14_	15_	16_	17_	18_	19_	20_
21_	22_	23_	24_	25_	26_	27_	28_	29_	30_	31_

Hint: The phrase reads: "Injuries map language areas of brain."

Women are more linguistically "balanced" than men

Arguments about the source of gender differences in human behavior and performance are often divided up simplistically along lines of "nature" vs. "nurture": are men from Mars and women from Venus because they are built differently, or because society has made them that way?

As with most things, the right answer lies somewhere in the middle. While many gender differences are culturally determined, the more we learn about the structure and mechanisms of the human brain, the more evidence we find that some of these differences have an innate biological basis.

It is by now common knowledge that the "language areas" of the brain are located in the left hemisphere. A recent experiment indicates that this may be more true for men than for women.

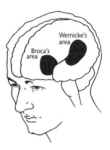

In the left hemisphere of the brain two areas have long been identified as main speech processors. Broca's area in the frontal lobe turns thoughts into words. Wernicke's area in the temporal and parietal lobes turns speech into thoughts.

When men perform the task of breaking down words into individual distinctive sounds, they rely heavily on the left side of the *inferior frontal gyrus,* an area of the brain which has long been known to be specialized for language. When women perform the same linguistic task, they use both sides of the brain about equally.

This important finding was enabled by the development of a new technology called functional magnetic resonance imaging, which provides a visual display of the parts of the brain being activated during the performance of a particular task.

For this experiment, 19 male and 19 female right-handers were given a rhyme-judgment task, which requires subjects to determine whether two nonsense words rhyme or not. Since the nonsense words were presented in written form, the task required visual and orthographic (letter recognition) processing as well as the mapping of the letter sequences onto phonological (sound) representations. They were also given a task of judging whether two sets of strings of letters featured the same patterns of lowercase-uppercase alternation.

Wherever the brain regions activated for the two tasks failed to overlap, these remaining regions were identified as the areas responsible for phonological processing alone. While the men showed an 11.7:5 ratio of left-right brain activation in this region, the women's ratio was a relatively equally-divided 9.4:12.

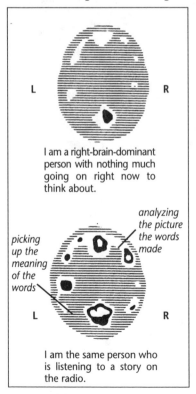

I am a right-brain-dominant person with nothing much going on right now to think about.

picking up the meaning of the words

analyzing the picture the words made

I am the same person who is listening to a story on the radio.

Men tend to do most of their word-processing only on the left side of their brains

This offers direct evidence in support of the hypothesis that language functions are more highly lateralized in men than in women — just as they are in left-handers as opposed to in right-handers. Left-handers tend to have their language competency more equally distributed across both hemispheres than right-handers. This means that if a left-hander suffers injury to the left hemisphere, any resulting aphasia (speech loss) is less likely to be permanent than with right-handers. But left-handers tend also to be less proficient in perceptual-spatial abilities, perhaps because the distribution of language ability across both hemispheres in effect displaces some right-brain-dependent functions such as the judgment of spatial relationships and Gestalt (whole-shape) perception.

Women, and left-handed men, tend to have more difficulty working with shapes and spaces than right-handed men

It has been shown that women and left-handed men have a culturally-independent tendency to perform slightly worse on certain tests of spatial relationships than right-handed men. This knowledge has prompted speculation that women may have just the sort of distribution of language ability across both hemispheres that left-handers have — a speculation confirmed by these new findings.

While no significant disparity emerged between men and women in their performance on the tasks involved in this experiment, the gender differences have both good and bad implications for each sex. The sort of left-hemisphere language specialization which is the norm for right-handed males may permit right-hemisphere spatial perception to function at a high level — to permit a simultaneous grasp of both the forest and the trees, as it were. Indeed, this is a dominant theory for the development of hemispheric lateralization in humans.

Women are less likely to suffer permanent language loss from effects of a stroke

Women's more even distribution of language across both halves of the brain may give them a sort of flexibility should something go awry. Less specialization may help women recover their linguistic abilities following a stroke or brain injury, and it may explain why girls seem to have an easier time than boys overcoming reading disabilities, including dyslexia.

EXERCISE: Language circleword

Directions: Just as one word leads to another, words lead into each other, or overlap. If you start with the correct word, you should have little trouble completing the circle with 10 additional overlapping words. Each word starts in a numbered slot that corresponds to the number of the clues.

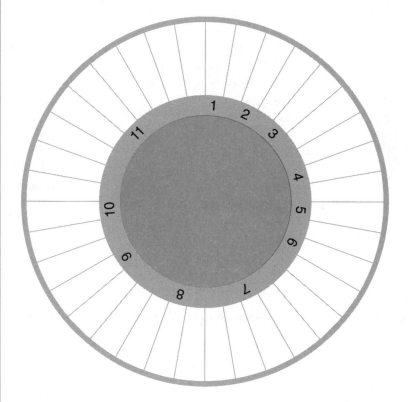

1. Bulrush
2. Man's name
3. Car park
4. Spy
5. Whole
6. Boring

7. Person
8. Car improvement
9. Employed
10. City in Jamaica
11. Monk's haircut

Hint: A man's name is Edgar.

Cortisol — as destructive to the brain as cholesterol is to the heart

Neuroscientists are closing in on a way to prevent loss of cognitive function in the elderly. A recent study shows that higher-than-average levels of the hormone cortisol are correlated with subclinical cognitive deficits in the elderly. A group of healthy elderly subjects were tested for blood-levels of cortisol, and then tested on a battery of cognitive functions, including memory, attention, and language ability. Those subjects who had relatively high cortisol levels and whose cortisol levels had been increasing over a four-year period scored the lowest on memory and attention tasks. Elderly subjects with *decreasing* cortisol levels, on the other hand, performed as well as healthy young subjects on the cognitive tasks. Also, it has been independently shown that high levels of cortisol correlate with Alzheimer's disease, a loss of cognitive abilities in the elderly, early symptoms of which are the inability to recall recent events and the names of friends.

How cortisol destroys memory

We've all had the experience of being unable to think clearly or to learn or remember things when under stress. One of the reasons for this is that cortisol, which is released in stressful situations, reduces the blood-sugar energy supply to the hippocampus and the rest of the brain. If the hippocampus is temporarily out of commission, short-term memories can't be created, so we feel mentally confused.

Another reason for mental confusion under stress is that cortisol interferes with the brain's neurotransmitters, prevent-

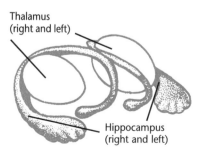

Thalamus
(right and left)

Hippocampus
(right and left)

The hippocampus and the two egg-like thalami are parts of the primitive "limbic system," where emotions and lasting memories are aroused and retrieved. The hippocampus is crucial to humans' ability to learn about things, ideas and the events that make up life—hence, damage to it affects memory. Without it, the mind cannot learn new data or access information learned in the past—precisely the kind of memory loss suffered by high-cortisol subjects.

ing you from laying down new memory pathways and from retrieving pre-existing memories from long-term storage. That's why it's precisely when under the pressure of an exam or public-speaking situation you're most likely to have difficulty accessing facts. One of the most important neurotransmitters involved in memory formation is *acetylcholine*.

Too much cortisol can even kill brain cells by causing an excess of calcium intake into neurons, and by stimulating the production of "free radicals." Free radicals are molecules that are destructive to the brain and body because they destroy brain cells and other neurons.

How you can lower your cortisol levels and enhance your prospects for brain longevity

Since the production of cortisol by your adrenal glands is stimulated by stress, exposing yourself to chronic stress kills brain cells and may hasten the onset of Alzheimer's. Learning to mitigate the stressors in your life, and learning to control your *response* to stress, will not only make you feel better, but will help your brain stay in good working order. Stress-reduction techniques, such as yoga, meditation, and biofeedback, can play a crucial role in helping you keep cognitively fit.

Regular aerobic exercise also helps counteract brain degeneration. Physically fit people tend to have a milder stress response, so their cortisol levels tend to be lower. Also, a half hour of sufficiently vigorous aerobic exercise can have a tranquilizing effect that lasts for several hours. Exercise can have the additional cognitive benefits of increasing blood flow to the brain, thereby promoting mental clarity, and of releasing neurotransmitters essential to good mood and memory.

Since excess cortisol also creates free radicals, you can to some degree compensate for cortisol's destructive effect by ensuring that your diet has enough "free radical scavengers," including the antioxidant vitamins A, C, and E. An adequate supply of choline in your diet helps ensure that you have enough of the essential building block of the "memory" neurotransmitter acetylcholine. A potent source of choline is lecithin, which may be puchased as a dietary supplement in any health food store.

EXERCISE: Unconstructible constructs

Sometimes, a perfectly reasonable question may be unaskable not because of social convention or nonsensical meaning, but simply because our mental grammar won't produce the structure underlying it. Here are examples of some such questions you'll never hear. Trying to decipher them produces a sensation similar to what you might feel when applying yourself to a very strange foreign language. This kind of exercise is excellent for challenging the kind of working memory faculty crucial for maintaining linguistic abilities into old age. Can you figure out what these questions are asking?

1. *Whom and your mother did you talk to?*
2. *Who did you know whether talked to your mother?*
3. *Whom did you talk to the woman who married?*
4. *Whom did the fact that you know bother John?*

Some sentences may be generatable in principle, but they're universally disfavored because they rely on structures that are very difficult for humans to process. With some effort, you can decipher them, but the effort required seems to be too much for everyday situations. Try your hand at translating the following examples into normal English.

5. *This is the woman whom the man whom you talked to yesterday abandoned.*
6. *This is the car that the man whom you saw talking to the woman you met yesterday parked.*
7. *This is the guy Richard sent the package that was in the room that you read the instructions through in to.*
8. *The fact that the man whom the guy you saw yesterday met told you about that I don't like you is disturbing.*

More impossibilities:
How would you ask the following question about more than one box?

9. *How big (of) a box do you need?*

How would you turn these passive sentences into their active counterparts?

10. *He was rumored to be a Mafioso.*
11. *She was reputed to be rich.*

SELF-TEST: Mental status for language ability

This can be used as a quick and simple test of verbal acuity, or of possible signs of age-related cognitive decline. Have a friend test you, or test a friend or family member who may be concerned about her mental status.

1. Explain to your friend that you're going to ask her to repeat a short phrase word for word. Then, read the following out loud:
"If you couldn't cook, I'd drop you quicker than a box of rocks."
> A. *She can't repeat it correctly.*
> B. *She makes a mistake the first time, but gets it right the second time.*
> C. *She does it perfectly the first time.*

2. Mention a common category, such as fruits, animals, or vegetables, and ask your friend to list as many members of that category as she can in 1 minute.
> A. *She can only think of 10 or fewer.*
> B. *She can only think of 11 to 15.*
> C. *She can think of 16 or more.*

3. Explain that you're going to read a sentence out loud, and that the task will be to write down the sentence word for word. Use the following sentence (or one of similar length and complexity from a newspaper article):
"New scanning methods have helped pinpoint the location of many brain functions."
> A. *She can't do it at all, or makes many mistakes.*
> B. *She makes a couple of mistakes, but the two versions are close.*
> C. *She makes no mistakes.*

4. Gather a collection of 6 familiar objects, such as a can opener, a corkscrew, a key, a paper clip, a thumbtack, and a shoelace. Point to each object in turn, and give your friend a couple of seconds to name each one.
> A. *She can only name two or fewer correctly.*
> B. *She makes a few errors, such as calling a shoelace a "string."*
> C. *She makes no mistakes.*

How a child begins to speak a complex language before it can even pull on its socks

Anyone who has raised a child from infancy knows that language acquisition is a mysterious, even miraculous, process. A 4-year-old child, who probably hasn't even learned to tie her shoes and may not be fully toilet-trained, will have mastered enough of whatever language she's been exposed to — whether English, Arabic, or Swahili — for her to be considered fluent. For an adult English speaker, achieving that level of proficiency in a language like Arabic would take years of focused, concentrated effort — and many adults would never attain fluency at all, no matter how long and hard they tried. Clearly, then, as infants we have some kind of language-acquisition faculty which we lose as we grow older. Understanding the details of this faculty — where it comes from, how long it lasts, what its stages are, and what biologically-determined expectations about "possible languages" it gives us as we enter the world — is the domain of the intersection of psychology and linguistics, called psycholinguistics.

The core question is whether humans are born with a specialized brain function dedicated only to acquiring language skills as opposed to general strategies for acquiring knowledge that may be applied to a number of tasks including language acquisition. There is no doubt that infants do bring to the task of language acquisition more than they're exposed to in their environment.

At least two kinds of evidence point to this. One is that we seem to have a biologically-given window of language acquisition (see "Critical window of opportunity..." p. 221). The other is that certain aspects of language development unfold in remarkably uniform ways for all children.

From babbling to multi-word phrases, all human infants go through predictable stages as they learn to talk

From about 4 to 6 months of age, infants produce brief, isolated consonant and vowel sounds, as well as clicks, coos, grunts, and sighs that often bear little or no resemblance to any speech sounds in any language. At about 6 months, they begin what's called the *babbling* stage — the production of a reduplicative sequence of consonant-vowel (CV), but almost no vowel-consonant (VC), sequences — such as "KOO" but not "OOK." (A compelling piece of evidence that this behavior is innate is that even congenitally deaf infants will start babbling at more or less the same age, with the same syllable-structure preferences — although, unlike hearing children, they may continue to babble until well beyond the babbling stage, sometimes until age 6 or 7.) Toward the end of the first year, the infant's repertoire of syllables increases, to include not just CV, but CVC and VC. The sequences of babbled syllables become less repetitive and more varied.

All infants babble the same way no matter what language their parents speak

The speech sounds the infant uses in these babbling stages are universal and independent of the speech sounds used in the *particular* language to which the infant is exposed. All infants favor oral stops (consonants we represent with the letters "p," "t," "k," "b," "d," "g"), nasal stops (especially "m" and "n"), glides ("w," "y"), and "h." Of the oral stops, voiced are more common than voiceless ones, and sounds produced toward the front of the vocal tract (e.g., "b," "d," "m," "n") are more common than ones produced toward the rear (e.g., "k," "ng"). (During the *pre*-babbling stage, on the other hand, back stops are much more common.) Fricatives ("s," "th," "f," etc.), affricates ("ch," etc.) and liquids ("r," "l") are strongly disfavored, although if the infant does produce one of these sounds it may be one that her parents' language doesn't have (e.g., the velar fricative found in German "Ach!" from a child with English-speaking parents). The most common vowel in the babbling stages is the sound in "lot" — perhaps because that sound can be made without using tongue or face muscles in a way that requires much practice.

The sounds that infants universally prefer in these early stages probably explain why it is that certain sounds tend universally to appear in different languages' words (or, even more frequently, "baby" words) for "mother" and "father" — e.g., *papa* and *mama* in English. This, combined with the babbling preferences, also gives rise to the mother or father's gratifying illusion that the child's "first word" is her or his own name.

THE WORLD BABBLES IN UNISON

Among all the world's languages there are more similarities in the sound of the words for *mama* and *papa* than would be expected by pure chance. They can't be explained through the inheritance of a common root because completely unrelated languages show these similarities, Chinese and English for example. To some extent, the explanation for the recurrence of certain sounds has to do with constraints on the infant's vocal apparatus during the early "babbling" period. Both oral and nasal stops ("p" and "m," for example) are strongly favored over other consonants, and front consonants ("p," "b," "t," "d," "m," "n") are favored over back consonants.

A more puzzling mystery is why nasals ("m," "n") are so strongly preferred for "mama" and orals ("p," "b," "t," "d") are so strongly favored for "papa." Again, there are exceptions — in Georgian, a Caucasian language spoken in the former Soviet Union, *mama* means "father." Somehow, there appears to be some kind of sound-symbolic association of nasals with "mother" and oral stops with "father."

Sound symbolism — the "natural" connection between a certain kind of sound and a certain kind of meaning — is a subtle but nevertheless real and fascinating motivating factor in the words used by languages to refer to things. Another universal sound-symbolic tendency is for small things to be referred to with words with high front vowels — like the vowel in *teeny* — and for large things to be referred to with low and/or back vowels — as in *large* or *huge*. By the general sound-change process known as the Great Vowel Shift, a Middle English word sounding similar to *teeny* became Modern English *tiny* — the high front vowel changed to a low vowel. Interestingly enough, while *tiny*, with its newly sound-symbolically inappropriate vowel, remains in the language as a word describing very little objects, speakers have "resurrected" the high front vowel in the word *teeny* — which simply, somehow, sounds more appropriate to many speakers, especially children, for denoting an *eentsy-weentsy* (more high front vowels!) object such as a "bikini."

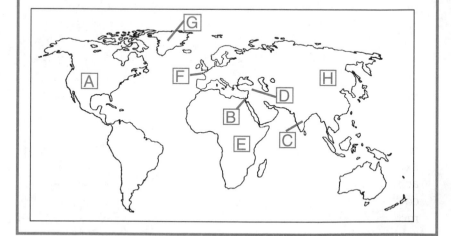

EXERCISE: Mama and papa

Children use words for "mama" and "papa" that are so similar from one language to another that something more than chance is at work. (See "The world babbles in unison," p. 215.)

Among the 16 words listed here in random order, one means "mama" and one means "papa" in each of the eight languages listed.

The task in this exercise is to identify which member of the pair of words for each language means "mama" and which means "papa." To test your knowledge of linguistic geography, locate the area on the world map in which each language is spoken. These eight areas are designated by the letters A through H in the boxes on the map.

i. Welsh   *mam*

                 tad, tada, dad

ii. Hebrew   *aba*

                 ima

iii. Swahili   *mama*

                 baba

iv. Tamil   *ammaa*

                 appa

v. Chinese   *pa pa*

                 ma ma

vi. Dakota   *ena*

                 ate

vii. Turkish   *annecigim*

                 baba

viii. Greenlandic

                 anaana(q)

                 ataata(q)

Hint: Remember that nasal consonants tend universally to be associated with "mama" words.

Educating babies

Human infants seem to be able to adapt to living conditions wherever they are born: For example, at 8,000 feet or at sea level; in third-world communities, to a daily calorie intake that is way below the starvation level of people living in industrialized countries; or to rare diseases found only in their community and nowhere else. A molecular biologist named Gerald Edelman traced the process that allows an infant's immune system to develop antibodies before it is born, which will attack and control the specific diseases it will encounter once it emerges into its outside world.

Edelman used some of those discoveries to build a theory called *neural Darwinism* to explain how a newborn infant's brain can master so much information so fast into its early childhood. Take language, for example. The rules of grammar are extremely complex and vary from one language to another, as does vocabulary. Most of us know the frustration of attempting to learn a new language as an adult. How does a newborn brain pull off that trick?

Edelman claims that the brain of a fetus is a sea of neurons grouped into areas of the brain that allow the infant to master different kinds of skills when these areas are exposed to experience. What happens is that when a newborn tries to achieve something (like moving across the floor to reach a cookie, for example) neurons that cause the specific body movements that get the infant going toward the cookie will "cluster" and remain. (The readiness of so many available neurons to devote themselves to new tasks helps explain, for example, how it is that a three-year-old can begin to be fluent

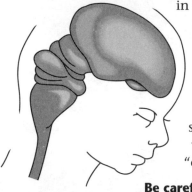
in a new second language so much more quickly than an adult.) The neurons that cause whatever other random actions that do not help achieve the desired goal die off. The developing brain has so many billions of neurons that it can afford a policy of "only what works survives."

6 months

Be careful what you say; your unborn child is listening

Learning word sounds probably begins before an infant is born. A group of expectant mothers eight months into term were divided into three groups. Every day the mothers in each group read aloud, to their as-yet unborn babies, a paragraph from the same three-paragraph-long children's story, with each group reading a different paragraph from the others. This went on for about a month. Two days after each baby was born, it was given a bottle with a special nipple that allowed it to suck faster or slower without changing the amount of milk it received. The baby was fitted with earphones linked to a tape recorder that played its mother's voice reading *all three* of the paragraphs from the story — not just the one she read while the infant was in the womb, but the other two as well. The special nipple was wired to the recorder in such a way that the infant could select which of the three passages it heard by changing its rate of sucking. All the newborns changed their sucking rate so they could hear the *same* paragraph their mother read to them during the month before they were born.

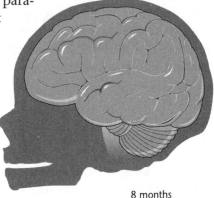
8 months

Around the turn of the first year, the infant moves beyond babbling and begins to produce recognizable words in the language spoken around him

Sometimes the stage of word formation is preceded by a "silent period" (which may cause considerable anxiety or relief for the parents, as the case may be).

Within about 6 months thereafter, the average child has a vocabulary of about 50 words. From there, she moves on to the "two-word" stage. Early multi-word speech is sometimes referred to as "telegraphic," since the same sorts of words are omitted that we omit when writing a telegram — words like *the* and *is*. After that, language acquisition moves on to a bewilderingly rapid explosion of progress.

Life sure was a lot easier when all we had to worry about was nouns and verbs

The child progresses to syntactically more complex structures by about age 3 — relative clauses such as "the dog that bit me," for example. By shortly after age 4, the child has developed a grammar — *real* grammar, not artificial prescriptive rules of grammar such as "Never end a sentence with a preposition" or "Never split an infinitive" — largely the same as that of an adult speaker.

The degree to which this progression is preordained shouldn't be exaggerated. In fact, every child is different, and a girl who begins reduplicative babbling at 6 months may have a brother who waits until 12 months to enter this same stage. But within these general parameters, all children, except those with special deficits, progress on schedule, and the acquisitional stages are never out of order. In these respects, language acquisition has been claimed to be similar to other biologically-programmed behavior in humans and other species, such as learning to walk or fly.

Of course, it remains a somewhat open question to what extent these stages are determined by some language-specific part of the infant's *brain* as opposed to the infant's physiology — in particular, the structure and development of the vocal tract. The reason that infants babble for months before they show any real evidence of copying the speech of their parents may simply be that their brains haven't yet developed enough. Two critical networks of neurons are involved in auditory analysis, ability to name objects and put meaning to spoken words (Wernicke's and adjacent areas) and speech-motor output (Broca's area); this means that the 6-month-old infant may be neurologically unequipped to monitor and imitate the speech sounds produced by adults.

The critical window of opportunity to learn languages easily and fluently closes at puberty

A major argument for the biologically-determined, innate nature of a specifically linguistic "module" of the brain has to do with the concept of the critical period. There is a series of windows of opportunity lasting between six months and puberty for the acquisition of language, beyond which language learning is impaired.

While there is some disagreement about exactly how long each window remains open, it seems to be true that, up until around puberty, humans can learn whatever language or languages they're exposed to in a relatively effortless manner leading naturally to native-like fluency. After about age 12, language acquisition is much more difficult, and even if vocabulary and usage of a second language is correct and fluent, the sound of the speech always carries traces of the native language learned in infancy — as in Henry Kissinger's speech. The rare cases where children have somehow progressed through the critical period without learning any language (see "The forbidden experiment," p. 225) show that, after this period, they cannot become fluent even in their first language.

Why don't we simply keep the window open all our life?
Most of us have had the experience of wishing that we had been exposed to more languages as an infant, or that we could somehow recapture our youthful gift of language acquisition. Why do we have a critical period at all?

The reason for this frustrating course of events is probably essentially the same as why most adults have difficulty digesting dairy products: if an enzyme — or neural circuitry — is not needed beyond a certain early stage in life, then it will be shut down, or recycled to other purposes. The neural circuitry of language acquisition is an especially good candidate for dismantling or recycling since the brain is such a greedy consumer of oxygen, energy, and nutrients. A child has completed its acquisition of its native language in the first few years of its life, except for learning additional vocabulary. After that the body would be wasting valuable resources if it continued to maintain, unused into adulthood, the vast circuitry laid down to acquire structure and pronunciation. The large number of additional brain cells that a child has available to develop speech and language skills seems eventually to become unavailable except for those that have been put to work.

This means, by the way, that you should beware of any language-instruction program that promises to help you learn a foreign language with the same ease, and by the same "just-listen-and-learn" exposure, with which you acquired your native language. Adult second-language acquisition by necessity relies on much more conscious, effortful strategies than child language acquisition.

"HYPERLEXIA": WHEN CHILDREN ARE LINGUISTICALLY RETARDED, BUT PRECOCIOUSLY LITERATE

Most children pick up spoken language effortlessly and with no deliberate instruction in their preschool years, and pick up reading and writing skills later, after the expenditure of considerable time and conscious effort. There are, however, a few children who seem to do it backwards, or do the latter without ever attaining normal ability in the former. Known as "hyperlexics," these children may be almost entirely mute, may show linguistic and other development in the moderately to severely retarded range, and yet have reading and writing skills well beyond those of their agemates. In most cases, their reading ability seems to emerge abruptly and spontaneously, with no conscious instruction on the part of the parents.

One case reported in the literature is that of "V," a 5-and-a-half-year-old child who was admitted to the UCLA Neuropsychiatric Institute because of severe behavioral and developmental problems. She had no expressive speech, but had advanced reading skills. (Indeed, almost the only way she could respond to cognitive-evaluation test questions was to point to the answer in a written text.) She responded perfectly to written commands (in contrast to most 5-year-olds, who can respond to oral commands but not written commands at all), and was just as avid a reader of hospital charts as children's books. She had also taught herself to use a typewriter, and occasionally used this skill to answer questions.

EXERCISE: Child speak

It takes a surprisingly long time for a child to learn to use some simple "concept" words in an "adult" way.

The following five pairs of sentences use the simple words *really, have to, still, since* and *while* in two different senses. A young child would have no hesitation identifying one member of each pair as something he or she might say, and the other not. This isn't because of the content of the utterance as a whole. Rather, it's because of the sense in which the words are used. A child may learn these words at a young age, but they are only used with a certain meaning. Other senses are acquired only later, and give the older child the more sophisticated sound of a grown-up.

Which of the two usages, A or B, would be less natural to a young child?

1.   A. *Daddy is* really *Santa Claus.*

       B. Really, *I don't think you should say that.*

2.   A. *He* has to *be Santa Claus—I saw him wearing a red hat.*

       B. *He* has to *go now.*

3.   A. Still, *I think you're wrong.*

       B. *Are you* still *up?*

4.   A. *He's been here* since *Friday.*

       B. Since *you're eating all the cookies, I'll drink all the milk.*

5.   A. *I'll fetch the cookies* while *you fetch the milk.*

       B. While *I like cookies, she likes milk.*

Hint: The later-acquired senses tend to be, for want of a better word, more abstract.

EXERCISE: Stages of language acquisition

Match the following 11 sounds, words and sentences (1-11) with the four stages (A, B, C, D) of a child's development of language ability

Stages: A: Babbling (6 months); B: First words (end of first year); C: Early multi-word speech (second year); D: More complex sentences (age 3 on).

Sounds and Words:

1. Will you help me?

2. hi mama, pants off

3. Why you smiling?

4. bababa

5. wawa

6. He was stuck and I got him out.

7. more cookie

8. mama

9. What cowboy doing?

10. nana

11. I want the ones that Mommy got.

EXERCISE: Letters into words

The letters stacked up in each column below go into the boxes directly under them, but not necessarily in the order in which they are shown in their stack. When all the boxes have been filled in, a sentence or phrase from the preceding article will appear.

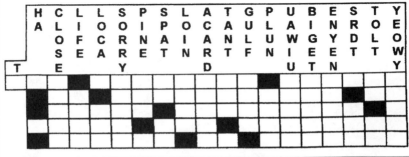

H	C	L	L	S	P	S	L	A	T	G	P	U	B	E	S	T	Y
A	L	I	O	O	I	P	O	C	A	U	L	A	I	N	R	O	E
	O	F	C	R	N	A	I	A	N	L	U	W	G	Y	D	L	O
	S	E	A	R	E	T	N	R	T	F	N	I	E	E	T	T	W
T		E		Y				D			U	T	N				Y

Hint: The first word is "the" and the last word is "puberty." The letters in the third column below will be rearranged in the column below them as: e, o, l, s, c.

224   BUILDING MENTAL MUSCLE

The forbidden experiment: What happens when a child is deprived of any linguistic stimulation?

Since the dawn of history, people have wondered what kind of language, if any, would be developed by a child completely isolated from environmental linguistic influence. Writing in the 5th century B.C., the Greek historian Herodotus relates the story of the 7th-century B.C. Egyptian king Psamtik I, who decided to conduct an experiment to settle the matter once and for all. According to Herodotus's account, Psamtik took two infants from their mother at birth and left them in an isolated hut in the care of a shepherd. The shepherd was instructed never to utter a word to the infants, and to pay particular attention to the first sound that came out of their mouths. One day when the infants were about two years old, upon returning to the hut from his daily chores, the shepherd was greeted with what sounded to him like "*bekos.*" Since *bekos* was the word for "bread" in Phrygian, an Indo-European language spoken in Asia Minor before the arrival of Turkic invaders, Psamtik concluded that Phrygian must have been the world's first language.

How much of what an infant does in the process of learning her first language is instinctive and how much determined by her surroundings?

While the methods of this experiment and Psamtik's conclusion from it obviously leave much to be desired, the basic question remains a compelling one: How much of language acquisition is "nature" and how much is "nurture"? If the genetic linguistic blueprint were permitted to express itself without any outside influence, what would it look like?

For obvious reasons of ethics, nobody nowadays can actually run an experiment on a human child that would answer this question. However, some sadly natural events do provide some insight. Congenitally deaf children who — because of ignorance about the "proper" parental response — are denied the opportunity to learn sign language (of which, by the way, there are many mutually-unintelligible varieties around the world with just as complete and legitimate a linguistic status as spoken languages like English and Cantonese), or even manacled to prevent them from using manual gestures, may pass through the window of first-language acquisition without really learning language at all, and may remain this way for the rest of their lives.

A "feral" child is an infant abandoned after birth and raised by social wild animals, such as wolves

When a "wild child" emerges from the wilderness after having been socialized by whatever animal raised him, any expressive noises — such as grunts, howls, and barks — will be those of the child's adoptive "parents." Even such biologically preordained behaviors as walking erect, grasping objects between the fingers and opposable thumb, and displaying sensitivity to extremes of heat or cold may be absent. Instead a feral child may walk or scamper on all fours, paw or scratch, pull hot potatoes bare-handed out of the fire or cavort naked in the snow. This shows that whatever genetic blueprint we have for many natural human abilities, including language, is either so general that it won't express itself as anything resembling human language in the absence of an appropriate environmental model, or that this blueprint will fail to express itself at all lacking relevant environmental input. If the latter conclusion is true, then language development is much like vision: if a newborn cat has a patch applied to one eye, then the eye will never develop as a visual organ; when the patch is later removed, the cat is blind in that eye, and will remain so for the rest of its life.

For the development of any of the body's "organs" — whether literal or metaphorical — exposure to appropriate stimuli *at the right age* is crucially important. This doesn't mean that the eye's capacity for vision derives from nothing but external stimuli rather than its innate biological structure, but rather that the division between "nature" and "nurture," or "empiricism" and "rationalism," is not as clear-cut nor even as real as we are sometimes led to believe.

Language, too, has its own critical period, beyond which the task of acquisition becomes at the very least considerably harder, and less likely to succeed, than it is for infants (see "How a child begins to speak a complex language...," p. 213).

Most of our understanding about this window of opportunity — closing, at different times for different specific abilities, by the age of about 12 — comes from evidence of the increased difficulty of acquiring a *second* (non-native) language as an adult. But what about *first* language acquisition? What would happen if a child were somehow denied the chance to learn any language at all until after the critical period had ended?

The Wild Boy of Aveyron

While any evidence that we could use to answer this question is, fortunately, rarely available, once in a while something of relevance does fall into our laps. Victor, the Wild Boy of Aveyron depicted in François Truffaut's film *The Wild Child*, was discovered in rural southern France in 1800. Nobody was sure exactly how old he was, but he seemed to be about 12. Nothing was known about his personal history beyond the fact that his throat had been cut in infancy, presumably when he had been left to die in the woods. The fact that he had survived probably meant that he had been raised by wild animals. He spoke not a word of language.

The best efforts of Jean-Marc-Gaspard Itard, a young physician at Paris's National Institute of Deaf-Mutes, resulted in an initial, promising flurry of language acquisition — the learning of names for individual objects, and even the ability to understand and formulate rudimentary multiword utterances — but nothing beyond this. Eventually, once the initial enthusiasm had faded over the opportunity Victor provided for testing certain Enlightenment ideas about human perfectibility, Victor was abandoned to obscurity in an inconspicuous home on the Impasse de Feuillantines, supported by a caretaker and a modest pension. He died there at age 40.

As if you were doing an acrostic puzzle, think of a synonym for each word in the left column that fits in the numbered spaces opposite that word in the right column. Write the correspondingly numbered letters into the numbered squares in the grid below. (If you are not an *experienced* genius, write in pencil.) The letters you write correctly into the grid below will reveal a phrase from the preceding article on feral children and language.

Clue								
CONTAMINATED	9	17	32	48	54	21	3	11
LARGE NUMBER	50	12	6	67	64	53	15	13
RABBIT FOOD				68	1	10	45	26
UNDISCIPLINED			58	62	20	39	27	63
JEWELED CROWN				33	59	5	4	66
LACKING HEARING					61	34	19	2
LIVING KINGDOM			56	28	16	65	41	60
MARK INDELIBLY				23	35	14	42	30
EXTENDED GRASP				38	29	22	7	8
POST-THURSDAY			18	44	37	43	24	51
FEDORA & BOWLER					57	46	49	52
TO FORCE EXILE			36	31	25	55	47	40

Grid (■ = shaded square):

1	■	2	3	4	5	6	■	7	8	9	10
11	■	12	13	■	14	15	■	16	17	18	19
20	21	■	22	23	24	25	26	27	28	29	30
■	31	32	33	34	35	■	36	37	38	39	40
■	41	42	43	■	44	45	46	47	48	49	■
50	51	■	52	53	54	55	56	57	■	58	59
60	61	■	62	63	64	65	66	67	68	■	

The tragic case of "Genie" from L.A., whose "language-learning" window was sealed shut from the age of 20 months to 13½ years

A recent case of a child who passed through her critical acquisition period without learning language is that of "Genie," a severely abused and neglected child discovered in 1970 in, of all places, Los Angeles. After a relatively normal early infancy, from about the age of 20 months until she was brought to the light of day at 13 and a half years of age, Genie had been confined to a small bedroom in the back of her parents' house, and often harnessed to an infant's potty seat or in a straight-jacket, with very little human contact or stimulation of any kind. From infancy on, almost the only exposure she had to human vocalization was when her father or brother barked or growled at her like a dog. The father forbade anyone in the family, including Genie's mother, to talk to her.

When she was discovered, Genie was malnourished, animal-like, and neither spoke nor understood language beyond a few words. (She was also near-sighted to precisely the distance — 10 feet — from one edge of her room to the opposite wall.) The only words she uttered, or seemed capable of uttering, were "stopit" and "nomore"; she appeared to understand about a dozen isolated words, including her own name, "door," "walk," "go," and "no." Presumably, despite the father's prohibition, Genie's mother had managed to teach her a tiny, rudimentary vocabulary — although it's possible that these few words were nothing more than a memory from a distant, relatively normal infancy.

Genie passed through what is generally considered the "critical period" with no language acquisition

From infancy until about 12 years of age Genie did not learn to speak. She could understand about as many words as a typical family dog. It was very much an open question whether she would ever be able to become a linguistically full-fledged adult. Perhaps unfortunately for Genie, she became the object of competing academic, scientific, and personal interests to the point where her needs as a human being were — despite good intentions all around — only questionably served.

While she was being studied by UCLA linguists (in particular Susan Curtiss, who turned her study into a doctoral dissertation), Genie did make some progress in her comprehension and production of language, albeit sometimes with a puzzling waxing and waning of specific abilities. To some degree, her progress followed that of a normal child in the early stages of language learning, although much more slowly. For the first two or three years, she spoke very little, and she always remained much more reticent, and less linguistically playful and exploratory, than a normal child in the first few years of language acquisition. And while normal children experience an explosion of learning after the two-word stage at around age three (see "Around the turn of the first year...," p. 219), Genie remained stuck in a "telegraphic" stage. For her, the normal developmental explosion simply never occurred.

Genie never learned simple grammatical structures the rest of us take for granted

Some of the seemingly unremarkable structures Genie never learned to use properly or, in test situations, to understand, were

- tense/aspect markers (e.g., walk*ed*)
- possessive markers (e.g., John*'s*)
- some prepositions (especially *under*)
- modal verbs (*may, can, must*, etc.)
- quantifiers (*many, most, few, fewest*)
- the conjunction *or*
- possessive pronouns (*my, your*, etc.)
- first- and second-person object pronouns (*me, you*)
- all third-person pronouns (*he, she, him, her*, etc.)
- relative pronouns ("the man *whom* I saw," "the cat *that* bit me")

She had ongoing difficulties matching the "actor" and "patient" with the subject and object of both active and passive sentences ("The cat is biting the dog" vs. "The dog is biting the cat"). While she understood "wh"-questions (e.g., "Whom did you see today?"), she never learned to produce them spontaneously.

Genie often seemed to understand language better than she could demonstrate in test situations

Genie could understand better than one would guess from her speech, but it wasn't clear to what extent this comprehension was due to contextual clues that don't depend on linguistic knowledge as such. Curtiss speculated that Genie, having missed language acquisition during her critical period, may have failed to develop the left-brain specialization for linguistic knowledge typical of humans. We all rely on contextual information and pragmatic expectations in our linguistic interactions with others, but perhaps Genie was more dependent on these right-brain faculties than most of us.

After being bounced from caretaker to caretaker, Genie moved into a home for mentally retarded adults, withdrew into a state of unresponsiveness and depression, and disappeared from the world of scientists and health-care providers who had studied her and argued over her for years. The only person from her past she continues to have contact with is her own mother, whom Genie visits once a week.

EXAMPLES OF GENIE'S SPEECH, WITH GLOSSES:

"At school scratch face": *Someone/I scratched my face at school/ I scratched someone's face at school* (after $2^1/_2$ years of language exposure)

"Not spit bus": *I didn't spit on the bus* (after $3^1/_2$ years)

"Mama is feed you": *Mama is feeding you/me* (after $3^1/_2$ years)

"I supermarket surprise Roy": *I surprised/will surprise/want to surprise Roy in the supermarket* (after $4^1/_2$ years)

Genie: "Genie have yellow material at school"

(M: "What are you using it for?")

Genie: "Paint. Paint picture. Take home. Ask teacher yellow material. Blue paint. Yellow green paint. Genie have blue material, teacher said no. Genie use material paint. I want use material at home." (after $4^1/_2$ years)

"I want you open my mouth": *I want you to open your mouth* (after $4^1/_2$ years)

"Mama not have baby grow up": *(meaning uncertain)* (after $4^1/_2$ years)

HOW PIDGINS BECOME CREOLES

In many ways, Genie's telegraphic, structurally impoverished speech resembles what are known as *pidgins*. Pidgins are rudimentary semi-languages jerry-built in situations where different speakers share no common language and quick communication is required — in situations of trade or slavery, for example. A pidgin, in other words, is nobody's native language, and is hastily assembled by adults well past the critical language-acquisition period who simply need to communicate with one another on a basic level. Such structures as tense and agreement markers, relative clause markers, morphological plural markers, and many "function" words are simply omitted from a communication system consisting largely of nouns and verbs strung together in a fairly unstructured manner.

One of the fascinating things about pidgins is that, when they are passed on to the subsequent generation, they change. Infants exposed to the parents' pidgin as their first language actually add complexity and structure, rather than simply learning or imitating what they hear. Of course, infants don't create the material for this increased complexity de novo, like Athena from the head of Zeus. Rather, they recruit "function" words and markers from other more "concrete" words they're exposed to. This process is recapitulated continuously in "normal" languages — consider the recruitment of English tense-aspect markers out of verbs like *finish* and *go* (as in, "He's *going* to leave" to express future), or the development of prepositions out of body-part nouns (e.g., *ahead [of]*).

A pidgin that has become more complex by developing into a subsequent generation's primary language is known as a *creole*. The creativity infants display in turning their parents' pidgin into a creole has inspired University of Hawaii linguist Derek Bickerton to look to creoles, or to the difference between creoles and pidgins, for evidence of our innate "bioprogram" — the genetic language-acquisition blueprint we bring as infants to the task of learning language.

EXERCISE: Translating from the pidgin

The following are examples of pidgins transcribed from the speech of Asian immigrants to Hawaii around the turn of the last century. The first is from a native Japanese speaker, the second a native Korean speaker, and the third a native speaker of Filipino. See if you can decipher them. Any Hawaiian-language words are underlined and translated in the lower line to help you out. The other words are English-based.

1. Ifu laik <u>meiki</u>, mo beta make time, mani no kaen <u>hapai</u>.
    "die"   "carry"

2. Aena tu macha churen, samawl churen, haus mani pei.

3. <u>Luna</u>, hu <u>hapai</u>? Hapai awl, <u>hemo</u> awl.
   "foreman" "carry"   "cut"

Tok Pisin (literally "pidgin-talk"), spoken in Papua New Guinea, is an English-based creole undergoing a gradual process of development. In this process, "grammatical" or "function" words and markers evolve their new uses out of pre-existing words. Take a look at the following examples of Tok Pisin speech, together with their translations:

Mi no stap long ples ol paitim em long-en
I no stop at   place they beat up him at it
"I wasn't there where they beat him up"

Husat i kukim dispela haus?
who   burn this   house
"Who burned down this house?"

In the following examples, long "at," longen "at it," and husat "who?" show evidence of having evolved into words with a different function. Can you decipher these and figure out the new function of long, longen, and husat?

4. Mi paitim em long diwai mi holim longen.

5. Bai mi toktok long ol asua husat bai i kamap sapos Tok Pisin i kamap nambawan tokples bilong Papua Niugini.

New technology for testing theories about language processing

A new kind of tool is now available for testing the validity of different theories about how we organize our mental grammar. In an experiment presented recently in the premier journal in the field of linguistics, Jaeger et al. (1996) report the results of PET scans (see "What is the brain so busy doing," p. 177) of the brains of volunteers performing past-tense-inflection tasks on three different kinds of verbs: regularly-inflected verbs, such as *ask*, irregularly-inflected verbs, such as *fall*, and made-up "nonce" verbs, such as *baff*. (The nonce words were carefully chosen so as not to resemble real irregular verbs; therefore, the past-tense forms supplied for them by the volunteers featured the regular inflection.) The PET images reveal that many of the parts of the brain activated in irregular past-tense formation are distinct from those activated in regular past-tense formation. Overall, irregular past-tense formation is not simply a more taxing task in requiring more time and resulting in more errors — irregular past tenses also require the involvement of much more of the brain, at a higher level of activation, than regular verbs.

The simplest conclusion from this is that we may indeed be relying on fundamentally different strategies for producing and processing irregular patterns, such as irregular past-tense forms, than we do for regular patterns. The evidence seems at least to suggest that the most efficient way for us to deal with irregular patterns is to store the various forms as listed entries in our mental lexicon, while the most efficient way for us to deal with regular, productive patterns is to store them as rules that may be applied to lexical stems (uninflected forms) in on-line fashion.

The PET scans do, admittedly, show overlapping activation for all three past-tense tasks centering on and around Broca's area — a traditionally-conceived locus of grammatical processing. In addition, however, an area at the extreme front of the left frontal lobe is activated only with the irregular and nonce past-tense tasks. Also activated only in irregular past-tense for-

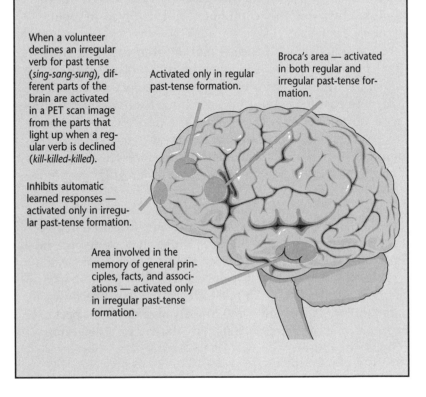

When a volunteer declines an irregular verb for past tense (*sing-sang-sung*), different parts of the brain are activated in a PET scan image from the parts that light up when a regular verb is declined (*kill-killed-killed*).

Activated only in regular past-tense formation.

Broca's area — activated in both regular and irregular past-tense formation.

Inhibits automatic learned responses — activated only in irregular past-tense formation.

Area involved in the memory of general principles, facts, and associations — activated only in irregular past-tense formation.

mation is an area in the left temporal lobe, and two areas in the parietal lobe. Two areas activated in just the regular and nonce inflection tasks are in the prefrontal cortex and cingulate cortex.

One of the areas involved in just the irregular and nonce past-tense tasks has been independently found to have a function of inhibiting automatic learned responses to stimuli. It is activated in novel learning tasks, but the activation disappears with practice and familiarity. Therefore, this region is probably responsible for suppressing activation of the regular past-tense formation rule — at least until it can be determined whether the regular rule should apply. Another area, activated only in the irregular past-tense task, is generally thought to be associated with auditory memory, especially long-term "semantic" memory — the memory of general principles, facts, and associations. It seems, then, that irregular past-tense retrieval is supported by a memory component not involved in regular past-tense retrieval.

An area activated in the generation of just regular and nonce past-tense forms is independently involved in the willful manipulation of items in long-term memory storage. The reason the past-tense inflection of nonce forms activated this region is presumably because, since the nonce verbs were carefully selected to avoid resemblance to real irregular verbs, the volunteers inflected them regularly. Therefore, this area seems to be the best candidate for the locus of the regular past-tense suffixation process.

One of the interesting implications of this research is that our rules of mental grammar will "migrate" from one region of the brain to another as the rules themselves undergo a natural process of evolution. The first time you use a word such as *re-shellack*, you'll process it in one part of your brain as a complex item composed of two parts. If the word becomes more familar, its use will come to activate a different part of the brain in accordance with its new status as a single, noncompositional unit.

SELF-TEST: Regular and irregular past-tense formation under time pressure

Even though irregular verbs comprise a large portion of our most common, everyday vocabulary, there are many different patterns represented by irregular past-tense forms. When supplying past-tense forms for a list of irregular verbs, getting the right form for each verb is a relatively slow and difficult process.

Below are two lists of common verbs — regular and irregular. For the regular list, give the past-tense forms as quickly as you can, and time how long it takes. Next, try the same thing with the irregular list. You'll need more time for the second list, and you'll probably make more errors.

Note: For an especially difficult exercise, try supplying not just the "simple" past-tense form (as in, "Yesterday I drank the wine") but the compound past form as well (as in, "I have drunk the wine," yielding drink-drank-drunk).

Regular list:	Irregular list:	Regular list:	Irregular list:
pass	think	love	flow
ask	draw	count	blow
rub	fall	name	feed
drop	dig	look	hear
load	catch	watch	bring
dress	sell	blow	keep
push	fight	pay	drink
plan	teach	kill	ride
burn	reach	tie	sing
jump	sleep	start	grow
walk	stand	add	bite
form	hold	laugh	sweep
list	fly	work	send
place	flee	visit	wear

We mixed one irregular verb in with the regulars, and two regulars with the irregulars. Did you spot them and inflect them properly?

EXERCISE: Word storage

The letters stacked up in each column below go into the boxes directly under them, but not necessarily in the order in which they are shown in their stack. When all the boxes have been filled in, a sentence or phrase from the preceding article will appear.

```
        T  U  M  T  R  G  G  T  L  D  L  S  P  F  C  F  S  S  R  S
        U  N  I  I  M  A  N  E  A  A  E  L  R  O  I  R  E  P  N  O
   F    G  D  A  N  E  B  A  N  R  E  Y  R  D  T  E  F  O  I  N
   W    E  S  R  R  E  T  U  G  I  R  Y  P  I  O  T  R  R  E
   N    D  C  A  Y        E  L  P        A  N  G        E  N  E
```

(grid of boxes to be filled in)

Hint: The fourth word is "relying." The letters in the second column will be rearranged in the column below them in this vertical order: e, u, t, d, g.

 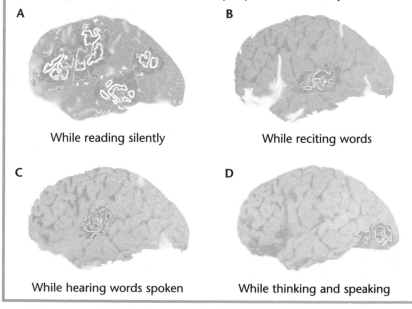

EXERCISE: PET (Positron Emission Tomography) brain scans

The photos (**A**, **B**, **C**, **D**) here are retouched brain scans that show what areas primarily become active while the brain is processing different language tasks. Their captions have been switched. Can you place them correctly?

A

While reading silently

B

While reciting words

C

While hearing words spoken

D

While thinking and speaking

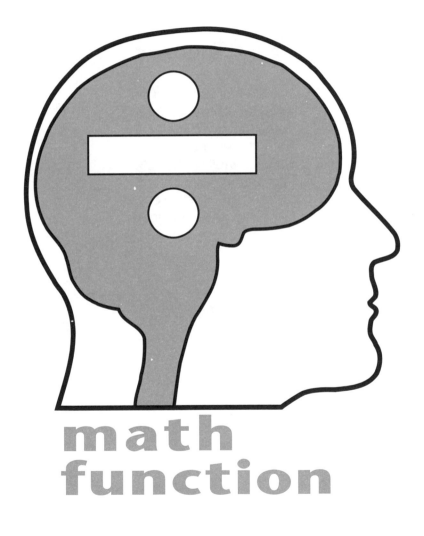

math
function

MATH

Almost all of us fall within the same range of basic mathematical ability. Why, then, do so many of us avoid mental arithmetic calculations and math-games with the excuse that we're just "not good at math"?

W e tend to think of math as something we're "good at" or "not good at." In fact, almost all of us are united by a common basic level of ability. For example, if you have a friend read aloud to you the sequence of numbers in the box in the center of this page, chances are great you'll be able to repeat back only about six of them. Very few people are able to recall only three or four, and even fewer — a vanishingly small number — can repeat over 10.

7, 12, 3, 5, 9, 11, 5, 1, 6, 2, 8, 7, 4, 15

Have a friend read aloud to you the first four numbers, then repeat them back. Repeat for five numbers, and so on, until you make a mistake. What's your limit? For almost all people, it's around six or seven.

But those of us who think of math as something we're simply not good at tend to leave the mental calculations to others. When we go out to eat, we let someone else perform the reckoning of the tip, or let someone else verify that the change returned is correct. By allowing ourselves to settle into this kind of pattern, we allow our mathematical acuity, and general mental alertness, to slip. This is, in fact, exactly why most of us who really are "not good at math" have become this way — because we've become comfortable *thinking* of ourselves this way.

That's why you should take a look at this chapter even if you're not one of those who are "good at math" — perhaps especially so. The more math-games you play, the better you become, and the more your self-perception shifts from one who isn't good at math to one who is.

Beyond keeping your mathematical ability from falling fallow, there's a lot you can do with your lifestyle to keep mathematically nimble. That's because math skills, more than perhaps any other facet of general intelligence, tend to fluctuate with your mood and momentary mental alertness. So good sleep and the right kind of nutrition are particularly important for mathematical performance. And the kind of lunch you should eat if you want to perform well on math tasks during the afternoon is not the same as what you should have in the evening if you want to ensure a good night's sleep. This chapter will tell you about those things too.

Some of the most revealing research into how the human mind manipulates numbers to achieve goals in the real world comes from study of how number concepts are learned by infants and how individuals with extraordinary mathematical skills solve problems. For example, even newborns are able to perceive a difference between three and four dots flashed onto a screen in front of them. Idiot savants who are able to perform complex calculations involving multi-digit numbers have developed different strategies to accomplish these feats. Some even involve visualizing numbers in terms of color, sound or shape; some break a calculation into component parts, solve those serially and retain the components in memory by visualizing them. In somewhat the same way people learn to remember names by linking some meaning of the name with a visual picture related to the way the person looks.

Why are musicians often also accomplished in mathematics? Could it have something to do with perceiving and manipulating intervals by seeing them with the mind's eye?

Are human infants born with number skills?

As with most domains of human cognitive ability, there's considerable debate about whether our arithmetic skills are simply learned through instruction and interaction with the environment, or whether we're born with specific mathematical skills on which we may build as we mature.

There is evidence that humans are indeed innately endowed with a rudimentary sense of numerical quantity. If a newborn infant is shown a picture of three dots, he will be initially attentive. After repeated showings, he becomes "habituated," and loses any interest in the picture. If the *number* of dots is changed, however — even after he's become bored with the first picture — he'll perk up again and treat the picture with a dot added or subtracted as if it were completely new.

This may show that human infants have an innate understanding of the difference between, say, 3 and 4 — years before they learn to "count" in the usual sense, or even to talk. It's interesting that the experiment only works for classes of items up to 3 or 4. Newborns don't seem to have the ability to distinguish, say, 6 from 7. Even at age 3, after learning to recite the names for numbers 1 through 10, children can correctly label a set of items as "three," but normally can't correctly assign the word "eight" to a set of eight items.

Are children of all cultures equally good in arithmetic?

At a basic level, there seems to be little cross-cultural variation in the mathematical abilities of children. Differences do emerge, however, due to the influence of school systems and even due to differences in the kinds of names different languages give to numbers.

In English, the learning of numbers higher than 10 is particularly difficult for children, since many number names are arbitrary and "opaque," rather than transparently and iconically motivated. To see how this works, consider the difference between "sixteen" and "eleven." Once a child has learned "six" and "ten," the new number-name "sixteen" would be relatively easy to learn because it's transparently composed of the smaller number-words. Perhaps even more importantly, this compositionality helps in the acquisition and reinforcement of the understanding of 16 as 6 plus 10. Thus, it's not only the case that sixteen is easy to learn as a new number-word, the very structure of the word helps to teach the child about the concept of addition.

On the other hand, "eleven" is quite arbitrary: it bears no relevant discernible resemblance to smaller number-words (such as "one" or "ten"), and must simply be learned as a completely new label with no compositionality or internal motivation. (The origin of "eleven," by the way, is "one-left," and "twelve" originally meant "two-left"; that is, after counting up to ten on your fingers, there is one item left.)

To imagine how difficult a *completely* arbitrary number-naming system would be, imagine that instead of "two hundred" we had a word "flart." Imagine further that, instead of "two hundred and one," we had "sneel," and that instead of "two hundred and two," we had "lentel," and so on. Obviously, such a system would require much more time and effort to learn, and it would fail completely to express an understanding of these larger numbers as composed of smaller numbers added or multiplied together.

In some languages, number-words are much more transparently compositional than in English. In Japanese, number-words below 100 are transparently composed of the words for 10 and for 1-9 (see p. 245). And even though the English number-word "ninety-seven" is fairly transparent and internally motivated by other names for smaller numbers, the French word for the same number is much more so: *quatre-vingt-dix-sept*, literally meaning "four (times) twenty (plus) ten (plus) seven." (At the same time, this difference points out a *disadvantage* of maximally transparent naming-systems: they tend to get quite cumbersome.)

Children learning languages with more transparent number-naming systems than English, then, tend to have an easier time learning the number-names and grasping the concept of larger numbers as being composed of smaller numbers. Inconsistencies in even the relatively transparent English number-names give rise to typical errors among young learners. While the number we write as "51" is logically enough

The transparent compositionality of the Japanese language's number-names helps a Japanese child understand the concepts of addition and multiplication. The word for 12 is "ten-two," the word for 20 is "two-ten," and so on.

iti "one"	*zyuuiti* "eleven"	
ni "two"	*zyuuni* "twelve"	*nizyuu* "twenty"
san "three"	*zyuusan* "thirteen"	*sanzyuu* "thirty"
si or *yon* "four"	*zyuusi* "fourteen"	*yonzyuu* "forty"
go "five"	*zyuugo* "fifteen"	*gozyuu* "fifty"
roku "six"	*zyuuroku* "sixteen"	*rokuzyuu* "sixty"
siti or *nana* "seven"	*zyuusiti* "seventeen"	*nanazyuu* "seventy"
hati "eight"	*zyuuhati* "eighteen"	*hatizyuu* "eighty"
ku or *kyuu* "nine"	*zyuuku* "nineteen"	*kyuuzyu* "ninety"
zyuu "ten"		

identified by the name "fifty-one," with the "five" before the "one," the opposite is true for "15." So young English-speaking children often write the spoken word "fifteen" as "51."

How do you know if your child *really* understands what the number-names mean?

Although it's second nature to adults, young children do not automatically understand that the number-word used to count the last item in a set of items may also be used to identify the *quantity* of the set as a whole. How can you tell if your child has successfully made this conceptual jump? Just ask her to count the number of fingers on your hands. Then, ask her how many fingers you have. If she has to re-count, then she doesn't really understand the significance of the last number-word mentioned in a counting sequence.

To make absolutely sure that your child truly understands this concept rather than simply having learned that repeating the last-counted item's number-name will evoke a favorable reaction from an adult, try this next simple test. Ask her to hand you a certain fairly small number of items — say, seven peanuts. If she counts out seven peanuts and then hands them to you, she's reached an understanding of *cardinality* attained by most 4- or 5-year-olds, but by only a minority of 3-year-olds. If she simply hands you a bunch of peanuts without counting, she's still at the typical 3-year-old stage.

Even for 4- and 5-year-olds, this understanding of cardi-

Which row has more marbles?
A four-year-old child will tell you, "The top row."

nality is rather tentative. Piaget showed that 5-year-olds are easily deceived into thinking that a more spread-out, longer row of a given number of objects has *more* items than a row of the same number of objects more tightly spaced. It usually isn't until 7 or 8 years of age that a child will consistently rely on cardinality alone in making these judgments, as opposed to relying on other, non-numerical perceptual cues.

EXERCISE: An algebraic dispute

A little girl and her brother are hunting Easter eggs.

The boy says to his sister:

"Give me seven of your eggs and I'll have twice as many as you!"

To which the little girl replies:

"Not fair! Give me seven of yours and we'll have the same amount."

How many eggs does each have?

Hint: Since the girl's quantity plus seven equals the boy's total minus seven, they are fourteen apart: He must have fourteen more eggs than she.

"Idiot" savants

Idiot savants (such as the character played by Dustin Hoffman in the movie *Rain Man*) have long intrigued psychiatrists because of their combination of low I.Q. (although not usually so low that they would be "idiots" according to the technical definition of the term) with impressive, sometimes phenomenal, feats of memory, artistic ability, or calculation. Some of the most famous savants have been calendar calculators, able to rapidly figure the day of the week for any date going back several decades; one celebrated pair of identical twin savants could reputedly perform such calculations over a span of 8,000 years. Another savant is reported to have had the ability to repeat a discourse of any length in any language without the omission of so much as a syllable.

Strangely, such skills may appear or disappear quite suddenly and unexpectedly

When savantism develops or disappears, it may do so in tandem with the loss or development of a seemingly unrelated and sometimes quite commonplace ability. Sometimes, impaired mental functioning may occur together with the appearance of a hitherto unglimpsed prodigious talent after a head trauma or illness.

Their loss of left-brain function may explain why so many savants show extremes of both ability and disability

One theory about the coexistence of such extreme ability and disability in many savants is that they suffer from left-brain deficit, which causes the right hemisphere to take over. This is a particularly plausible hypothesis in the case of one autistic child whose linguistic development (primarily associated with the left brain hemisphere) displaced a phenomenal artistic skill (right hemisphere). Another intriguing perspective on the savantism puzzle is that the impressive concrete memory together with poor powers of abstract reasoning that savants typically display may actually be caused by an inability to sort through and selectively *forget* sensory input, rather than any increased ability to remember per se. (Also see "If you want to remember complex data," p. 91.)

EXERCISE: Numberlocker

Directions: The digits 1 through 9 are used; there are no zeros. Only one digit may be placed in each box, and a digit may be used more than once in a combination. Where it appears that more than one combination of digits is possible, look for additional clues in interlocking numbers.

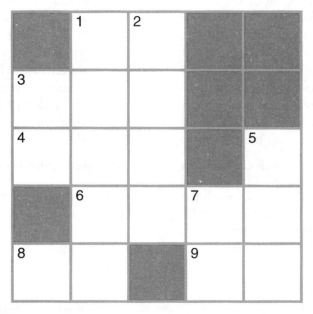

ACROSS

1. The square of the third-smallest prime number.

3. The square of an Arabic number that looks like a Roman 2.

4. An odd number that is 30 less than it would be upside-down.

6. Onion Market Day in Bern, Switzerland.

8. The square of a prime number larger than the root of 1 Across and smaller than the root of 3 Across.

9. The next square after 8 Across.

DOWN

1. The last two digits added equal the sum of the first three.

2. The second and fourth digits are alike.

3. The square of an even number that itself is a square.

5. The next square after 3 Across.

7. The sum of its digits is the square root of 9 Across.

Brain-changing nutrition and the "post-lunch dip"

Given the phenomenon of the "post-lunch dip" (a fall-off in alertness and performance after lunch, due at least in part to internal circadian body rhythm), much research has been devoted to the question of the optimal type of lunch to increase performance, or at least minimize the dip.

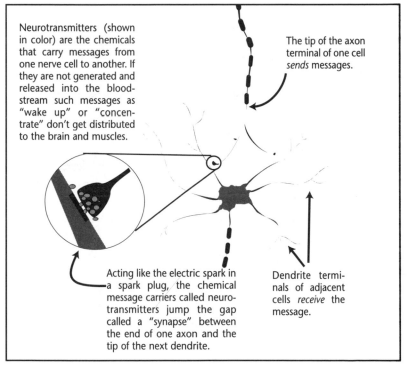

Neurotransmitters (shown in color) are the chemicals that carry messages from one nerve cell to another. If they are not generated and released into the bloodstream such messages as "wake up" or "concentrate" don't get distributed to the brain and muscles.

The tip of the axon terminal of one cell *sends* messages.

Acting like the electric spark in a spark plug, the chemical message carriers called neurotransmitters jump the gap called a "synapse" between the end of one axon and the tip of the next dendrite.

Dendrite terminals of adjacent cells *receive* the message.

Since the 1970's, some interesting studies have focused on the effects of certain "brain-modifying" nutrients, including the amino acids tryptophan and tyrosine, and a component of lecithin called choline. It makes sense that these substances would interact with mental function, since they are all *precursors of neurotransmitters:* they are converted into substances that convey messages across the synapse between one neuron and another.

Different neurotransmitters, and therefore their precursors, have different effects. Tryptophan is converted into the neurotransmitter serotonin, which, among other things, is conducive to calmness or mental alertness (depending on factors such as time of day, personality type, etc.). Tyrosine is used in the synthesis of dopamine, norepinephrine, and epinephrine, which help you remain mentally alert, energetic, and motivated. Choline is converted into acetylcholine, crucial to memory function.

Tryptophan and tyrosine are especially plentiful in foods rich in protein, while egg yolks, liver and soybeans are especially rich in choline. Perhaps, then, a meal high in protein (since protein is rich in tryptophan and tyrosine) would result in elevated levels of serotonin, dopamine, norepinephrine, and epinephrine, thereby (ideally) making you simultaneously more calm, focused, and alert. However, things are not quite so simple.

The important thing is a good balance of protein and carbohydrate, not protein alone

It turns out that a high-protein meal may actually *decrease* serotonin levels while a meal with moderate amounts of protein and carbohydrates *increases* them.

The paradox is explained by the fact that protein contains many other amino acids which compete with and beat out tryptophan for transmission across the blood-brain barrier. Even though a meal high in carbohydrates fails to introduce as much tryptophan into the blood-stream as one high in protein would, it stimulates the production of insulin, which transports most of the amino acids other than tryptophan into the muscle cells. Any tryptophan in the blood is therefore relatively unimpeded for access to the carrier cells for transport into the brain.

The best lunch for minimizing the post-lunch dip, then, seems to be one that features lean protein, little fat, moderate carbohydrate, and, overall, moderate calories

Protein is important for the synthesis of the "alertness" neurotransmitters which your brain would otherwise be running low on. Low fat and moderate calories are important because a heavy meal that's hard to digest diverts blood from your brain to your stomach and is conducive to grogginess. If the carbohydrate-to-protein ratio is moderate, little enough serotonin will be synthesized to avoid the sleepiness which might otherwise occur when that "calming" neurotransmitter interacts with your early-afternoon circadian dip.

How NOT to meet your protein requirements

The amino acid tryptophan is the chemical from which the body makes the neurotransmitter serotonin. Amino acids are also the building blocks of protein, and tryptophan is one of the "essential" amino acids, meaning that it can't be manufactured by the body and must be obtained from foods. Some foods, such as gelatin, contain many of the amino acids required for complete protein but lack tryptophan. If you try to satisfy your protein requirements with such foods, your body will use any available tryptophan for protein synthesis, leaving little or nothing for the production of serotonin. In an experiment on the effects of a gelatin-protein diet, subjects had a tendency to become tired, irritable, and depressed.

A good way to calm down is to go for the sweets

When tense or unfocused, or if you are trying to fall asleep when overly anxious, have a meal or snack consisting of nothing but glucose-containing carbohydrates, including most "sugars" (including table sugar, corn sweetener, and honey, but not fructose or purely fructose-containing foods, i.e., fruits) and "starch," which is composed of long chains of glucose molecules. Such foods will release insulin into your bloodstream, and hence tryptophan from your blood plasma into your brain, resulting in serotonin production and a sensation of calm. This is one reason why we think of pasta as a "comfort" food, and may be part of the explanation for why women often reach for sweets during their premenstrual period.

You can set up your own experiment by trying the concentration exercises on the following pages during, and again after, lunches with and without protein.

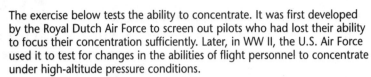

SELF-TEST: Concentration

The exercise below tests the ability to concentrate. It was first developed by the Royal Dutch Air Force to screen out pilots who had lost their ability to focus their concentration sufficiently. Later, in WW II, the U.S. Air Force used it to test for changes in the abilities of flight personnel to concentrate under high-altitude pressure conditions.

Repeated trials of this kind improved the attention span of pilots, so similar exercises have become part of many training programs. To lengthen your concentration span, repeat the exercise with combinations of other letters and numbers.

Instructions:

Do not look at the grid below, yet. First, set your timer for 30 seconds. Start the timer, then study the grid. Count the number of 4's and g's you can locate without marking the grid or making notes. Write down your answer when the 30 seconds is up.

a	7	3	d	g	t	p	9	6	2	x	d	e	o
e	w	q	d	c	5	6	o	i	d	g	v	c	d
w	3	6	7	9	w	d	z	x	j	g	e	2	3
7	b	f	d	x	c	k	l	p	o	u	t	e	e
4	c	v	b	n	m	s	w	e	r	u	i	o	p
h	4	f	d	s	a	q	w	6	r	t	y	u	i
7	o	e	r	t	y	u	i	4	d	e	r	g	f
r	t	y	u	i	c	s	w	r	d	w	2	5	3
4	4	d	3	s	w	e	d	3	5	h	t	c	e
3	c	d	f	g	h	y	w	s	q	x	d	7	a

Lack of sleep, especially the phase when you are dreaming, reduces problem-solving ability

The fact that sleep plays a critical role in effective cognitive functioning is obvious. Beyond the common-sense knowledge that a bad night's sleep is detrimental to optimal performance the next day, there have been experiments showing that the learning of conditioned-avoidance tasks in rats is followed by an increase in REM sleep (rapid eye movement, associated with dreaming in humans). Their learning is impaired by lack of REM sleep, as well. A human study of mathematics graduate students shows that they are unable to perform even the simplest calculations if awakened from recovery sleep following a 48-hour period of sleep deprivation.

That part of your brain that regulates sleeping and alertness patterns is very similar in all mammals

As shown in the diagram below, the primary alertness and sleep-control centers are located in a peg-shaped area at the top front of the brainstem, the most most primitive part of the brain. At the top of this area a cluster of cells called the *locus coeruleus,* controls secretions which put the brain into deep sleep, including REM (Rapid Eye Movement). Other clusters of cells control the secretion of *norepinephrine* ("norepi," for short) alerting the brain, especially to the unexpected, even in sleep.

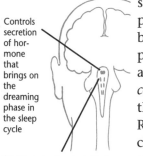

Controls secretion of hormone that brings on the dreaming phase in the sleep cycle

Secretes a chemical that brings on light sleep—the phase in which a disrupted sleeper is easily awakened

It is a flood of norepinephrine, released into the brain during moments of acute stress, that gives rise to the "slow motion" effect we experience during an automobile accident, for example. It makes our brain *so* alert that it's as if we were taking in several times the normal amount of information that we normally would in the same span of time.

When sleep starts, production of norepinephrine falls to half its normal levels. At about 100 minutes into each sleep cycle it shuts down completely during the phase of deep sleep when dreaming and rapid eye movement (REM) sleep take over. In the diagram on p. 253 the row of smaller dark-colored cells below the locus coeruleus represents the *raphe nuclei*, which secrete a substance causing a state of light sleep.

The body's internal "clock" is hidden deep inside the brain at the top of its most primitive parts

This diagram below represents the brain sliced in half to show the location of the *pineal gland*. (Note that both the *thalami* have been removed from this diagram for clarity.) It is located at the very top of the brainstem. It sets the *circadian rhythm* "clock," which controls timing of sleep and wakefulness by secreting the hormone *melatonin* in response to a number of factors including daylight and darkness. Melatonin is produced from serotonin, and appears to counteract the production of the "alertness" hormone norepinephrine (a.k.a. noradrenaline). Some research suggests that an "S" chemical builds up gradually when humans are awake until it reaches a saturation level which starts the sleep cycle. When the "S" chemical is drawn from humans and injected into laboratory rats they become drowsy.

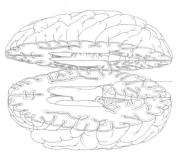

Pineal gland that controls the body's internal "clock"

EXERCISE: Numberlocker

Directions: The digits 1 through 9 are used; there are no zeros. Only one digit may be placed in each box, and a digit may be used more than once in a combination. Where it appears that more than one combination of digits is possible, look for additional clues in interlocking numbers.

ACROSS

1. Two more than 8 Down.
3. Ten more than 1 Across.
5. The first day of winter.
7. John Milton's Birthday.
8. Christmas Day.
10. The square of an even number which itself is a cube.
11. A multiple of 1 Across.

DOWN

2. The square of an odd number.
3. The first three digits are alike, so are the last two.
4. The sum of the first two digits is equal to the third.
6. Boiling point.
8. The square of an even number.
9. The second digit is double the first.

Hint: The poet John Milton was born on the ninth of December in 1608.

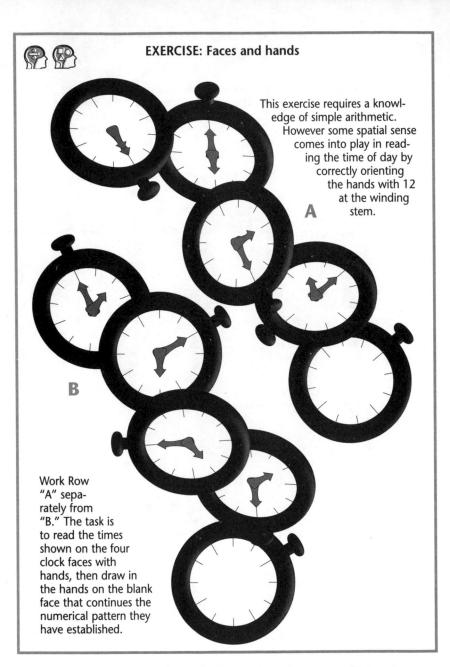

EXERCISE: Faces and hands

This exercise requires a knowledge of simple arithmetic. However some spatial sense comes into play in reading the time of day by correctly orienting the hands with 12 at the winding stem.

A

B

Work Row "A" separately from "B." The task is to read the times shown on the four clock faces with hands, then draw in the hands on the blank face that continues the numerical pattern they have established.

Hint for Row A: Try multiplying the second time by the first. Don't forget that the hands go completely around every 12. **Hint for Row B:** Try working the problem from right to left so that each time to the left is double the number of hours of the time to its right. Don't forget that the hands go completely around every 12 hours.

The genius who thought in pictures but expressed his ideas in math

Since the publication of an article some 25 years ago, it has been popular to refer to the young Albert Einstein as "learning disabled," possibly dyslexic or even aphasic. ("Aphasia" is a language impairment resulting from damage to some part of the brain's language areas.) Others have more recently pointed out that such diagnoses are difficult enough for living people, let alone dead ones, and that the evidence for them in the cases of Einstein, Edison, Rodin and others is often flimsy at best.

Be that as it may, the evidence does show that Einstein was relatively weak in certain left-brain abilities, opening the door to speculation that his phenomenal genius may be partly attributed to right-brain compensation for a poorly developed left hemisphere. Most notable are his early difficulties with language — a largely left-brain skill — some aspects of which continued throughout his life. By the report of his sister, as well as his own recollection, he only began to speak at age three, and by all accounts had difficult, labored speech until about age ten. Throughout his adult life, Einstein admitted to being a poor speller, reader and writer: "When I read I hear the words. Writing is difficult, and I communicate this way very badly."

Words and math were both difficult for Einstein

It may come as a shock to learn that Einstein was also no genius at left-brain-dependent mathematical calculations. As a schoolboy, arithmetic was almost as much a struggle for him as foreign languages, and even during his residency at Princeton, after winning the Nobel Prize for physics, he had difficulty helping high-school students with their calculus homework.

Einstein did, on the other hand, have an unusual gift for visual conceptualization, and for kinds of math involving — or which he could translate into — spatial configurations (a right-brain-dependent ability). When his uncle Jakob Einstein, an engineer, introduced him to geometry's Pythagorean Theorem, Einstein thought the theorem so obvious from simple visual inspection that it failed to require proof. He did, however, devise a formal proof quite different from the standard one which would have been taught in school — and he did this before the age of ten. It was only after leaving the authoritarian German school system and enrolling in the Kanton School at Aarau, Switzerland, that his unique gifts began to blossom. The school at Aarau was founded by the Swiss education reformer Pestalozzi, who believed that a flexible, radically visually-oriented curriculum was the way to let young minds develop freely.

Einstein always maintained that, for him, thought was essentially imagistic and non-verbal, and that words or language entered his mind only during the late stage of translating his insights into a communicable form. "For me," he claimed, "it is not dubious that our thinking goes on for the most part without use of words."

EXERCISE: The math-mind's eye

This exercise requires the use of both math and spatial thinking. Below are two rows of cubes with numbers printed on their six faces, like a child's block. Each row shows a different cube rotated to show four different views of its sides.

Work with row "A" and row "B" separately. When you rotate each view in your mind's eye to *spatially* orient all four views in the same way you will notice that the placement of the numbers on one of them does not match the other three.

A

B

When you work with the numbers on the visible faces of each view to find a consistent *arithmetical* pattern among them, again you will see that one does not fit the pattern established by the other three. That one will be different from the *spatially* inconsistent one in that row.

Hint for Row A: Multiply the numbers on the visible faces of each cube. One produces a product that differs from the other three. Notice the orientation of the 5 and 8 on the other cubes compared to the one which is mathematically inconsistent. **Hint for Row B:** Add the numbers on the visible faces of each cube. One produces a sum that differs from the other three. Notice the orientation of the 12 and 36 on the other cubes compared to the mathematically inconsistent one.

EXERCISE: Now don't get mad!

Study the three groups of black numbers marked A, B, and C. Above them are three colored numbers. Your task is to decide which of the colored numbers belongs with which of the three lettered groups. When you do figure this out in a blinding flash of rage and anguish, try it on your local Einstein.

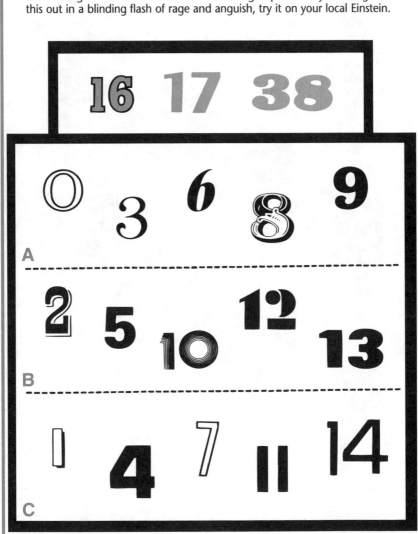

Hint: Note that there are two symbols next to the title of this Exercise. One indicates that the subject is math and the other indicates a spatial subject. In this puzzle the numerical values are irrelevant.

260   BUILDING MENTAL MUSCLE

The magical number 7: How it limits us, and how we can overcome it

Have you ever wondered what it is about the number 7 that makes it recur so frequently in lists of important things? There are seven days of the week, seven wonders of the world, seven ages of man, seven notes on the musical scale. Telephone numbers have seven digits, and psychological tests frequently employ a 7-point rating scale.

There may be something more than just coincidence lying behind the ubiquity of the number 7. Our brain seems to have a built-in limitation organized around this number in its span of judgment, attention, and memory. The limitation isn't hard and fast, but again and again our discriminatory abilities seem to hover around seven categories or points on a scale, give or take a few.

Let's say you hear two musical tones, one after the other. You're told that the lower-pitched tone is "tone number 1," and the higher-pitched one is "tone number 2." If you then hear one of the tones played again, you'll have no problem assigning the correct number to it. You can try this with a larger range of tones, and you'll soon reach the point where you make a lot of mistakes. That point, for almost all people, seems to be around six.

This doesn't just have to do with the larger number of tones being closer to each other in pitch, and therefore inherently easier to confuse. If you try the experiment with five high-pitched tones, it's easy to avoid errors. Confusion is equally unlikely with five low-pitched tones. But combine the five high-pitched tones with the five low-pitched ones in a single sequence, and you'll have to resort to guesswork, resulting in frequent mistakes. So there's something about the absolute number of categories we have to discriminate that represents a limit to our abilities.

Below 7, you count — above 7, you guess

The same numerical limit shows itself in experiments requiring people to perform quick estimates of the number of dots flashed on a computer screen. Below six or seven dots, people make no errors. At seven or above, errors become routine, as

estimations of the number of dots replace accurate instantaneous counts.

If there's really this numerical limit to our discriminatory
abilities, then how is it that we're able to differentiate so
many words, so many faces, and so on? The answer seems to
be that, with faces and words, we're increasing the number of
dimensions we're relying on for our categorical judgments, or
stringing several units along in succesion and thereby dramatically increasing our discriminatory capacity. If the distinctive
characteristic of faces were simply one single variable such as
darkness or color, then we would indeed have difficulty distinguishing the faces of over seven people. But every face consists
of many more than one variable: different noses, eyes,
mouths, ears, and two-dimensional spatial relationships
among all these features. And words consist of not just a single distinctive sound, but of many such sounds strung together. Each single sound is typically, in any given language, defin-
able in terms of about seven binary distinctive features (plus
or minus consonantal, plus or minus voiced, and so on), and
arranging such sounds in sequence results in our ability to distinguish thousands of different words.

"Chunking" helps you memorize more data

Another way around the limit imposed by the number 7 on
our memory capacity is by what is sometimes called "chunk-
ing." A telephone number including the area code consists of
10 digits. We can make the task of memorizing such a long
string of numbers easier by memorizing the area code separately from the rest, or by rearranging the numbers into a
shorter sequence of two-digit numbers — as when we memorize
an area-code sequence of 5, 1 and 0 as "five-ten."

The same motivation may underlie the rhythmic breath-
groups into which we arrange the letters of the alphabet. If
you recite the alphabet, you'll find you pause after "g" (the
seventh letter), after "p" (the ninth letter after that), and finally "v" (the sixth letter after that), before finishing the
sequence. On the one hand, these pauses may simply be
viewed as a holdover from the rhythmic groupings in the

alphabet song we learn as children. On the other hand, one reason the song makes the alphabet easier to learn is that it breaks down an unmanageably long sequence of items into groups consisting of an easily-managed sequence of 7 letters, give or take a couple.

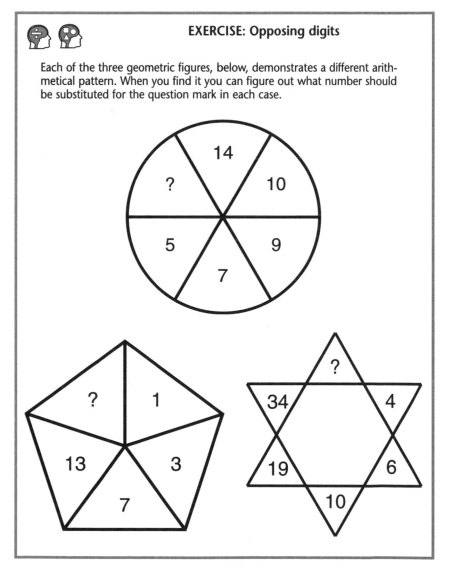

EXERCISE: Opposing digits

Each of the three geometric figures, below, demonstrates a different arithmetical pattern. When you find it you can figure out what number should be substituted for the question mark in each case.

Hint: Most people find the six-pointed star the most difficult until they realize that it is made up of two, overlapping, geometric figures.

EXERCISE: Times tables

Most people find effective solutions by looking for a pattern that relates to past experience. (Don't be too proud; rats find their way through mazes that way too.) Each of the top three rows of numbers demonstrates the same arithmetical pattern. When you find it you can figure out what number should be substituted for the question mark.

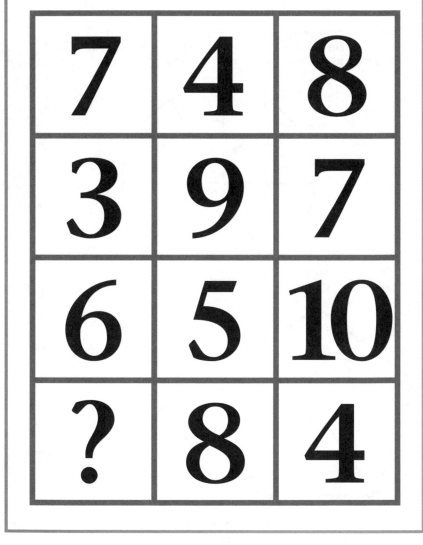

Hint: First multiply the first two numbers in each row.

spatial function

SPATIAL

Your visuo-spatial ability is in fact many different *kinds* of ability, ranging from picking out details, to perceiving the arrangement of those details into patterns, to fitting those patterns into a knowledge base so you know what to do with them.

The study of vision has yielded some of the most fascinating insights (no pun intended) into the nature of human consciousness. Even though we rely most heavily on our visual sense in our interpretation of the world around us, psychologists have been telling us for decades that what we think we see out there may not really be out there at all. Take a look, for example, at the white blob in the box in the middle of this page. White blob? In reality, all there is is a circular arrangement of irregular black blobs. Our brain constructs the white blob, complete with an imaginary border separating that imaginary blob from the white space outside it, out of nothing but negative space. If your brain is playing this kind of trick on you, what else might it be doing behind your back?

Focus on the top dot. Are you aware of a white shape defined by the black images? Now focus on the bottom dot. Are you more aware of the white shape, or less? Most people see it more clearly.

It's easy to miss the fact that there are different *kinds* of ability underlying what we think of as a unified visual awareness. We have a largely left-brain-dependent awareness of visual details — the trees in the forest — and a right-brain perception of the pattern into which the details fit — the overall shape of the forest. The illusion of the white blob is your right brain playing tricks on you, creating a shape out of hints provided by bits and pieces of detail. Usually, we rely on both atomistic and configurational awareness in our processing of the world of visual stimuli around us. The communication lines between different parts of our brain are so rapid that we don't even notice that these various facets of awareness are separate things. But if you meet someone whose vision is just as good as yours, but who somehow cannot fit visually-perceived objects into any kind of knowledge base that would allow her to recognize what those objects are and what to do with them, then you begin to realize what a complex and multifaceted faculty visual awareness is.

Like your other faculties, your visuo-spatial intelligence can be maintained or left to deteriorate. Visual close-ups can challenge you to project those details onto a larger pattern, thus exercising your right-brain-dependent holistic-imaging skills. Familiar patterns with a subtle detail or two out of place can test your attention to objective minutiae. And tasks demanding mental rotation of three-dimensional visual objects can be a real brain-buster, until you learn to get the hang of it.

Seeing both the forest and the trees: Different parts of the brain are specialized for different visual tasks

When you look at a person's face, or a mosaic design, or the stars in the night sky, there are at least two levels of visual awareness you can have. You can focus on the individual tiles, or facial features, or stars, as discrete items of detail, or you can perceive the parts as forming a more inclusive, patterned whole. Usually, you have to switch from one mode of seeing to the other, rather than doing both simultaneously. But both options are available to us.

Not so for people who have suffered damage to either the left or the right visual cortex. The right hemisphere, in vision as in other aspects of our interpretation of the world around us, is the creative department of the brain, best at getting the big picture and grasping global patterns. The left hemisphere is the brain's accounting department, nit-pickingly focused on details. So when the left visual cortex is damaged, the ability to perceive and focus on detail suffers, while right-hemisphere damage impairs the integration of those details into a global whole.

The right hemisphere corresponds to your left visual field (that is, everything to the left of whatever point you're focusing your eyes on), and the left hemisphere to the right visual field. So in theory, you should be better at seeing the details of objects in your right field, and at perceiving patterns in your left field. But you rarely ever notice any difference, mainly because, simply put, you look at what you're looking at — things you're focusing on cross the center of your visual field and spread into both the left and the right fields. Also, communication across both halves of the brain is so automatic and instantaneous that the bias in specialization is pretty much neutralized.

Things are different, however, for those who have a severed corpus callosum—the bundle of fibers connecting the right hemisphere to the left. (Sometimes, epilepsy patients have their corpus callosum deliberately severed in an operation designed to control their seizures.)

These individuals can perceive *only* details in their right field of vision, and only global patterns in their left field. So if, say, a picture of a mosaic design is moved from the left side of their visual field to the right, a dramatic switch occurs halfway across: what began as a pattern becomes an unpatterned assortment of random individual tiles.

V or L? Your right brain shows you the large letters, your left brain the small ones — but not both at the same time.

Your upper and lower visual fields are specialized too

Psychologists have long been interested in a phenomenon referred to as *illusory contours*, whereby the human mind projects a boundary onto an image where no boundary actually exists. This kind of projection illustrates dramatically that what we see in the world around us is not so much an objective image of the world "out there" as an automatic subconscious organization of visual stimuli into actively created images.

For some reason, the *lower* visual field is better at perceiving illusory contours than the upper visual field — despite the fact that neither the upper nor the lower field is better at perceiving images *in general*. One can only speculate about the reasons for lower visual-field specialization for such a narrow skill. Perhaps it has to do with the kinds of visual perception that, in our evolutionary past, was especially useful for objects on the ground as opposed to objects at or above eye level.

SELF-TEST: Something's fishy

Giuseppi Arcimboldo (Italian, 1537-93) painted portraits using combinations of objects from nature such as the one shown below composed of marine life. If the nerve cells connecting the right and left halves of your brain were destroyed, you would see only fish, not the image of a man, if this picture were held to your right as you looked straight ahead. The left lobe processes what's seen in the right field of vision and vice versa. The left lobe handles details but the right lobe perceives the big picture.

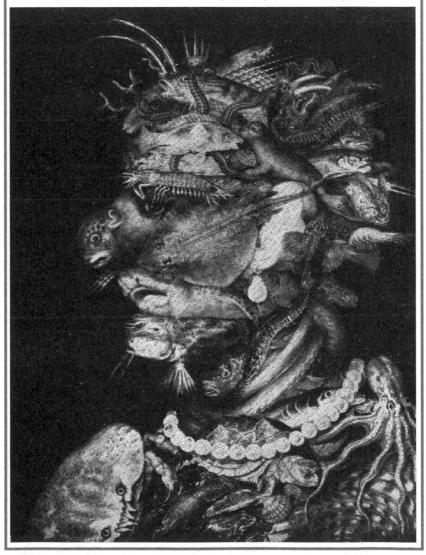

EXERCISE: Shapes in space

What we see is partly governed by what we expect to see related to past experience. Research on monkeys isolated specific areas in different parts of the brain that respond only to food (a yellow banana but not a yellow flower, for example), another area that responds to objects seen before, but not new ones (a large red balloon but not a small blue one), and a still different area that recognizes different faces.

The brain can perceive only one interpretation of a shape at one time. Our experience may lead us to expect that the "background" is less significant than what we see as a "shape" in the "foreground." We try to identify shapes with familiar objects ("If it looks a lot like a wrench, it's a wrench") and we can be wildly mistaken. The images on this page demonstrate some of those tricks of the mind.

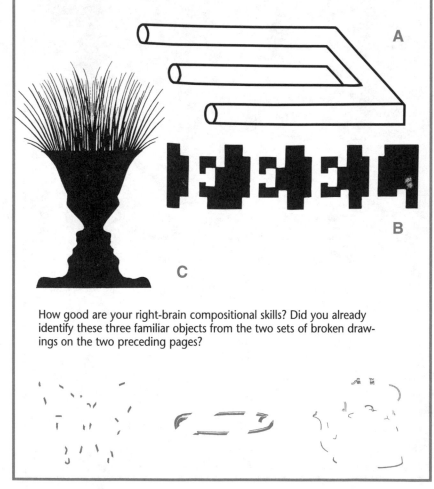

How good are your right-brain compositional skills? Did you already identify these three familiar objects from the two sets of broken drawings on the two preceding pages?

Facial recognition depends on visual-spatial processing by the right side of your brain — but that's not all

We've all had the experience of remembering a face without recalling the name attached to that face. When we find ourselves in the mildly embarrassing situation of forgetting the name of someone who greets us by name, we may fall back on the excuse that we're good at memorizing faces, but not names. In fact, virtually all people are better at memorizing faces than names. Facial recognition relies on a right-brain-based visual-spatial ability which develops during the first ten years of life, but which somehow also lets us memorize faces even better than we can memorize other, otherwise comparable, visual images. It's an impressive gift that we sometimes take for granted.

We humans have a prodigious ability to store other human faces in our long-term memory, and to access those stored images years later. In one study, subjects were asked to identify a high-school classmate from among five photographs taken from yearbooks from the same period. Recognition rates were 90% — regardless of the time elapsed since graduation (from three months to 35 years) and class size (90 to 800). Over the three or four years of high school, in other words, it is just as easy to memorize 800 faces as 90 — and it is just as easy to remember them for 35 years as for three months. All this is done largely unconsciously, with no deliberate effort or mnemonic tricks.

Face recognition must be fluid enough that we can identify a face from different angles, and through changes of hairstyle, expression, aging, and weight loss or gain. Damage to the right brain may result in a complete or partial loss of facial recognition abilities under changing conditions of lighting, paraphernalia such as eyeglasses or earrings, or angle of view. Since faces may be thought of as visual patterns, and since the right hemisphere is the general locus of visual-spatial abilities, it makes sense that facial recognition may be right-hemisphere-dependent. But there's more to it.

Some kinds of changes make it harder to recognize a face

If you turn a photograph of a familiar face upside-down, it's much harder to recognize. You might think this is just because the inverted representation is so different from the way you would have stored the visual image in your mind. But other visual images — stick figures, costumes, various inanimate objects — are almost as easy to recognize upside-down as rightside-up. And that's not all. If you try to memorize novel faces presented upside-down, your performance will be, on average, 30% worse than if the faces are presented rightside-up. In other words, even though you'll later be shown the same upside-down face among other upside-down faces, you won't have anything near your usual ability to recognize which one is the same as the one presented earlier. So whatever ability we're using to encode, memorize, and retrieve facial images, it's more specific than, or somehow different from, the equivalent ability when applied to other kinds of objects.

In memorizing and recognizing upside-down faces, adults are forced to fall back on the piecemeal processing strategy children rely on in analyzing rightside-up faces. That means that we focus on the specific components only, not on their spatial configuration, and our performance on facial recognition tests is poor.

Children rely on different strategies to memorize and recognize faces

Faces are complex visual images, and in theory we might rely

Do you notice anything unusual about this face? Take a look at it for a few seconds, then turn the book upside-down.
For upside-down faces, we process the individual component parts, but we're not very good at noticing distortions in the orientation of these specific features.

on either (or both) of two different kinds of information in memorizing them: piecemeal information about individual components or features (eyebrows, a mole, etc.), or configurational information about the spatial relations among the component parts of the overall facial pattern. In general, we may rely on either strategy in processing visual forms. Adults seem to rely on both strategies when memorizing faces, but the relational-configurational strategy seems to be particularly important. Children under the age of 10, on the other hand, seem to rely primarily on the componential strategy. Evidence for this comes from experiments that show that 6-year-old children are no better at memorizing rightside-up faces than they are at processing inverted faces, with 8-year-olds falling halfway between the 6-year-olds and adults.

In both tasks, children are relying primarily on information about specific facial features rather than the overall configurational gestalt. For adults, performance is much better on upright faces. We can immediately recognize, for example, the difference between two otherwise identical upright faces with some kind of facial distortion among the individual features. Spatial distortions are difficult to perceive for upside-down faces, so we fall back on a reliance on examination of individual features only.

Do you notice anything unusual about this face? Take a look at it for a few seconds, then turn the book upside-down.

We're *much* better and quicker at recognizing spatial distortions of upright faces than of inverted faces. What looks grotesque rightside-up looks relatively normal upside-down.

The difference between 6-year-olds and adults, then, is not that children are better at processing upside-down faces, but that they're worse at processing rightside-up faces. (Children are also much more easily thrown off by facial expressions — two faces might be identified as the same if they're both smiling, for example — and extraneous paraphernalia such as eyeglasses and earrings.) By the age of 10, children have developed the spatial-configurational ability to discriminate, identify, and memorize faces at the adult level.

Do you recognize these famous faces?

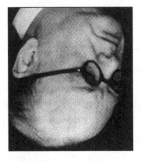

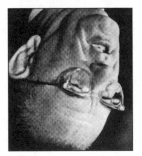

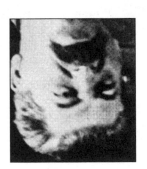

Hint: Four of the five were pivotal figures in monumental political events of the 20th century related to senseless deaths.

EXERCISE: Eyeball busters

The brain draws on experience to recognize objects. When a closeup detail of an object is all that is visible, and the shape of the entire object cannot be seen, even familiar objects are difficult to identify. The hints may help.

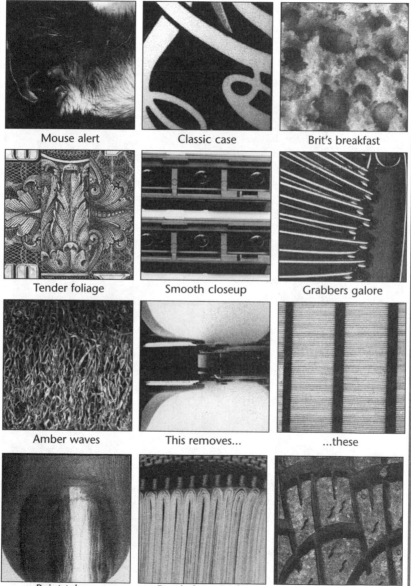

Mouse alert

Classic case

Brit's breakfast

Tender foliage

Smooth closeup

Grabbers galore

Amber waves

This removes...

...these

Point taken

Bonded servitude

Hit the road

SELF-TEST: Facing nature

A stained glass artist from Milan, Giuseppi Arcimboldo, became court painter to a long line of 16th-century Hapsburg kings. He sometimes made surrealistic-looking pictures using combinations of familiar objects.

The brain finds the overall pattern of a face easier to recognize when the face is right side up. What do you think you will see when you turn this photo upside down?

A gene for visual-spatial ability

Advances in chromosomal mapping techniques have led to the identification of a single gene responsible for pattern-construction tasks — building a model, for example, or assembling different-colored blocks into a design. This discovery represents what is reported to be the first identification of a gene involved in cognition.

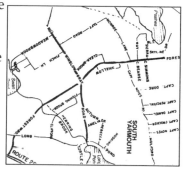

Depending on how much of the "pattern" gene — LIM-kinase1 (LIMK1) — and an adjacent gene — Elastin — are missing or defective, an affected person may have anything from limited physical and cognitive abnormalities to full-blown Williams syndrome, a disorder featuring vascular disease, elfin facial features, and mental retardation, but (for some as-yet unknown reason) curiously strong rote memory and language abilities.

People with a limited deletion of LIMK1 may have a more-or-less normal overall IQ, and will be able to cope adequately with the routine demands of everyday life. However, even they will have great difficulty with the simplest exercises requiring visual and spatial representations, so they cope with their problem by going through life avoiding any tasks involving such reasoning or images. Sketching a map of the neighborhood, then, would be as arduous a chore for them as dismantling and re-assembling a VCR would be for those of us with full expression of the gene.

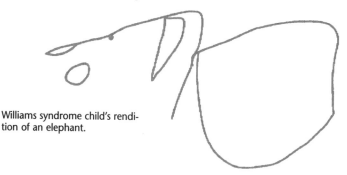

Williams syndrome child's rendition of an elephant.

Can complex human behavior really derive from a single gene?
The media are speculating that the discovery of other genes
responsible for higher cognitive functions, such as spatial,
may be just around the corner. A "spatial gene" represents
something of a holy grail for some neurolinguists and evolutionary anthropologists, who have gone so far as to venture
that the development of such a gene may have been responsible for the meteoric rise in dominance of our species during
our recent evolution. Is it in fact likely that such a gene will
soon be found?

Probably not. While the human spatial faculty does
indeed have a genetic basis, it involves many different kinds
of ability distributed over a sizeable region of the left hemisphere. Many different genes, then, must be responsible for
different facets of this ability. Consider, too, that while there is
admittedly (as far as we can tell, at least) a clear qualitative
difference between human spatial function and the communication systems of other animals, it is not possible to draw as
decisive a line as we might like between what we do and what
some other animals do. As is well known, chimpanzees and
gorillas can readily learn to recognize and manipulate arbitrary symbols to receive and send information. While people
may argue about whether what they do is "really" spatial, the
point may be moot: regardless of what label you give to such
behavior, it is clearly a prerequisite for what we do call spatial
in humans.

**A single genetic defect may disrupt a complex ability, but a
single gene alone doesn't account for it**
Imagine if there were a gene crucially responsible for such
symbol manipulation — say, a gene responsible for the ability
to associate a given form (either visual or auditory) with a
given meaning to which it has no necessary or inherent connection. This gene, then, would be responsible for precisely
the sorts of arbitrary associations — the association between
the concept "tree" with the word *tree* in one spatial function,
and with the word *arbre* or *baum* in another — that we consider to lie at the core of spatial function. If this gene were damaged or ill-formed, then spatial function as we know it would
be impossible. Would such a gene, then, be the "spatial gene"?

No. As neurolinguist Steven Pinker has written, "A single gene [may] disrupt grammar, but that does not mean a single gene controls grammar."

The same objection applies to the identification of the "spatial" gene discussed above. When the gene is defective or missing, spatial ability is indeed severely impaired. Does this mean that a single gene is responsible for spatial reasoning? No. For one thing, although those with the defective LIMK1 gene will never become engineers, many spatially-oriented abilities are intact — otherwise, they couldn't so much as walk or eat with a fork. Also, the fact that a defective LIMK1 gene will disrupt spatial ability to some degree doesn't mean that it alone is responsible even for those specific abilities it affects. Pinker's analogy with reference to the possibility of a "spatial gene" is apropos here: "Removing the distributor wire prevents a car from moving, but that does not mean a car is controlled by its distributor wire."

Williams syndrome child's attempts (bottom) at copying a simple line-drawing image (top).

Williams syndrome child's attempts (bottom) at arranging blocks in the configuration shown at top.

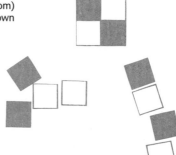

EXERCISE: Fitting the pieces together

This exercise uses the visual skills that people with Williams syndrome lack. The nine boxed designs along the top and right sides match squares in the picture of the antique jug. The grid on the picture, with letters down the left side and numbers across the top, allows you to identify which design matches which square in the grid. The designs may have to be rotated to fit. Write your answer in the blank square next to each design.

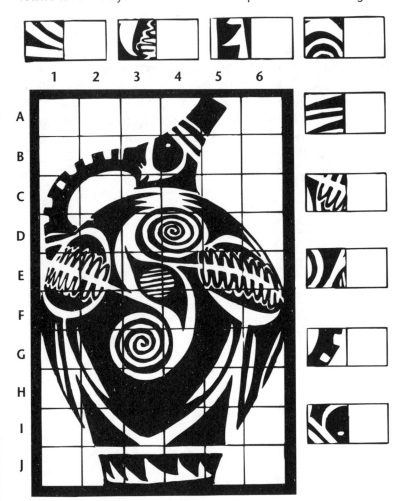

Hint: For example, the first design on the top row, far left, matches square 5-H on the grid when the design is rotated 90 degrees counterclockwise.

Nicotine improves spatial memory, learning, and information processing. Some research also suggests that it lessens memory deficits associated with aging and Alzheimer's

Shakespeare wrote that "there is some soul of goodness in things evil, would men observingly distill it out." The bard's pithy wisdom seems particularly relevant to recent studies showing that the psychoactive compound in tobacco, nicotine, has a wide range of potential benefits for learning and memory, and may even help forestall Alzheimer's and Parkinson's diseases. This has prompted efforts to synthesize nicotine-like compounds that have all the advantages of nicotine for the brain without any of its unwanted side effects.

Cigarette smoking is, despite what the tobacco companies would have you believe, immensely destructive, responsible for millions of deaths each year through cancer, heart disease, stroke, and other diseases. At the same time, it has long been known that tobacco has at least two valued effects on the mind: one, it induces a sense of well-being, and two, it at least seems to enhance memory and alertness. These effects and their neurological bases have now been confirmed in a series of experiments on animals and humans.

Nicotine — a new "smart" drug?
Nicotine affects the brain by binding to receptors that stimulate the release of a host of neurotransmitters, including dopamine and acetylcholine, thereby facilitating transmission of signals between brain cells. Recent evidence indicates that a locus with a particularly high density for nicotinic receptors is the hippocampus, a part of the brain which plays a central role in learning and memory.

In experiments with rats, nicotine has been shown to steepen the learning curve in maze-mastering exercises and to improve memory — in some cases, up to four weeks after the nicotine is administered. In tests on humans, nicotine improves rapid information processing. It also improves short-term recall, spatial memory, and reaction times in Alzheimer's patients.

The cortical nicotinic receptors that appear to be involved in these cognitive tasks are precisely the ones that decline in concentration in patients with Alzheimer's, and experimental drug-induced blockade of neurons that produce or respond to acetylcholine has been shown to mimic the effects of the disease in healthy young test subjects. There's even some indication that nicotine may not only enhance transmission across nerve cells involved in memory-formation, but may counteract the formation of toxic plaques responsible for the development of Alzheimer's.

The source of a cigarette's hedonistic allure

Nicotine also interacts with dopamine — the "hedonistic" neurotransmitter — and dopamine receptors. In fact, there appears to be a precise region of the forebrain that is activated by nicotine, cocaine, amphetamine, and morphine alike. Lest this lead to bewilderment at the perversity of nature, let it be understood that it is not the case that we have evolved these receptors specifically to make us a drug-addicted species; rather, the compounds in these drugs simply mimic the chemical structure of compounds that are naturally produced in the brain itself. Anything that stimulates dopamine transmission is associated by the brain with a powerful, pleasurable reward, and the brain will want to return to that stimulus again and again — hence the strongly psychologically addictive nature of these drugs.

Why smokers are 50% less likely to develop Parkinson's

By stimulating the release of dopamine, nicotine appears to have the potential to lower the risk of developing Parkinson's disease, and to lessen the severity of the disease in those who already have it. Parkinson's is a degenerative brain disease which kills the brain cells that manufacture dopamine. This results not only in a dour, stoic demeanor, but loss of body control — tremors and, ultimately, complete immobilization.

Many of the advances in the burgeoning field of neurotransmitter research result from improving the specificity of drugs that interact with the neurotransmitters or the receptors to which they bind. Drugs that have a broad, imprecise effect are called "dirty," while more specific versions are relatively "clean." Now that the potential benefits of nicotine have been proven, a lot of research money will be devoted to synthesizing nicotine-like compounds that affect just the receptors affected by a particular ailment. Among other things, this will mean fine-tuning the chemical structure of the nicotine look-alike so as to interact with just the relevant brain cells, rather than also acting in undesired ways on the central nervous system.

EXERCISE: A practical, boring joke

Sir Rodney Koala was rearranging the books on his bookshelf when he discovered a bookworm perched on his two-volume copy of War and Peace.

"You're not thinking of making lunch out of my beloved Tolstoy, are you?" asked Rodney.

"Tolstoy, schmolstoy," replied the worm with a derisive sneer, "it's all the same to me. All I know is," he continued, sizing up the novel with a hungry eye, "if all your authors had his problem of not knowing when to clam up, I'd be set for a lifetime of lunches — my wife and kids, too."

Sir Rodney, being the type to prefer the power of the mind to that of the clenched fist, decided to negotiate.

"All right then, let's make a deal. You must eat to live. But I equally live to read — and that Tolstoy edition is the most prized possession of my collection, even if the binding is a bit worse for wear. The deal is this: Each volume of War and Peace is 550 pages long. If I let you eat your way from the first page of the first volume to the last page of the second, will you promise to leave the rest of the novel alone?"

The worm chortled with delight. "Eat my way from the first page of the first volume to the last page of the second! Are you nuts? I go through about ten pages a day. I'm no mathematician, but at that rate I'll be kept in my cups for more weeks than I can count." The bookworm shook his head with mock pity. "You know, bear, you may read a lot, but you sure don't have much street smarts. It's a deal!"

How long would it take the bookworm to eat the number of pages agreed to in the deal?

Hint: The answer is immediately clear once you visualize the volumes the way they would normally be placed on the shelf.

EXERCISE: A geometric paradox

Sir Rodney Koala had a delicious conundrum he was sure would stump even the keenest mind. He decided to pay a visit to his friend Whitney, a white-cheeked gibbon living out his golden years in the London Zoo. Whitney was formerly known for his prowess as a mental calculator, but Rodney suspected that the impoverished environment of the zoo might have made him lose some of his acuity. Rodney stood in front of Whitney's cage, tossing an apple into the air and catching it.

"Take a look at this apple, Whitney."

"I have, Rodney, and a tasty apple it looks. May I eat it?"

"Not just yet. First, you have to answer a question." Rodney pulled a ball of string out of his pocket, and fed out just enough to encircle the apple. "If you wrap a string around it, you need 25 centimeters' worth of string to go completely around."

"That's the circumference of the apple, then — 25 centimeters. May I have it now?"

"That's right," said Rodney. "And no, not yet. Now, if I add a meter of string to the 25 centimeters — like so — you can see that there's a good bit of distance between the apple and the string."

"I dare say. It wraps around the apple now the way your belt would wrap around my waist: loose as the morals of the English nobility."

"Very good, but we're supposed to be applying ourselves to the task at hand; let's not get personal. Now, as we agree there's a good bit of distance between the apple and the string when we add a meter's worth of string to what's needed just to wrap around the apple."

"When we add a meter to the apple's circumference, and imagine this to form a circle around the apple."

"Yes, exactly."

"Not only," added Whitney with a sniff, "is there a good bit of distance, as you so precisely put it, but I can tell you exactly how much distance there is."

"Ah so? Tell me then."

(cont'd on next page)

"Any fool knows that the circumference of a circle is two times pi times the radius of the circle. In this case, the circumference of the circle formed by the string is 125 centimeters. So, the radius of that circle — the distance between the string and the core of the apple — is 125 divided by twice pi. Let's take pi to be 3.14. This gives us 125 divided by 6.28, which is" (he calculated rapidly in his head) "about 20 centimeters. Now, to find the distance between the string and the skin of the apple, we simply subtract the radius of the apple from the radius of the string. Repeating the same procedure for an apple of circumference 25 centimeters, we get" (he paused) "a radius of about 4 centimeters for the apple itself. 20 minus 4 is 16, ergo the distance between the apple and the string is about 16 centimeters. May I eat the apple now?"

"Very good. I can see you haven't lost your edge. But no, not yet. Now, here is the real question. Imagine that, instead of the apple, we had a very large globe."

"A globe like the earth?"

"Perfect," continued Rodney. "Let's imagine, as you suggest, that instead of the apple we have this very globe on which we stand. Imagine further that you wrap a piece of string around the entire earth."

"A piece of string around the entire earth? That won't do! A flimsy bit of string would be sure to break somewhere, and then we'd have to start all over again. Let's use some nice sturdy twine."

"All right, fine. We wrap some sturdy twine around the circumference of the entire earth. Now, let's imagine that we do what we did before. Let's add one meter to the length of our piece of twine. The question, then, is this: After I add the extra meter, how far out from the earth would the twine be?"

"You mean, how loose would that twine be?"

"Yes, exactly."

"My dear Sir Rodney, you disappoint me."

"I disappoint you? How so?"

"You are repeating yourself, and wasting both your time and mine."

(cont'd on next page)

"Repeating myself?"

"Yes, and stop echoing whatever I say. I have already answered your trivial question: the twine would be 16 centimeters from the surface of the earth."

The squirrel monkey in the adjacent cage could contain himself no longer. "You ninny!" he screamed. "You really have lost it! Anyone can see that an extra meter more or less won't make any difference to a length of twine wrapped all around the entire earth! Sixteen centimeters my eye! That twine would scarcely be slack enough to let a microbe pass under it — which, judging by your answer, would be about the same size as your brain. Now, let me have that apple!"

Whitney cast a sidelong glance at the squirrel monkey. "That, my high-strung little friend, is confirmation of the several rungs separating us on the evolutionary ladder. The apple always goes to the primate who can reach the highest." He reached out his hand to Rodney. "May I have it now?"

Did Sir Rodney give the apple to Whitney, or to the squirrel monkey?

Hint: In actual fact, Whitney didn't need to take the step of subtracting the radius of the apple from the radius of the circle formed by the string around the apple. If he had simply calculated the radius of a circle with a circumference of a meter, that would have given the right answer of about 16 centimeters. Presumably, he walked Sir Rodney through that extra step simply for the sake of clarity.

"Blindsight," a suprising finding, and other curiosities: The riddle of consciousness

No one would deny that the collective cognitive sciences have made tremendous strides in understanding the material underpinnings of many aspects of our experience of life and the world around us: vision, memory, spatial, fear, even love. But the biggest questions remain elusive: What ties it all together? What accounts for our ability to ask these questions at all? What, in other words, is the locus of consciousness?

Many kinds of brain injury may disrupt some aspect of consciousness, but no single locus serves as the seat of consciousness per se. In patients with something called "blindsight," there is a clear separation of vision (and response to visual stimuli) and awareness. True, even though we can say that their injury has affected their awareness, it is only one *aspect* of their awareness that's affected. But curiosities such as blindsight might still help us get our foot in the door of the question of the neurological nature of consciousness.

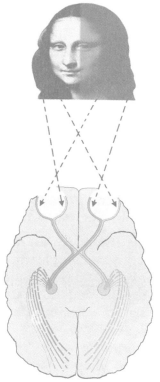

Blindsight: vision without awareness

What is blindsight? People who have lost their primary visual cortex have no awareness of visual objects, and no ability to identify visual

In a person with normal sight, the occipital lobes in the brain convert all the patterns, forms and colors from the outside world into meaningful objects.

objects, while they nevertheless follow such objects with their eyes. In some sense, they "see" the objects despite being absolutely unaware of that fact.

Different animals suffer different degrees or types of visual impairment from loss of the primary visual cortex. Tree shrews and cats seem to retain most of their visual ability, and remain able to avoid obstacles and discriminate between visual patterns. New World monkeys suffer more extensive impairment, but can still visually follow and even reach out for visually presented objects — even though they indicate that "no object was present" in a learning task. Old World monkeys and humans experience the most profound loss of the ability to be aware of and use the vision which still in some sense remains at least partly intact. An indirect visual pathway still remains from the retina through the midbrain and thalamus, but without the mediation of the primary visual cortex, there is no visual awareness.

Where do "gut feelings" come from?

This kind of evidence makes us wonder how many of our "gut feelings" and "instincts" derive from parts of the brain that partly or wholly lack connection to structures, such as the primary visual cortex, that mediate in fully conscious awareness. This is similar to the possibility that iron particles in our brain cells may still play some vestigial role in helping us to orient ourselves with respect to the earth's magnetic field.

A brain divided against itself

Consider, too, people whose epilepsy is so severe that doctors sever their corpus callosum, the bundle of fibers connecting the two halves of the brain. If you place their left hand in a bowl of ice water and ask them if their hand feels cold, they answer both "yes" and "no" in turn. Give them a piece of paper with the words "yes" and "no" written on it, and their left hand will point to one answer while their right hand points to the other. They have, in effect, two centers of consciousness.

But having two centers of consciousness of a stimulus presented to one or the other side of the body is different from having no consciousness at all — from being an unreflecting automaton. Of course, you can make someone unconscious in the sense of shutting down the activity of everything but the brain stem. But this shuts down most or all of the "higher" brain functions, so it's not the case that they are acting in ways that they're not conscious of. Also, this is different from saying that consciousness derives from the integration of the brain's functions in some single defined area.

The "blindsight" evidence shows that even something as apparently unified as visual perception in fact involves many facets that we distinguish only when they become dissociated by injury. In forming a perception — visual, olfactory, or what have you — there's no single site where everything is integrated. Different neurons fire in different regions of the brain, and the mystery is how they're experienced subjectively in a unified way. This is what's known as the "binding problem."

Why aren't we unreflecting automatons?

Many tentative solutions have been proposed to the binding problem, none of them very satisfactory. One is that widely scattered neurons might be subjectively associated if they oscillate at the same frequency. Another is that this sort of association may happen when neurons fire at the same time. Neither of these approaches appears to handle the facts very well, though, since the activated neurons corresponding to a subjectively unified experience usually fire at neither the same frequency nor the same time. Others speculate that the apparently chaotic firing of neurons at various sites may in fact contain a hidden pattern which might somehow explain their integration — if only their code could be cracked.

There are also those, of course, who remain deeply skeptical that a material explanation will ever be found for the problem of consciousness. From one common-sense perspective, we should simply accept that our brain, having evolved to meet the demands of our material environment, has inherent limitations just as does the brain of any other biological organism. Some questions may by their nature — or ours — be inherently unanswerable. The fact remains, though, that we do feel satisfied to have developed an understanding of other points, which presumably have little survival value to understand and which a dog or geranium would presumably be incapable of understanding — the structure of DNA, for example, or the essential features of the reconstructed ancestor of all the Indo-European languages.

What's the survival advantage of self-awareness?

Even if the material underpinnings of consciousness are eventually identified, however, this will not necessarily answer what may be the ultimate, and hardest, question the study of consciousness faces: *Why* do we have a subjective integration of experience? Why, in other words, are we self-aware? This seems to be as hard, and perhaps as intractable, a question as the other chestnuts that have thus far resisted being cracked by Western science: How can life emerge out of inert matter? Will the universe ever cease to exist? And, while we're at it — What is the key to true wisdom?

EXERCISE: Yard sale

Have you ever seen any of these old-time household objects? This exercise requires a combination of visual memory, "tool naming," and luck.

Seeing without understanding: Visual object agnosia

One of the most frequent complaints among the middle-aged and elderly is an inability to remember the name of an object. In a momentary lapse, a mailbox may be called "the thing you put letters in," or a corkscrew may be referred to as "the little metal coil for the wine."

This kind of mental lapse, which is by no means necessarily a sign of the onset of dreaded Alzheimer's, is sometimes referred to as "benign senescent forgetfulness" — which sounds much nicer than the old-fashioned term "senility." Although it may be mildly disconcerting, normal age-related forgetfulness is *nothing* compared with the considerably rarer phenomenon known as *visual object agnosia* — a disorder affecting not just the *naming* of objects but the very recognition of their identity or function.

There are two basic kinds of visual object agnosia: apperceptive and associative. Apperceptive agnosics have, according to the standard tests, relatively good visual capabilities, such as color vision and brightness discrimination. But they not only cannot name or recognize a visually perceived object; they cannot even reproduce it in a simple sketch.

Apperceptive agnosic's attempt to copy a simple line drawing of a house. An apperceptive agnosic has good visual perception, but can neither recognize nor reproduce an object such as the house on the left.

Associative agnosics, on the other hand, can muster reasonably faithful line-drawing copies of pictures. And yet, they are no better than apperceptive agnosics at naming or recognizing what they've drawn. Their perception of objects is all detail, and no pattern. They are much like illiterate counterfeiters who painstakingly reproduce every line and curve of a document or signature without having any idea what it says.

Other characteristics of associative agnosia are equally bizarre. An associative agnosic will be utterly unable to name or identify an object by sight alone, but will immediately recognize it upon feeling it. He will have no idea what the foods on his dinner plate are, or even whether they are edible, until putting them in his mouth.

You might think that agnosia simply involves some kind of dissociation between the visual and spatial centers of the brain. This theory would be disproved, however, by the fact that it isn't just *naming* that's affected, but the very recognition of the object at the most basic level.

A better theory implicates the role of internally-stored visual images used in the task of object recognition. If these stored images were somehow to become destroyed or inaccessible, then an external visual image would have nothing to match up to. In effect, it would be as if the most commonplace objects were being seen for the very first time.

An even better theory might rest on an understanding of recognition and memory as stored in connections between neurons forming a network: the stronger the connections, the stronger the memory. When an associative agnosic makes a line-drawing copy of a picture, he does so slowly, painstakingly, and with no recognition of the pattern the individual features of the picture represent. If associative agnosia derives from a destruction of a neural network, without any damage to the neurons themselves, this would explain why it is the overall patterns of the images, not the details, that are inaccessible.

SELF-TEST: Right brain inattention

Damage to the right hemisphere may result in a problem called *visual inattention* or *neglect*, involving a loss of awareness of visual stimuli in one half of the visual field. For example, someone with a right-brain stroke may eat only the food on the right half of his plate, and then complain about having been served an inadequate helping.

Dotting the circle

Place this page directly in front of you on a flat surface. With a pencil, place a dot inside the circle and then return your hand to a resting position in your lap. After practicing this a few times, close your eyes and continue placing dots inside the circle, returning your hand to its resting position after each attempt. After five tries with your eyes closed, open your eyes and see how you did.

(cont'd on next page)

Counting the dots

In 10 seconds, count as many of the dots as you can. As you count a dot, check it off with a pencil.

Results:

Dotting the circle: Placing the dots consistently to the right of the circle may indicate damage to the right hemisphere.

Counting the dots: Under-counting the dots in the left or right half of the square may indicate damage to the hemisphere opposite to the neglected side.

A circadian rhythm and sunlight tell us when to sleep

Humans have a built-in "neural pacemaker" which regulates our daily cycle of sleeping and waking. If uninfluenced by the solar cycle or an externally-imposed schedule, we naturally fall into a cycle of rest and activity slightly in excess of 24 hours — in other words, we go to sleep and wake up a little later each day. There has been serious speculation that all of human civilization, from the creative stimulus to destructive acts, is a response to the tension created by this disharmony!

Normally, however, our internal pacemaker is "entrained" by the sun: our internal clock adjusts itself on an ongoing basis to the length of the day. The exact manner in which this happens is only just coming to be understood. It turns out that we probably have a special set of retinal photoreceptors specifically involved in governing circadian rhythms. These receptors project through the optic nerve to the hypothalamus of the brain, which appears to be the physical locus of our neural pacemaker.

Melatonin levels, supposedly affected by sunlight, change as normally in some blind people as they do in the sighted

Compelling evidence that the photoreceptors involved in this process are distinct from those normally used in vision comes from a recent study of blind people with no conscious perception of light. It has long been known that, while some blind people suffer from bouts of insomnia due to a presumed inability to adjust their internal clocks to the shifting cycles of the sun, others never have such problems. A number of such subjects were shown to display increased melatonin levels — which is independently associated with exposure to light — precisely when exposed to bright light, and only when their eyes were uncovered. Thus, their eyes, while otherwise quite useless, seemed to have retained a special type of photoreceptor in perfect working order.

EXERCISE: Time intervals

Examine the sequence of times shown in the first four of these these five clock faces. Reading upper left to lower right, can you identify the logic behind the time intervals shown by their hands?

When you think you have uncovered it, draw the hands into the fifth clock face that correctly continue the pattern.

Hint: Don't be fooled by the fact that the third clock has been rotated. It reads 6:00, not 2:45. It might help to work backwards from the fourth clock.

EXERCISE: False faces

The white pattern shown above the pile of seven numbered blocks shows the location and orientation of the letters on their six sides — but not for *all* seven blocks. Which of the numbered blocks could *not* have been formed from the pattern?

Hint: If you can't fold the sample cube with your mind's eye, try unfolding the others. Notice which end of a letter faces which side of another letter — the open side of the C and the H for example.

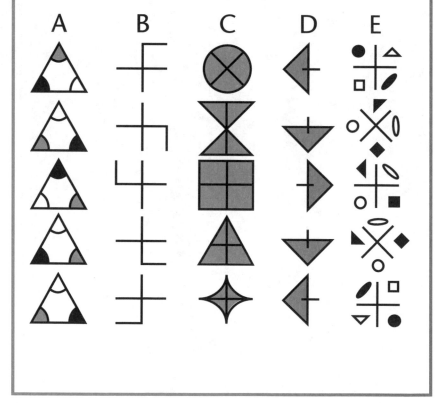

EXERCISE: Spatial intelligence?

Here is an exercise set for the right hemisphere of the brain (assuming you are right handed).

Pictured below are five groups of similar figures labeled A, B, C, D and E. They are a component of a classic test called the "Stanford-Binet," after its original compilers. Your task is to spot the similarities and differences among these five figures in each column. In each case one figure breaks the "correct" pattern — that is, the most consistent and predictable pattern. It is not wrong, of course, just different — much like the only boy in the school-yard with his shoelaces neatly tied.

Most people find that the challenge becomes progressively more difficult as they move from A toward E.

A   B   C   D   E

Hint: On A and D try rotating the figures and see how they line up. On E look at how the figures relate to one another when the lines are diagonal vs. horizontal and vertical.

SOLUTIONS

Abandon hope all ye who enter here. — Dante Alighieri

EXECUTIVE & SOCIAL

p. 18-21 **Mixed-up toons**

Panels are shown below in correct order. Numbers correspond to mixed-up order.

p. 22 Mixed-up toons

Panels are shown below in correct order. Numbers correspond to mixed-up order.

p. 24 Judgment of emotion

The right-hand image is reversed.

p. 28 Right-brain pattern abstraction/abstract reading

1) 9	11) smart
2) I	12) bill
3) check	13) 9
4) ray	14) G
5) to	15) cud
6) on	16) 352897
7) stop	17) nip
8) do	18) F
9) 1324	19) 9
10) lit	20) sure

p. 26 "Right" side of a person

Neither positive nor negative, hence neutral emotion. The right side of a person's face is more likely to display positive emotions. The left side displays negative attitudes. When you see the stranger face-to-face the right hemisphere of your brain (which is the dominant hemisphere for the perception of emotion) picks up the expression on the half of his face to the left of his nose as you face him. For him, that is the right half of his own face, which, normally, is controlled by the left (positive feelings) hemisphere of his brain, not his right hemisphere (negative feelings). So, you are more likely to miss any signs of the negative "side" of his personality.

p. 31-32 The eyes have it

1. Condescending eyes with smiling mouth
2. Neutral eyes with smiling mouth
3. Angry eyes with smiling mouth

p. 37 A familial dilemma

First, he drives his mother over to the restaurant. Next, he drives back and picks up his mother-in-law, and drives her to the restaurant. When he drops off his mother-in-law, he tells his mother to get back in the car with him and takes her back home. When he and his mother get home, he lets his mother out, picks up his wife, drives back to the restaurant, and leaves his wife at the restaurant with his mother-in-law. Finally, he drives back home to pick up his mother again, and returns to the restaurant with her.

p. 36 **Case of confused identity**

Part 1 No — at least, not if one of the twins really is the murderer. Either both will answer "Yes," or both will answer "No," and it will be impossible to tell who is telling the truth and who isn't. There are two variables here — one brother is a liar and the other is a truth-teller, and one brother is a murderer and the other is not. If the first is a liar and answers "Yes," then he, not his brother, is definitely the murderer. This means that his brother is an innocent truth-teller, in which case he will also answer "Yes" in response to the question of whether his brother is a murderer. If the first brother is a liar and answers "No," then the other brother is the murderer — but that means the second brother is a murdering truth-teller, and will likewise answer "No" in response to the question of whether his brother is the murderer. Either way, both brothers will give the same answer, and it will be impossible to know who is telling the truth — and who is the murderer.

Part 2 Assuming the truth of the premise that one brother is a consistent liar and the other always tells the truth, then there are only two possibilities. The first is that the eye-witness must be mistaken — neither brother can have committed the murder. Here's the logic: If the first brother is a liar and answers "Yes," then the second brother cannot be the murderer. Also, if the first brother is a liar, the second must be telling the truth. But then, if the second brother answers that his brother did not commit the murders, the first brother must be innocent. Hence, both are innocent.

The second possibility is that both brothers committed the murders. Let's assume that it's the first brother who is the truth-teller. Then, the second brother must be guilty. That means the second brother is a lying murderer. But the second brother answers "No" to the prosecutor's question whether the first brother committed the murders, meaning (since the second brother is a liar) that the first brother must be guilty. Hence, both brothers must be guilty.

Part 3 The first trick is to find out which twin is the liar. This may be done by asking the first twin any question to which you both already know the answer. "Do you have a twin brother?" will do. If the first twin answers "Yes," then you know the second twin is a liar. Then you can ask the second twin, "Did you commit the murders?" If he says "Yes," then you know (since he's a liar, and assuming that one of the twins is indeed the murderer) that the first twin is the murderer.

If, on the other hand, the first twin answers "No" to the first question, you know the second twin is a truth-teller, and will truthfully answer a direct question about his guilt.

p. 38 **Fox, goose and grain**

Take the goose over first, then return to pick up the fox. Take the fox over, put the goose back in the boat and return with the goose to the first bank. Leave the goose there, put the grain in the boat, and take the grain to the other bank and leave it there with the fox. Finally, return to pick up the goose.

It doesn't matter whether Antonio picks up the wife or the mother-in-law second, or whether the farmer picks up the fox or the grain second; the only crucial thing is that the first one over is the one which is least compatible with the others, i.e. the mother in the first story or the goose in the second.

p. 39 **Anders' dilemma**

It would take three travellers. One assistant carries four days' supplies, and after the first day's trek, he gives one day's supplies to the other assistant and one to Anders. This gives them each four full days' supplies again. The first assistant, with his day's supply remaining, then returns home. The other two complete another day's trip, at the end of which the other assistant gives one day's supplies to Anders, who again has four days' supplies, sufficient to reach the outpost. His assistant still has enough to reach home in two days.

p. 68 **The fastest track**

1-F; 2-B; 3-D; 4-A; 5-E; 6-C
Assuming the rate of improvement between the years of 1906-1960 but starting from the under-10-sec. time in 1984, the under-9-sec. time will happen around the year 2038.

p. 40 **Menu, please**

JENKINS   JENNINGS

JORDAN   JACKSON

JONES

1. Joe Jackson had a martini, roast beef and cake. 2. Jerry Jones had scotch, pheasant and cheese pie. 3. John Jordan had a martini, steak and cake. 4. Jack Jenkins had a cola, roast beef and pie. 5. Jamie Jennings had scotch, steak and ice cream.

p. 58 **If-then thinking**

The fourth statement is the only one that could be true because it correctly identifies all the others as false.

p. 54-58 **Frontal lobe logic**

Part1 If it is true that only one envelope has correct instructions, then that envelope has to be B, meaning that A is wrong — therefore, A does not have a contract renewal inside. Imagine A were right. Then, B would have to be wrong. But, assuming the correctness of the premise that one of the envelopes has a pink slip, B must be right. **Part 2** The right envelope. Let's imagine the left envelope contains a contract renewal. Then its instructions must be correct, and we may conclude (since the instructions say it makes no difference which envelope is picked) that the right envelope must also contain a contract renewal. But if that were true, then what's written on the right-hand envelope must be false, since we're told that the statement on the right envelope is false if a contract renewal is inside. Therefore, it's false that the left envelope has a contract renewal, which contradicts the first assumption, so that first assumption must be false: the left envelope cannot contain a contract renewal. **Part 3** Envelope A. Let's say envelope A is true, and it really does contain a pink slip. Then, the others must be false. If envelope B is false, it contains a pink slip too. So far, so good. If envelope C is false, then envelope B contains a contract renewal, not a pink slip — a contradiction, so envelope A must be false. Therefore, envelope A contains a contract renewal, not a pink slip.

p. 76 **Card senses**

p. 79 **Circleword**

1. Grater
2. Terse
3. Secret
4. Retire
5. Red herring
6. Ringmaster
7. Sterno
8. Noticing
9. Icing
10. Ingrate

p. 86 **Memory terms**

p. 90 **Addlock**

p. 98 **Divvy digit**

p. 100 **Numberlocker**

p. 101 **Numberlocker**

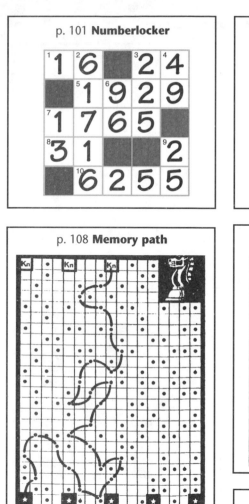

¹1	²6		³2	⁴4
	⁵1	⁶9	2	9
⁷1	7	6	5	
⁸3	1			⁹2
	¹⁰6	2	5	5

p. 102 **Analock**

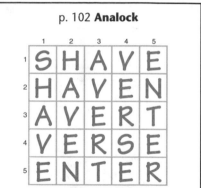

	1	2	3	4	5
1	S	H	A	V	E
2	H	A	V	E	N
3	A	V	E	R	T
4	V	E	R	S	E
5	E	N	T	E	R

p. 108 **Memory path**

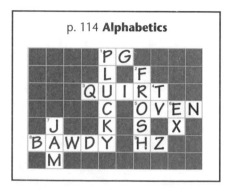

p. 116 **Geographics**

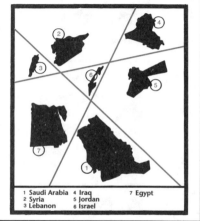

1 Saudi Arabia 4 Iraq 7 Egypt
2 Syria 5 Jordan
3 Lebanon 6 Israel

p. 114 **Alphabetics**

(grid puzzle with letters: PG, L, F, QUIRT, OVEN, J, C, K, S, X, BAWDY, HZ, M)

p. 120 **Neuron and off**

A	X	O	N		E	T	U	I		O	B	I
R	E	V	E		T	E	N	S		R	O	T
E	D	E	R		A	N	D	S		E	R	E
	R	O	M		N	E	U	R	O	N	S	
T	E	A	S	E	D		L	E	A			
E	R	G		D	E	T	E	R	M	I	N	E
A	S	E	S		N	A	T		S	N	I	T
R	E	S	T	U	D	I	E	D		S	N	O
		A	P	R		D	E	M	E	A	N	
C	H	A	B	L	I	S		S	E	C		
L	A	B		I	T	E	M		C	U	B	A
A	C	E		F	E	T	A		C	R	A	M
D	E	L		T	S	A	R		A	E	R	O

p. 122 **Personal pairs**

(One Possibility)	(Another Possibility)
flower — bee	carved bust — music
carved bust — chisel	bell buoy — marine signal flags
bell buoy — ship	ship — glass
milk — glass	milk — cow
cow— butter	butter — saltshaker
watering can — saltshaker	knife — bread
marine signal flags — music	acorn — tree
hatchet — tree	leaf — watering can
oak leaf — acorn	hatchet — chisel
knife — bread	bee — flower

p. 128 **A mental trick**

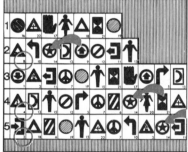

When you're told "rows 2, 4, and 5," look at the small numbers in the first column at the left. The small numbers next to the first symbol in rows 2, 4, and 5 are 8, 4, and 2. These total 14. Now look for the symbol with number 14 in its lower right-hand corner — it's the star in the circle!

p. 130-131 **Strategies**

The optimal strategy is to break the grid down into ever-smaller halves, in any order. A sample sequence: "Is it in the top half of the grid?" ("No" — you know it's in the bottom half.) "Is it in the right half of the bottom half?" ("Yes.") "Is it in the top half of that section?" And so on. Using this strategy, you'll still need two questions with a small 2 X 2 grid, but with larger grids the advantage over the row-by-row method is dramatic. For an 8 X 8 grid, you'll never need more than six questions, and for a 100 X 100 grid — with 10,000 squares — you'll always get the answer in 12 questions!

p. 132 **Eliminating possibilities**

Select the box with the cover marked "six and six." If you blind-picked a banana, a dozen bananas must be in that box (because the covers were switched). The box with the "twelve bananas" cover must contain twelve lemons. The lemons box, therefore, contains the six lemons and six bananas. If on the other hand, you blind-picked a lemon from the box marked "six and six," a dozen lemons must be in that box, the dozen bananas in the "twelve lemons" box, and the lemons and bananas in the bananas box.

p. 135-136 **Singles only**

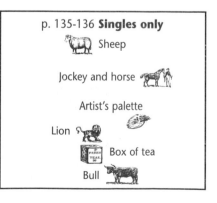

Sheep

Jockey and horse

Artist's palette

Lion

Box of tea

Bull

p. 155 **Facial expressions and emotions**

Happiness   Sadness   Anger

Disgust   Surprise   Fear

p. 159 **Pick the punch line**

The original punch line to the story was #3. The point is that loss of memory is associated with aging. If the residents of the retirement house forget their own name they know they can go to the caregiver at the front desk who will remind them.

p. 165 **Humors**

p. 156 **Emotions**

p. 164 **Melencolia I**

The central figure of the angel symbolizes the frustration and despair of the inquiring, creative mind. Her wing, trapped behind the hourglass, suggests that time imposes its strict limits on the efforts of artist and artisan.

All the measuring devices are tools of design and construction: hourglass, dividers in her hand, scales and a straight-edged board with holes in either end for drawing a circle.

Other tools and materials of construction visible include the saw and plane at her feet, nails, a pattern for cutting decorative moldings, a hammer, a fire with a crucible for melting metal, a stone wheel and cube with two opposing corners lopped off (which looks, at first glance, like a prism).

Many of these objects are also icons of geometry and mathematics as is the sphere at her feet, the magic square above her head and the arc of the rainbow.

The keys and purse attached to her belt symbolize power and wealth; perhaps as rewards from the pursuit of knowledge and skill or, perhaps, to symbolize their irrelevance before the "melancholy" caused by creative effort and pursuit of knowledge.

p. 182-183 **Thinking ahead**

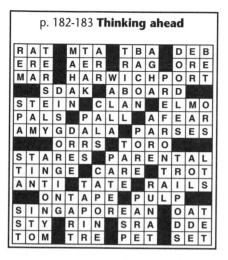

p. 184 **Terms test**

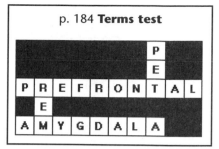

LANGUAGE

p. 202-203 **Language areas**

p. 204 **Damaged language**

1. scion = icons
2. knead = naked
3. janes = jeans
4. ruses = users
5. lager = regal
6. finer = infer
7. sited = edits
8. snail = slain
9. charm = march
10. tacos = ascot
11. grape = pager
12. brail = libra
13. sonar = arson
14. nerve = never
15. sarge = gears
16. surge = urges
17. later = alter
18. luger = gruel
19. spice = epics
20. ideal = ailed
21. dirge = ridge
22. lease = easel
23. wakes = askew
24. curbs = scrub
25. canoe = ocean
26. rifle = flier
27. gable = bagel
28. spore = ropes
29. blame = amble
30. trine = inert
31. stone = notes

"injuries map language areas of brain"

p. 208 **Language circleword**

1. Reed
2. Edgar
3. Garage
4. Agent
5. Entire
6. Tiresome
7. Somebody
8. Bodywork
9. Working
10. Kingston
11. Tonsure

p. 200 **Confused speech**

A. Wernicke's
B. Broca's
C. Apraxia

p. 211 **Unconstructible constructs**

1. You talked to your mother and someone else; who is that someone else?

2. You know whether a given person talked to your mother; who is that person?

3. You talked to the woman who married someone; who is that someone?

4. It bothered John that you know a certain person; who is that person?

5. This is the woman who was abandoned by the guy whom you talked to yesterday.

6. This is the car that was parked by the man whom you saw talking to the woman you met yesterday.

7. This is the guy to whom Richard sent the package that was in the room in which you read through the instructions.

8. The fact that I don't like you — which was told to you by the man who was met by the guy you saw yesterday — is disturbing.

9. You just can't do it using the same construction. Instead, you have to switch to a different construction altogether: What size boxes do you need?

10 & 11. You just can't do it. Rumored and reputed are passive "orphans" — their active-voice transitive counterparts no longer exist.

p. 212 **Mental status for language**

For each "A," give 1 point, for each "B," give 2 points, and for each "C," give 3 points.

Totals:

7 points or fewer: You may want to get a professional evaluation.

8-10 points: You have some signs of mild cognitive decline. You should work a little harder to keep yourself mentally fit.

11-12 points: You're in good shape. Keep it that way!

p. 223 **Child speak**

1. B; 2. A; 3. A; 4. B; 5. B

p. 224 **Stages of language acquisition**

1. D, 2. C, 3. D, 4. A, 5. B, 6. D, 7. C, 8. A, 9. D, 10. B, 11. D

p. 216 **Mama and papa**

Word pairs:

i. Welsh mam "mama"
   tad "papa"

ii. Hebrew aba "papa"
    ima "mama"

iii. Swahili mama "mama"
     baba "papa"

iv. Tamil ammaa "mama"
    appa "papa"

v. Chinese pa pa "papa"
   ma ma "mama"

vi. Dakota ena "mama"
    ate "papa"

vii. Turkish annecigim "mama"
     baba "papa"

viii. Greenlandic anaana(q) "mama"
      ataata(q) "papa"

Linguistic geography:

A. Dakota; B. Hebrew; C. Tamil; D. Turkish; E. Swahili; F. Welsh; G. Greenlandic; H. Chinese

p. 224 **Letters into words**

"The critical window of opportunity to learn languages easily and fluently closes at puberty."

p. 228 **The forbidden hidden**

contaminated = infected

large number = billions

rabbit food = salad

undisciplined = wanton

jeweled crown = tiara

lacks hearing = deaf

living kingdom = animal

mark indelibly = brand

extend grasp = reach

post-Thursday = Friday

fedora & bowler = lids

to force exile = banish

"A feral child is an infant abandoned after birth and raised by social wild animals."

p. 238 **Word storage**

"We may be relying on fundamentally different strategies for producing and processing irregular patterns."

p. 238 **PET brain scans**

A: Thinking and speaking. B: Hearing words spoken. C: Reciting words. D: Reading silently.

p. 233 **Translating from the pidgin**

1. Ifu laik meiki, mo beta make time, mani no kaen hapai.

   if like make more better die time money no can carry

   "If you want to build (something), you should do it just before you die, you can't take it with you!"

2. Aena tu macha churen, samawl churen, haus mani pei.

   and too much children small children house money pay

   "And I had many children, small children, and I had to pay the rent."

3. Luna, hu hapai? Hapai awl, hemo awl.

   foreman, who carry? carry all, cut all

   "Who'll carry it, boss? Everyone will cut it and everyone will carry it."

4. Mi paitim em long diwai me holim longen.

   I beat him with stick I hold at it/that.

   "I beat him with the stick that I was holding."

5. Bai me toktok long ol asua husat bai i kamap...

   I future talk-talk about problems who/that come up

   . . . sapos Tok Pisin i kamap nambawan tokples bilong Papua Niugini.

   suppose Tok Pisin come up munberone language belong Papua New Guinea.

   "I will discuss the problem that would arise if Tok Pisin (Pidgin Talk) became the national language of New Guinea."

p. 246 **Algebraic dispute**

The girl has 35; the boy 49. Since there are 14 eggs (lots of chickens) between them, when the girl says, "Give me seven of yours and we will be even" she is not only accurate, she is responding at a level of social accommodation that may save all our bacon. Francis Bacon might agree.

p. 248 **Numberlocker**

p. 256 **Faces and hands**

Row A

The blank face should show 2:15. That is half the number of hours shown on the face to its left, and so on. 2:15 is half of 4:30, which is half of 9:00, which is half of 18 hours (during which the hands rotated 12 hours plus 6 more to 6:00), which is half of 12:00.

Row B

The blank face should show 4:00. Multiply the time shown on the second face by the time shown on the first. (2 x 4 = 8) and that number will show on the third face. The prior two faces multiplied together equal 64. The remainder, after the hands have gone around five times, is 4.

p. 252 **Concentration**

There are five 4's and four g's.

p. 255 **Numberlocker**

p. 259 **The math-mind's eye**

Row A

Multiply the numbers visible on the face of each view of the cube. They all total 40 except the third from the left, which totals 80: the math culprit.

Notice the orientation of the 5 and 8 on the faces of that cube and on the first cube on the left. Since a different cube is spatially inconsistent from the one that is mathematically inconsistent, the first cube is the spatial culprit.

Row B

Add the numbers visible on the face of each view of the cube. They all total 72 except the third from the left, which totals 76: the math culprit.

Notice the orientation of the 36 and 12 on the faces of that cube and on the last cube in the row. The cube that is spatially inconsistent is a different cube from the one that is mathematically inconsistent. Therefore the last cube in the row is the spatial culprit.

p. 263 **Opposing digits**

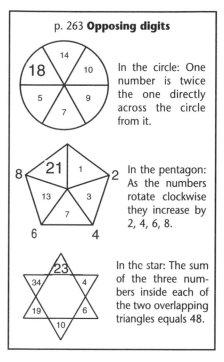

In the circle: One number is twice the one directly across the circle from it.

In the pentagon: As the numbers rotate clockwise they increase by 2, 4, 6, 8.

In the star: The sum of the three numbers inside each of the two overlapping triangles equals 48.

p. 260 **Now don't get mad!**

The numbers in group A are all shapes with only *curves*. Group C has only *straight lines*. Group B contains *both* curved and straight lines. So 38 belongs in group A; 16 in group B; and 17 in group C. Now calm down! You *promised* you wouldn't get mad.

p. 264 **Times table**

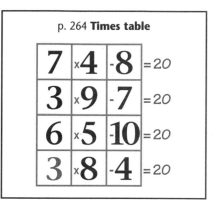

$$7 \times 4 - 8 = 20$$
$$3 \times 9 - 7 = 20$$
$$6 \times 5 - 10 = 20$$
$$3 \times 8 - 4 = 20$$

SPATIAL

p. 272 **Shapes in space**

A. We *want* it to be a 3-pronged fork, but the artist, Escher, makes that middle prong appear and disappear.

B. Do you see a row of abstract puzzle pieces or the letters of a word? How do you FEEL now?

C. Do you see a vase of grasses or pro-files of two human faces looking at each other? Most people see the vase first because their experience tells them that the "foreground" object is black.

p. 276 **About faces**

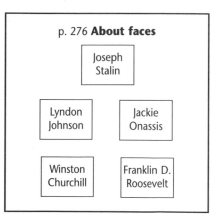

Joseph Stalin

Lyndon Johnson

Jackie Onassis

Winston Churchill

Franklin D. Roosevelt

p. 277 **Eyeball busters**

Row 1: Cat's ear
Row 2: $10, $1, $20 bills
Row 3: Shredded wheat
Row 4: Fingernail

Coke logo
Razor blade cartridges
Staple remover
Book spine

English muffin
Safety pins
Staples
Tire tread

p. 282 **Fitting pieces together**

Top row, left to right:
5H, 6F, 4J, 3D

Right side, top to bottom:
1G, 2E, 3F, 1C, 4B

p. 285 **A practical, boring joke**

Not long. In fact, the bookworm is the one who made the bad deal. If you visualize a book facing you spine-forward (the way it sits on a bookshelf), you'll realize that page one would be to the right as you face the book, not to the left (as it would be if you pulled the book off the shelf and turned it around to read it). The last page of the book, meanwhile, would be to the left. Since the first volume is placed to the left of the second on the bookshelf, the worm would eat from the right side of the rightmost page of the first volume to the left side of the leftmost page of the second. According to the agreement, then, he's only permitted to eat through the bindings of the two volumes — and, as Rodney mentioned, the books' covers are in bad condition anyway.

p. 286-288 **A geometric paradox**

The apple goes to Whitney. No matter what the size of the globe around which the twine is encircled, the twine's radius will always be 16 centimeters greater than that of the globe when a meter is added to the length of the twine.

p. 298 **Time intervals**

1:30. Each clock registers half the number of hours shown on the clock face to its left. Reading the intervals of time from left to right in hours: 24, 12, 6, 3, 1.5.

p. 292 **Yard sale**

A. Cherry pitter; B. Rug-hooking tool; C. Ceramic "pig" (hot-water bottle); D. Candle snuffer with wick trimmer; E. Holder for wooden kitchen matches (bird's sharp beak picks up matches); F. Apple peeler that also cores it; G. Water dispenser for chickens (sits in a shallow pan; the pointed top prevents chickens from climbing up onto it and fouling the water); H. Pincers that break up rock salt and sugar; I. Sewing caddy with spindle to hold spools of thread.

p. 299 **False faces**

Three of the cubes could not have been made from the pattern. In number 2, the T should be rotated 90 degrees as shown. In number 6, the T should be an O. In number 7, the C is backwards.

p. 300 **Spatial intelligence?**

A. The fourth figure's brown and black corners have been reversed; B. The fourth figure's tail has been reversed. C. The fourth figure's areas are not symmetrical. D. The fourth figure is not rotated in the proper direction. E. The third figure's circle and oval should be black and the square and triangle should be white.

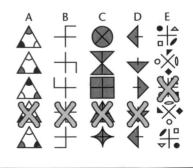

REFERENCES

p. 15 Part of your brain
Calvin, William H. and George Ojemann (1994): *Conversations with Neil's Brain: The Neural Nature of Thought and Language.* Reading, MA: Addison Wesley.

Stuss, Donald T. (1992). "Biological and psychological development of executive functions." *Brain and Cognition* 20:8-23.

Stuss, Donald T., Catherine A. Gow, and C. Ross Hetherington (1992). "'No longer Gage': frontal lobe dysfunction and emotional changes. *Journal of Consulting and Clinical Psychology* 60/3:349-59.

p. 23 Right frontal lobe
Davidson, Richard J. (1992). "Anterior cerebral asymmetry and the nature of emotion." *Brain and Cognition* 20:125-51.

Dimond, S.J. and L. Farrington (1977). "Emotional response to films shown to the right or left hemisphere of the brain measured by heart rate." *Acta Psychologica* 41:255-60.

Elias, J.W. (1979). "Lifespan perspective on cerebral asymmetry and information processing with an emphasis on the aging adult." *Century Systems and Communication in the Elderly* 18:187-201.

McDowell, Christine L., David W. Harrison, and Heath A. Demaree (1994). "Is right hemisphere decline in the perception of emotion a function of aging?" *International Journal of Neuroscience* 79:1-11

Sackeim, Harold A., Ruben C. Gur, and Marcel C. Saucy (1978). "Emotions are expressed more intensely on the left side of the face." *Science* 202:434-6.

Suberi, M. and W.F. McKeever (1977). "Differential right hemisphere memory storage of emotional and non-emotional faces." *Neuropsychologia* 8:757-68.

p. 27 How the brain views faces (self-test)
From *The Origin of Consciousness in the Breakdown of the Bicameral Mind* by Julian Jaynes. Copyright © 1976 by Julian Jaynes. Reprinted by permission of Houghton Mifflin.

p. 29 How to read deceit
Ekman, P. (1971). *Universals and Cultural Differences in Facial Expressions of Emotions.* University of Nebraska Press.

Ekman, P., W. Friesen, and P. Ellsworth (1972). *Emotion in the Human Face.* Pergamon Press.

Ekman, P., R. Levenson, and W. Friesen (1983). "Autonomic nervous system activity distinguishes among emotions." *Science* 221:1208-10.

Ekman, Paul (1992). "Facial expressions of emotion: new findings, new questions." *Psychological Science* 3/1:34-8.

Ekman, Paul, Wallace V. Friesen, and Maureen O'Sullivan (1988). "Smiles when lying." *Journal of Personality and Social Psychology* 54/3:414-20.

p. 33 DHEA
Herbert, J. (1995). "The age of dehydroepiandrosterone." *The Lancet* 345:1193-4.

Morales, A.J., J.J. Nolan, J.C. Nelson, and S.S.C. Yen (1994). "Effects of replacement dose of dehydroepiandrosterone in men and women of advancing age." *Journal of Clinical Endocrinology and Metabolism* 78/6:1360-7.

Skolnick, Andrew A. (1996). "Scientific verdict still out on DHEA." *Journal of the American Medical Association* 276/17: 1365-7.

"Researchers test 'hormone of youth.'" *San Francisco Chronicle,* Jan. 13, 1995.

p. 43 Middle-aged man
"Clue to the irrational nature of dreams." *New York Times,* July 12, 1994, p. C1.

p. 46 Feynman (exercise)
Feynman, Richard Phillips (1985). *"Surely You're Joking, Mr. Feynman": Adventures of a Curious Character.* New York: W.W. Norton.

p. 47 How self-conscious
Fenigstein, Allan, Michael F. Scheier, and Arnold H. Buss (1975). "Public and private self-consciousness: assessment and theory." *Journal of Consulting and Clinical Psychology* 43/4:522-7.

p. 51 Immoral and lazy
Kagan, Jerome, J. Stephen Reznick, and Nancy Snidman (1988). "Biological bases of childhood shyness." *Science* 240:167-71.

Rothbart, Mary K. and Stephen A. Ahadi (1994). "Temperament and the development of personality." *Journal of Abnormal Psychology* 103/1:55-66.

p. 59 "Show me the child"
Benjamin, Jonathan et al. (1996). "Population and familial association between the D4 dopamine receptor gene and measures of novelty seeking." *Nature Genetics* 12:81-4.

Cloninger, C. Robert (1987). "A systematic method for clinical description and classification of personality variants." *Archives of General Psychiatry* 44:573-88.

Cloninger, C. Robert (1994). "Temperament and personality." *Current Opinion in Neurobiology* 4:266-73.

Cloninger, C. Robert, Rolf Adolfsson, and Nenad Svrakic (1996). "Mapping genes for human personality." *Nature Genetics* 12:3-4.

Ebstein, Richard P. et al. (1996). "Dopamine D4 receptor (D4 DR) exon III polymorphism associated with the human personality trait of novelty seeking." *Nature Genetics* 12:78-80.

Lesch, Klaus-Peter at al. (1996). "Association of anxiety-related traits with a polymorphism in serotonin transporter gene regulatory region." *Science* 274: 1527-31.

p. 65 Physical exercise
Neeper, S.A., F. Gomez-Pinilla, J. Choi, and C. Cotman (1995). "Exercise and brain neurotrophins." *Nature* 373:109.

p. 73 Your "memory" is
Squire, L.R., B. Knowlton, and G. Musen (1993). "The structure and organization of memory." *Annual Review of Psychology* 44:453-95.

p. 77 Memory-enhancing
Bartsch, D. et al. (1995). "Aplysia CREB2 represses long-term facilitation." *Cell* 83:979-92.

Carew, Thomas J. (1996). "Molecular enhancement of memory formation." *Neuron* 16:5-8.

Yin, J.C.P. et al. (1995). "Creb as a memory modulator." *Cell* 81:107.

Birge, Stanley J. (1996). "Is there a role for estrogen replacement therapy in the prevention and treatment of dementia?" *Journal of the Am. Geriatrics Society* 44:865-70.

p. 83 You can still use
Weiskrantz, L. (1986). *Blind–sight.* Oxford: Clarendon Press.

Schachter, Daniel L. (1992). "Implicit knowledge: new perspectives on unconscious processes." *Proceedings of the National Academy of Sciences* 89:1111-37.

p. 87 Cause of forgetting
Underwood, Benton J. "Forgetting." *Int'l. Encyclopedia of the Social Sciences.*

p. 91 Want to remember
Bernstein, Jeremy (1993). "In many tongues." *The Atlantic Monthly* (Oct.):92-102.

Hunter, Ian M.L. (1977). "An exceptional memory." *British Jl. of Psychology* 68:155-64.

Hunter, Ian M.L. (1978). "The role of memory in expert mental calculations." In M.M. Gruneberg, P.E. Morris, and R.N. Sykes (eds.), *Practical Aspects of Memory.* New York: Academic Press, pp. 339-45.

Luria, A.R. (1968). *The Mind of a Mnemonist.* NY: Basic Books.

Sacks, Oliver W. (1990). *The Man Who Mistook His Wife for a Hat and Other Clinical Tales.*

New York: Harper Perennial Library.

Hunt, Earl and Tom Love (1972). "How good can memory be?" In Arthur W. Melton and Edwin Martin (eds.), *Coding Processes in Human Memory.* Ann Arbor: V.H. Winston & Sons, pp. 237-60.

p. 99 Background noises
Squire, Larry R. (1987). *Memory and Brain.* New York and Oxford: Oxford Univ. Press.

p. 103 Why stories
Bower, G.H. and M.C. Clark (1969). "Narrative stories as mediators for serial learning." *Psychonomic Science* 14:181-2.

Crovitz, Herbert (1979). "Memory retraining in brain-damaged patients: the airplane list." *Cortex* 15:131-4.

Harris, John E. (1978). "External memory aids." In M.M. Gruneberg, P.E. Morris, and R.N. Sykes (eds.), *Practical Aspects of Memory.* New York: Academic Press, pp. 172-9.

Higbee, K. (1977). *Your Memory: How it Works and How to Improve It.* Englewood Cliffs: Prentice-Hall.

Chase, W.G. and H.A. Simon (1973). "Perception in chess." *Cognitive Psychology* 4:55-81.

p. 109 A little stress
McEwen, Bruce S. and Robert M. Sapolsky (1995). "Stress and cognitive function." *Current Opinion in Neurobiology* 5:205-16.

p. 115 "My Prozac?"
Devanand, D.P. et al. (1996). "Depressed mood and the incidence of Alzheimer's disease in the elderly living in the community." *Archives of General Psychiatry* 53:175-82.

Zarit, Steven et al. (1981). "Memory training in community aged: effects on depression, memory complaint, and memory performance." *Educational Gerontology* 6:11-27.

p. 117 Mental activity
Shimamura, Arthur et al. (1995). "Memory and cognitive abilities in university professors: evidence for successful aging." *Psychological Science* 6.5:271-7.

p. 123 As they age
Shimamura, Arthur et al. (1995). "Memory and cognitive abilities in university professors: evidence for successful aging." *Psychological Science* 6.5:271-7.

p. 133 New hope
"Tantalizing data suggest estrogen may prevent or delay Alzheimer's." *New York Times,* July 31, 1996.

p. 141 Cheaper than gin
Ekman, Paul and Richard J. Davidson (1993). "Voluntary smiling changes regional brain activity." *Psychological Science* 4/5:342-5.

Ekman, Paul et al. (1987). "Universals and cultural differences in the judgments of facial expressions of emotion." *Journal of Personality and Social Psychology* 53/4:712-17.

Levenson, Robert W., Paul Ekman, and Wallace W. Friesen (1990). "Voluntary facial action generates emotion-specific autonomic nervous system activity." *Psychophysiology* 27/4:363-84.

p. 143 Distracting thoughts
Wegner, Daniel M. and Ralph Erber (1992). "The hyperaccessibility of suppressed thoughts." *Jl. of Personality and Social Psychology* 63:903-12.

Wegner, Daniel M., Ralph Erber, and Sophia Zanakos (1993). "Ironic processes in the mental control of mood-related thought." *Jl. of Personality and Social Psychology* 65:1093-1104.

p. 147 Self-illusions
Langer, Ellen J. (1975). "The illusion of control." *Journal of Personality and Social Psychology* 36:886-93.

Marks, Gary (1984). "Thinking one's abilities are unique and one's opinions are common." *Personality and Social Psychology Bulletin* 10/2:203-8.

Taylor, Shelley E. and Jonathon D. Brown (1988). "Illusion and well-being: a social psychological perspective on mental health." *Psychological Bulletin* 103/2:193-210.

p. 153 Recognizes fear
Adolphs, R. et al. (1994). "Impaired recognition of emotion in facial expressions following bilateral damage to the human amygdala." *Nature* 372:669-72.

Allman, J. and L. Brothers (1994). "Faces, fear and amygdala." *Nature* 372: 613-14.

p. 157 Marx brothers
Ader, Robert et al. (1995). "Psychoneuroimmunology: interactions between the nervous system and immune system." *The Lancet* 345:99-103.

Griffiths, Joan (1992). "The mirthful brain." *Omni* 14/11:18.

Seaward, Brian L. (1992). "Humor's healing potential." *Health Progress* (Apr. 1992):66-70.

"Immune system may benefit from the ability to laugh." *Journal of the American Cancer Institute* 87/5:342-3.

"Laughs are rhythmic bursts of social glue." *New York Times,* Feb. 27, 1996, pp. C1-5.

"A universal language." *New York Times,* Feb. 27, 1996, p. C5.

p. 161 Are you phlegmatic
King, Raymond E. and Christopher F. Flynn (1995). "Defining and measuring the 'right stuff': neuropsychiatrically enhanced flight screening (N-EFS)." *Aviation, Space, and Environmental Medicine* 66/10:951-6.

McCrae, Robert R. and Paul T. Costa (1990). *Personality in Adulthood.* New York: Guilford.

Sulloway, Frank J. (1996). *Born to Rebel: Birth Order, Family Dynamics, and Creative Lives.* New York: Pantheon.

Kramer, Peter D. (1993). *Listening to Prozac.* New York: Viking.

Seaward, Brian Luke (1992). "Humor's healing potential." *Health Progress* (Apr.):66-70.

p. 166 Self-inventory
King, Raymond E. and Christopher F. Flynn (1995). "Defining and measuring the 'right stuff': neuropsychiatrically enhanced flight screening (N-EFS)." *Aviation, Space, and Environmental Medicine* 66/10:951-6.

McCrae, Robert R. and Paul T. Costa (1990). *Personality in Adulthood.* New York: Guilford.

Sulloway, Frank J. (1996). *Born to Rebel: Birth Order, Family Dynamics, and Creative Lives.* New York: Pantheon.

p. 173 Women affected
Norden, Michael J. (1995). *Beyond Prozac: Brain-Toxic Lifestyles, Natural Antidotes and New Generation Antidepressants.* New York: Regan Books.

Wehr, Thomas A. et al. (1995). "Suppression of men's responses to seasonal changes in day length by modern artificial lighting." *American Journal of Physiology* 269:R173-8.

Wehr, Thomas A. et al. (1993). "Conservation of photoperiod-responsive mechanisms in humans." *American Journal of Physiology* 265:R846-57.

"Modern life seems to suppress ancient seasonal body rhythm." *New York Times*, Mar. 14, 1995, p. C1.

p. 176 Gender differences
Gur, Ruben C. et al. (1995) "Sex differences in regional cerebral glucose metabolism during a resting state." *Science* 267/5197:528-31.

Witelson, Sandra F. et al. (1995). "Women have greater density of neurons in posterior temporal cortex." *Journal of Neuroscience* 15:3418-28.

"Man's world, woman's world? Brain studies point to differences." *New York Times,* Feb. 28, 1995, p. B5.

p. 177 Brain so busy doing
Sandys-Wunsch, H. and C. Smith (1991). "The effects of alcohol consumption on sleep and memory." *Sleep Research* 20:419.

Smith, C. (1995). "Sleep states and memory processes." *Behavioral Brain Research* 69:137-45.

Smith, C. (1993). "REM sleep and learning: some recent findings." In A. Moffitt, M. Kramer, and R. Hoffmann (eds.), *The Functions of Dreaming.* New York: SUNY Press, pp. 341-61.

Smith, C. and L. Lapp (1991). "Increases in number of REMs and REM density in humans following an intensive learning period." *Sleep* 14:325-30.

Maquet, Pierre et al. (1996). "Functional neuroanatomy of human rapid-eye-movement sleep and dreaming." *Nature* 383:163-6.

Smith, C. and K. Weeden (1990). "Post training REMs coincident auditory stimulation enhances memory in humans." *Psychiatric Journal of the University of Ottawa* 15:85-90.

p. 179 Brain scans
Figure 1, Allen et al. (1991). "Sex differences in the corpus callosum." *Journal of Neuroscience* 11/4:935.

p. 185 Experiences
Berry, Diane S. and James W. Pennebaker (1993). "Nonverbal and verbal emotional expression and health." *Psychotherapy* 59:11-19.

p. 189 Why not surprised
Ader, Robert, Nicholas Cohen, and David Felten (1995). "Psychoneuroimmunology: interactions between the nervous system and the immune system." *The Lancet* 345:99-103.

Mason, Jeffrey Moussaieff and Susan McCarthy (1995). *When Elephants Weep: The Emotional Lives of Animals.* New York: Bantam Doubleday Dell.

Reichlin, Seymour (1993). "Neuroendocrine-immune interactions." *The New England Journal of Medicine* 329.17:1246-53

"Which comes first: depression or heart disease?" *New York Times,* Jan. 14, 1997, p. B9.

p. 197 Injuries help map
Damasio, A. R. (1992). "Aphasia." *The New England Journal of Medicine* 326/8:531-9.

Kellogg, Margaret Kimberly (1992). "Conceptual categories underlying noun and verb categorization: evidence from paraphasia." *Proceedings of the Eighteenth Annual Meeting of the Berkeley Linguistics Society,* pp. 300-309.

p. 200 New language area
Dronkers, Nina F. (1996). "A new brain region for coordinating speech articulation." *Nature* 384:159-61.

p. 205 Women are more
Shaywitz, Bennett A. et al. (1995). "Sex differences in the functional organization of the brain for language." *Nature* 373:607-9.

Levy, Jerre (1972). "Lateral specialization of the human brain: behavioral manifestations and possible evolutionary basis." In *The Biology of Behavior.* John A. Kiger Jr. (ed.). Corvallis: Oregon State University Press, pp. 159-80.

Gur, Ruben C. et al. (1995). "Sex differences in regional cerebral glucose metabolism during a resting state." *Science* 267/5197:528-31.

Witelson, Sandra F. et al. (1995). "Women have greater density of neurons in posterior temporal cortex." *Journal of Neuroscience* 15:3418-28.

"Man's world, woman's world? Brain studies point to differences." *New York Times,* Feb. 28, 1995, p. B5.

p. 209 Cortisol destructive
Lupien, S. et al. (1994). "Basal cortisol levels and cognitive deficits in human aging." *Journal of Neuroscience* 14/5:2893-2903.

p. 213 How a child
Sweetser, Eve (1990). *From Etymology to Pragmatics: Metaphorical and Cultural Aspects of Semantic Structure.* Cambridge: Cambridge University Press.

Traugott, Elizabeth Closs (1989). "On the rise of epistemic meanings in English: an example of subjectification in semantic change." *Language* 65/1:31-55.

p. 216 Mama and papa (exercise)
Crystal, David (ed.) (1987). *The Cambridge Encyclopedia of Language.* Cambridge: Cambridge University Press.

p. 219 Turn of first year
Goodluck, Helen (1991). *Language Acquisition.* Oxford: Oxford University Press.

Locke, John L. (1983). *Phonological Acquisition and Change.* New York: Academic Press.

p. 225 The forbidden experiment
Elliott, Dale E. and Rosa M. Needleman (1976). "The syndrome of hyperlexia." *Brain and Language* 3:339-49.

p. 229 Case of "Genie"
Curtiss, Susan (1977). *Genie: A Psycholinguistic Study of a Modern-day "Wild Child."* New York: Academic Press.

Rymer, Russ (1993). *Genie: An Abused Child's Flight from Silence.* New York: Harper Collins.

p. 234 New technology
Jaeger, Jeri, Alan Lockwood, David Kemmerer, Robert Van Valin, Jr., Brian W. Murphy, and Hanif Khalak (1996)."A positron emission tomographic study of regular and irregular verb morphology in English." *Language* 72/3:451-97.

p. 243 Are human infants
Geary, David C. (1994). *Children's Mathematical Development.* Washington: American Psychological Association.

p. 246 Algebraic dispute (exercise)
Squire, Larry R. (1987). *Memory and Brain.* New York: Oxford University Press.

p. 247 "Idiot" savants
Treffert, D. A. (1988). "The idiot savant: a review of the syndrome." *American Journal of Psychiatry* 145:563-72.

p. 249 "Post-lunch dip"
Lloyd, H. M., M. W. Green, and P.J. Rogers (1994). "Mood and cognitive performance: effects of isocaloric lunches differing in fat and carbohydrate content." *Psychology & Behavior* 56:51-7.

Spring, B. (1986). "Effects of foods and nutrients on the behavior of normal individuals." In R. J. Wurtman and J. J. Wurtman (eds.), *Nutrition and the Brain,* vol. 7. New York: Raven Press.

Wurtman, R. J. (1982). "Nutrients that modify brain function." *Scientific American* 246:50-59.

p. 253 Lack of sleep
Hobson, J. A. (1990). "Sleep and dreaming." *Journal of Neuroscience* 10/2:371-82.

Mikulincer, M. et al. (1989). "The effects of 72 hours of sleep loss on psychological variables." *British Journal of Psychology* 80:145-62.

p. 257 The genius
Adelman, Kimberley A. and Howard S. Adelman (1987). "Rodin, Patton, Edison, Wilson, Einstein: were they really learning disabled?" *Jl. of Learning Disabilities* 20/5:270-79.

Patten, Bernard M. (1973). "Visually mediated thinking: a report of the case of Albert Einstein." *Journal of Learning Disabilities* 6/7:15-20.

p. 261 Magical number 7
Miller, George A. (1956). "The magical number seven plus or minus two: some limits on our capacity for processing information." *The Psychological Review* 63/2:81-97.

p. 269 Seeing both the forest and the trees
Rubin, Nava, Ken Nakayama, and Robert Shapley (1996). "Enhanced perception of illusory contours in the lower versus upper visual hemifields." *Science* 271:651-3.

Fink, G.R. et al. (1996). "Where in the brain does visual attention select the forest and the trees?" *Nature* 382:626-8.

p. 273 Facial recognition
Carey, Susan and Rhea Diamond (1977). "From piecemeal to configurational representation of faces." *Science* 195:312-14.

Searcy, Jean H. and James C. Bartlett (1996). "Inversion and processing of component and spatial-relational information in faces." *Journal of Experimental Psychology: Human Perception and Performance* 22/4:904-15.

Yin, R.K. (1969). "Looking at upside-down faces." *Journal of Experimental Psychology: Human Learning and Memory* 7:181-90.

p. 279 Visual-spatial ability
Frangiskakis, J. Michael et al. (1996). "LIM-kinase1 hemizygosity implicated in impaired visuospatial constructive cognition." *Cell* 86:59-69.

Pinker, Steven (1994). *The Language Instinct*. New York: W. Morrow and Co.

Wang, Paul P. et al. (1995). "Unique profile of visuo-perceptual skills in a genetic syndrome." *Brain and Cognition* 29:54-65.

"Odd disorder of brain may offer new clues to basis of language." *New York Times*, Aug. 2, 1994, p. C1.

"Researchers track down a gene that may govern spatial abilities." *New York Times*, July 23, 1996, p. B6.

p. 283 Nicotine
Gray, Richard, Arun S. Rajan, Kristofer A. Radcliffe, Masuhide Yakehiro, and John A. Dani (1996). "Hippocampal synaptic transmission enhanced by low concentrations of nicotine." *Nature* 383:713-16.

Levin, Edward D. (1992). "Nicotinic systems and cognitive function." *Psycho–pharmacology* 108:417-31.

Levin, Edward D., Sandra J. Briggs, Nadine C. Christopher, and Jed E. Rose (1992). "Persistence of chronic nicotine-induced cognitive facilitation." *Behavioral and Neural Biology* 58:152-8.

Levin, Edward D., Jed E. Rose, and Leo Abood (1995). "Effects of nicotinic dimethlaminoethyl esthers on working memory performance of rats in the radial-arm maze." *Pharmacology, Biochemistry, and Behavior* 51/2:369-73.

McGehee, Daniel S., and Lorna W. Role (1996). "Memories of nicotine." *Nature* 383:670-71.

Pontieri, F.E., G. Tanda, F. Orzi, and G. Di Chiara (1996). "Effects of nicotine on the nucleus accumbens and similarity to those of addictive drugs." *Nature* 382:255-7.

"Researchers investigate (horrors!) nicotine's potential benefits." *New York Times*, Jan. 14, 1997, p. B11.

p. 289 "Blindsight"
Cowey, A. and P. Stoerig (1995). "Blindsight in monkeys." *Nature* 373:247-9.

Kaas, J. H. (1995). "Vision without awareness." *Nature* 373:195.

Stoerig, P. and A. Cowey (1995). "Visual perception and phenomenal consciousness." *Behavioral Brain Research* 71:147-56.

p. 293 Without understanding
Farah, Martha J. (1992). "Visual object agnosia." In L. Squire (ed.), *Encyclopedia of Learning and Memory*. New York: Macmillan, pp. 627-30.

p. 297 Circadian rhythm
Czeisler, C.A. et al. (1995). "Suppression of melatonin secretion in some blind patients by exposure to bright light." *The New England Journal of Medicine* 332/1:6-11.

Moore, R. Y. (1995). "Vision without sight." *The New England Journal of Medicine* 332/1:54-5.

CREDITS

Cartoons pp. 18-22 from "The Little King" by Otto Soglow, copyright © 1933,1961 by Otto Soglow. Reprinted by permission of Henry Holt & Co., Inc.

Art on pp. 8-10, 41-2, 135, 153, 162, 197, 218, 289 is reproduced with permission of LifeART Collection Images, copyright © 1989-97 TechPool Studios, Cleveland, OH.

Charts on pp. 62-4 are reproduced by permission of Robert Cloninger, Wash. Univ. Sch. of Medicine, St. Louis, MO.

Longevity data and 100-meter sprint times on pp. 67-8 were compiled by Richard Latta, Plainfield, IL.

Crosswords on pp. 120 and 202 were compiled/edited by Tom Underhill, Chatham, MA.

MRI scans on p. 179 reprinted by permission of *The Journal of Neuroscience* 11/4 (1991): 935, Washington, DC.

Exercises on pp. 204, 224 (bottom), 228, 234 (top), 238 (top) were compiled by Don Franks, Seattle, WA.

Translations on p. 233 were adapted from *An Introduction to Historical Linguistics* by Terry Crowley, 1992, Oxford University Press.

Some technical art has been adapted with the kind permission of The Diagram Group, London, England.

Some Exercises originally appeared in the syndicated feature *Playspace* or the book *Diabolical Diversions*, ©1978, 1979, 1980 by Allen Bragdon and Leonard Fellows.